AMERICA ENCOUNTERS JAPAN:

FROM PERRY TO MAC ARTHUR

AMERICA
Encounters
JAPAN

From Perry to MacArthur

BY WILLIAM L. NEUMANN

The Goucher College Series

THE JOHNS HOPKINS PRESS
BALTIMORE AND LONDON

To Arnold R. Verduin, 1905–1960,
a great teacher.

PREFACE

THE IDEAS AND ATTITUDES which shaped and influenced American foreign policy in respect to Japan and the Far East over the past century and a half are the primary concern of this book. It is not a diplomatic history in the traditional sense, devoted to detailed summaries of diplomatic negotiations. Japanese policy is treated only secondarily and when necessary for the understanding of American reactions. Particular emphasis is given to those ideas, attitudes, and events which are related to the coming of war in 1941.

This is a critical history; critical in the sense that the writer does not hold the view that what happened had to be. There were alternatives possible which merit discussion. As the late C. Wright Mills reiterated so vigorously, history is not the product of Fortune, Chance, or Fate. To the extent that historical events are understandable, they are the result of human decisions, small and large. To explain the course of American relations with Asia in terms of destiny or inevitability is to abdicate a major intellectual task. Accidents have their place in the course of human affairs and accidents affected the Japanese-American exchanges, but fundamentally this relationship was shaped by leaders and active elements among the people of Japan and the United States.

The research upon which this history is based has been carried on for over a decade in a great diversity of materials; to footnote all sources and quotations would distract too many readers. For the benefit of students and other interested readers, a critical bibliography is appended which can open the way to further reading. Scholars will find the chapter bibliographies a guide to the sources drawn upon. Japanese names are presented in the western forms.

Arthur A. Ekirch, Walter Scholes, Percy L. Greaves Jr., Robert W. Tucker, Gerald Wheeler, and Kenneth O. Walker have all been generous enough to read all or part of the manuscript and to help me prune out some of the judgments most difficult to defend. For those which remain, the onus is mine alone.

I am indebted to the William Volker Fund and to Goucher College for financial assistance in completing my research and writing.

William L. Neumann

Timonium, Maryland

CONTENTS

AMERICA ENCOUNTERS JAPAN:
FROM PERRY TO MAC ARTHUR

Chapter I

THE FIRST ARRIVALS

TOKYO'S REACTION to Americans began with panic. Terrified families gathered their household goods and fled to the hills as news spread of a foreign invader. Four black ships had sailed into the Bay of Tokyo, two of them belching black smoke, the first steamships to visit Japan. At their masts was the flag of the United States. The date was July 8, 1853. Commodore Matthew C. Perry had arrived to open Japan to the commerce and culture of the western world.

Some 80 years later, far across the Pacific, another city experienced a wave of fear and again men fled to the hills to await an invader. A deadly attack had surprised Honolulu's neighboring naval base at Pearl Harbor. Squadrons of alien bombers roared out of the western skies, their wings marked with the Rising Sun of Japan, bringing death and destruction to the men and ships of the United States Pacific Fleet. The date was December 7, 1941. A westernized Japan was striking at the outpost of American power in the Pacific. The attack was planned by Admiral Isoroku Yamamoto and his aides. He had enlisted in the Japanese Navy as a boy because, he said, "I wanted to return Commodore Perry's visit."

Between these two points in time many Americans and

Japanese crossed the Pacific and mingled on friendly terms. American sea captains and merchants, naval officers and diplomats, missionaries and engineers came to Japan's shores. Japan sent diplomats and military men, businessmen and students to the United States. Thousands of Japanese came to Hawaii and to the Pacific Coast to settle and prosper.

Trade flourished as Japanese silk graced the legs of American women and American cotton fed the spindles of Japanese textile mills. Communications and cultural contacts multiplied and expanded. Hollywood movies brought visions of occidental ways of life to Japan. Japanese prints found a place on the walls of American homes and Japanese architecture left its mark on the American landscape. Baseball was played within sight of Fujiyama and judo was introduced into the White House by Theodore Roosevelt.

Each country formed vague images of and attitudes toward the other. For many decades these concepts were predominantly benevolent as Japan recovered from the trauma of the Perry mission and subsequent western imperialism. Feelings of friendship and respect were cultivated in both nations by lecturers and official missions. Organizations and authors on both sides of the Pacific devoted themselves to the reinforcement and perpetuation of friendly relations between the two countries. Japanese xenophobia was submerged by a wave of enthusiasm for things western, while America's initial disregard for Japan's culture was tempered by a growing respect for oriental art and crafts.

But suspicion and animosity also grew with time. By the first decade of the twentieth century anti-Japanese feelings erupted among west coast Americans, and anti-Americanism was openly voiced in Tokyo. In the second decade of this century the American Navy moved its major strength to the Pacific. Japanese warships, sliding off the ways in increasing numbers, threatened America's drive for Pacific hegemony. Professional propagandists sounded the cry of "Yellow Peril" for American ears, and "Asia for Asiatics" was proclaimed by Japanese nationalists.

In the decade, 1931–1941, animosities drowned amities. Anger toward Japan was no longer limited to west coast Americans. The caricature of the toothy, ruthless Japanese was in standard usage in the American political cartoon and became the common image held by many Americans. The Land of the Rising Sun evoked the labels of "aggressor" and "militarists." For many Japanese the United States had become the "white peril," challenging Japan's Monroe Doctrine and plans for Asian leadership.

The last stage of animosity began with war in 1941. For three and one half years a gigantic struggle of steel and blood was waged across the Pacific. "Japs" became a hate word for Americans, evoking an image of treacherous little yellow men. Loyal Americans of Japanese ancestry were ordered out of their homes and concentrated behind barbed wire in remote camps. Even the famous cherry blossoms of Washington's Tidal Basin bowed before the wartime temper and concealed their ancestry as "Oriental" cherry trees. In Japan and the United States history was rewritten to prove that the relationship begun by Perry was doomed from the beginning by the malevolence of the other nation.

The actual story of the relations of the two peoples cannot be related in blacks and whites nor diagrammed as the steady convergence of two national forces, meeting at Pearl Harbor. Even its beginning cannot be ascribed to Matthew Perry. Americans had already met Japanese on many occasions when the bluejackets of Perry's fleet watched the Japanese officials climb over the railing of the flagship *Susquehanna* in 1853. Perry's achievement was to regularize and expand a relationship which had previously been limited to a series of isolated contacts.

The Japanese-American association was born out of an American faith in destiny. From the earliest days of the Republic, some Americans were confident that their nation's future was to be fulfilled in the Far East. Yankees were not only to be the heirs of Columbus with ready access to the wealth of the Indies, but also to the fabled island of Chipangu (Japan) which the Great Navigator had sought in vain. American goods were destined to stock the markets of the Orient and Yankee ships to return laden with gold and the rarities of another world.

Commercial gain was not the only component of the American dream of the national future in Asia. As a Christian nation with messianic-minded preachers and laymen, its ships were also to carry the Gospel to the yellow pagan and rid him of his idolatry. The young American republic had another export upon which it placed high value, the ideals of 1776. The republican form of government with its obvious superiorities was to spread across the Pacific, overthrowing oriental tyrannies and tradition-bound political systems. From this happy identity of gain, religion, and political progress came the faith which moved Americans and their ships confidently into the Far East.

The economic interest was the most obvious. "The first Americans went to Asia because they had to go—they had to go everywhere" said Tyler Dennett in his pioneering work, *Americans in Eastern Asia*. Despite its agricultural and mineral potential the new nation was commercially poor. Unable to satisfy even their tastes in food and drink from their own soil, Americans had to find means of paying for their imports. A merchant fleet and a carrying trade was a ready answer for men who lived along the seacoast and who could build their ships from the timber of their own forests. Ranging the seas, Yankee skippers could not only dispose of their own country's raw materials, but could earn good profits in carrying the manufactures of Europe to distant lands.

"Geography points us to China, Persia, India, Arabia, Felix and Japan," said a hopeful New Englander, Congressman

James Elliott of Vermont in 1803. His fellow congressmen had reason to accept his optimism, since by that date American ships were not only engaged in a lucrative trade with China, but were also trading with Japan under Dutch charters. American trade with Asia was launched in 1785, when the *Empress of China* unloaded its Canton cargo on the docks of New York's East River. Before the Revolution American colonists knew of Asia's products through British imports, but the arrival of the *Empress of China* opened the direct trade and created a sensation in shipping circles. The voyage netted a respectable 30 percent profit and sent other ships on the same quest. Special tariff privileges, extended by the states and later by the federal government, helped to make larger profits possible. The *Betsy* returned to New York from Canton in 1798 with a cargo that brought the owners a profit of $53,000 on an investment of little more than $7,000. Risks were high; wrecks and unstable markets ruined many a merchant, but the high profits for the fortunate few assured a flow of capital into the China trade. In 1819 the administration of President Monroe recognized the importance of the Asian trade by dispatching the frigate *Congress* to Chinese waters to protect American ships from pirates.

For those Americans who had read Marco Polo, trade with Japan offered even more exciting prospects. The travelling Venetian had assured his readers that Chipangu was a land of riches to satisfy the dreams of the hungriest of gold-seeking westerners.

> And I can tell you the quantity of gold they had is endless; for they find it in their own islands and the king does not allow it to be exported. Moreover, few merchants visit the country because it is so far from the main land, and thus it comes to pass that their gold is abundant beyond all measure.

Among the wonders of Japan described by Polo was the palace of the emperor, "entirely roofed with gold" while the floors were paved with gold slabs "a good two fingers thick." Skeptics five centuries later could point out that the glib Venetian had never visited Japan and that the few Occidentals who had penetrated the isolated land did not confirm Polo's tales. There remained, nevertheless, enough mystery about the country's wealth to stir western curiosity and cupidity.

When the first American ships finally anchored in Japanese waters, that country's foreign trade had been a Dutch and Chinese monopoly for over 150 years. First encountered by Portuguese sailors in 1542, Japan was visited by Spanish, Dutch, and British traders in the next century. With the traders came Christian missionaries, attacking the traditional faiths of the Japanese and intriguing against each other for special advantages. The religious disturbances created by the missionaries and the avarice of the traders led to the curtailment of relations with the West. A series of government edicts culminated in the expulsion of foreigners from Japan by 1639. Only the Chinese and the Dutch who had refrained from proselytizing were allowed to continue their trade and under narrow restrictions. Japan remained subsequently almost completely isolated from the outer world, the Land of Great Peace, in the centuries when dynastic wars raged in Europe.

American whalers and traders had sighted the islands in cruising the North Pacific, but it was not until 1791 that an American ship entered Japan's closed waters. The brigantine, *Lady Washington,* under Captain John Kendrick and the sloop, *Grace,* entered a convenient Japanese harbor that year, claiming shelter from a storm. Attempts were also made to trade, but the local officials were firm in their adherence to the law. The Americans left, but not without grasping the uniqueness of their exchange. Captain Kendrick left behind a note in Chinese and Dutch, explaining the circumstances of his visit and calling attention to the fact that his ship belonged to "the Red Hairs from a land called America." The *Lady Washington* sailed eastward across the Pacific, and in 1794 Captain Kendrick visited Hawaii where he was, fittingly enough, the first American to fly his country's flag in the harbor formed by Pearl River, the site of America's future naval base.

The Napoleonic Wars provided the next opportunity for Americans to visit Japan. When the Netherlands fell into the hands of France, Dutch ships were driven from the seas by the British Navy. Dutch East Indies Company officials chartered neutral Yankee ships in order to maintain their monopoly by sending an annual cargo to Nagasaki. Between 1797 and 1809 Americans were frequent visitors to the Dutch warehouses on the small island of Deshima in the harbor of Nagasaki, where other foreigners were forbidden to enter.

A New Yorker of great persistence, William R. Stewart, was the first American to sail under a Dutch charter. His adventures illustrate the courage and ingenuity of the pioneer traders. Stewart entered the Pacific as an officer on the *Eliza* of New York, rose to her command, and began trading between the Dutch East Indies and the ports of British India. After losing two ships to creditors, he entered Nagasaki under Dutch charter in the summer of 1797. When the Japanese officials noted that his crew spoke English and not Dutch, they suspected a British ruse to open trade, but they were assured that these men were "a different kind" of English-speaking peoples.

Stewart won the favor of the Dutch and Japanese officials and was commissioned to bring a second cargo from Dutch Batavia in 1799. On leaving Japan with a cargo of copper and camphor wood, his *Eliza* struck a reef and sank while being towed back to Nagasaki. Stewart and the crew were saved but left destitute. He appealed to the Japanese authorities for help and was given men and equipment without charge to raise the *Eliza*. Their efforts to salvage the sunken ship were a failure, and two Japanese divers were reported to have died from the effect of the dissolving cargo of camphor. A wealthy local fisherman then offered his services to Stewart and by an ingenious system of floats raised the American vessel. Succeeding where his government had failed, the fisherman asked no reward and went further to repair the ship without billing Stewart for the expenses. This act of generosity came to the attention of the prince of the province. He conferred a noble's rank on the fisherman, giving him the privilege of wearing the two doubled-edged swords. For his coat of arms the new noble is reported to have chosen the marks of an American, the beaver hat and two crossed tobacco pipes.

Bad luck or poor seamanship continued to harass Stewart and he again lost the *Eliza* on his southward voyage off the coast of the Philippines. Landing on the Spanish islands, the destitute Stewart by some act of legerdemain managed to raise money for his fourth ship. Naming it the *Emperor of Japan,* out of gratitude—or for diplomatic reasons—Stewart returned to Nagasaki in 1800, claiming to be the Dutch chartered vessel for that year. While he was in the harbor, the *Massachusetts* of Boston arrived, not only carrying the Dutch charter papers but also a new Dutch director for Deshima. Stewart was arrested for flying Dutch colors without authorization, his ship and cargo confiscated, and he was sent back to Batavia for trial. Even this misfortune failed to crush the New Yorker; on reaching Java he escaped and fled to India on an American ship. One contemporary charges him with stealing this ship while its captain was on shore.

In India Stewart again found financial backing and was able to return to Japan in 1803 in a vessel he had hopefully named the *Nagasaki Maru,* and with papers declaring that he had been commissioned by "Prince Thomas Jefferson, the Shogun of the United States." Unusual gifts were carried for high Japanese officials, a camel, an Indian buffalo and a donkey. With these bribes and a bogus official commission, Stewart asked permission to open an American trading post. To avoid arousing the opposition of the Dutch by competing for Japanese copper and camphor, he proposed purchasing dried sea-slugs and seaweed which he would sell in Canton. Despite the skilled staging, the Japanese saw this bid for unusual cargoes as a ruse by which to slip in the door in the hopes of future, more profitable cargoes. Stewart's request was rejected, and this clever second American attempt to break through Japan's isolation failed.

For the duration of the Napoleonic Wars, American ships continued to come to Nagasaki under Dutch charter. Each entrance was accompanied by an elaborate ritual in which the East Indies Company officials instructed their American contractors. When the ship entered the Japanese harbor, a table was to be prepared on deck with cushions ready for the Japanese officials when they came on board to examine the ship's manifests. All books, particularly those of religious nature, were to be sealed in a cask and deposited on shore along with all firearms until the ship was ready to leave. A series of salutes—49 guns in all—were to be fired on making anchorage. The Dutch flag was to be flown on entering the harbor, but once moored the ship could be dressed with any colors except the Spanish and Portuguese, since these nations still remained in disgrace for their misbehavior in Japan two centuries earlier. American ships were able to take this opportunity to fly their own flags.

The first of the chartered vessels to bring Japanese goods back to the United States was the *Franklin* of Boston. Stopping in the Dutch East Indies in 1799 to acquire a cargo of Java coffee, the captain could not turn down a lucrative offer to make the charter run to Nagasaki before returning home. When the *Franklin* unloaded its cargo at Deshima—cotton goods, sugar, tin, pepper, cloves, and 2,000 pounds of elephant teeth— the captain not only filled his hold with the Dutch cargo of copper and camphor but also some Japanese articles for business of his own. In May of 1800 the *Franklin* reached Boston, 123 days out of Batavia, with coffee and spices along with the first Japanese goods brought directly to the United States. Advertisements drew attention to this unique collection of goods for sale, "Mats, Kuspidors, Nests of Pans" and a variety of Japanese lacquered goods.

The Netherlands resumed trade in its own ships in 1813, after giving Americans their first glimpses of Japan as official guests. Captain Stewart was not the only one to enjoy the friendliness of pre-Perry Japan. George Cleveland, a clerk on the *Margaret* of Boston, recorded in his journal a visit to Nagasaki with the officers of his ship in 1801. At the home of a Japanese merchant they dined sumptuously on "pork, fowls, meso, eggs, boiled fish, sweetmeats, cake, and various kinds of fruits," as well as on "saky and tea." After visiting local temples, they ended the day at a local tea house where they were entertained by dancers and acrobats. Western faces were such a rarity that when the *Margaret's* officers returned to the harbor in the evening, they found the streets jammed with Japanese trying to get a glimpse of the visitors.

Despite this friendliness, Japan held strictly to the terms of the Dutch monopoly. When the *Eclipse* of Boston appeared in Nagasaki harbor in June of 1807 under Russian colors, having been chartered in Canton by the Russian-American Company, the Dutch advised Captain Joseph O'Cain to put away the Russian flag and to hide the Russian supercargo. The Japanese were bitter over Russian raids on the northern islands and wanted no dealings with this expanding neighbor. When the Dutch advice was followed, the Japanese officials supplied the *Eclipse* with fish, hogs, vegetables, and water, without cost, but asked the captain to leave the closed waters as soon as possible.

Official American interest in establishing treaty relations with Japan lagged behind the traders. When the *Rebecca* of Baltimore left Nagasaki in 1809, a period of almost 30 years began without recorded American visits to Japan's harbors. In 1832 the Department of State authorized an executive agent, Edmund Roberts, to visit the Far East and to negotiate commercial treaties with a number of nations, including Japan. Roberts succeeded in concluding a treaty with Siam and the Sultan of Muscat, but lacked the funds to visit Japan. In 1835 he was again authorized to visit Japan, but contracted a disease in Bangkok and died before his ship sailed for the northern islands. Britain and Russia both failed to secure trading privileges in Japan in the 1830's, and there is nothing to suggest that Roberts would have been more successful. After a few unpleasant experiences with foreign ships which threatened to bombard Japanese ports, the Japanese government closed the door still further in 1825 by issuing an edict which ordered coastal batteries to fire upon any foreign vessel—Dutch and Chinese excepted—which came within their range.

It was zeal for the conversion of pagans which combined with business interests to promote the next American attempt to enter Japan. If the average American mind had any impressions of Japanese religion they were negative in character. One of the earliest and most widely read American geography texts, first published in 1784, spoke of the Japanese as the "grossest idolaters and irreconcilable to Christianity." The urge to remedy the situation may have come to many evangelical-minded American Christians, but the first to act upon it was David W. C. Olyphant, head of Olyphant & Company, a leading commercial house trading in the Far East and well known for its support of Protestant missionary work in China. Olyphant had helped to finance the first American missionaries to reach Canton in 1830 and was noted for his refusal to take part in the opium trade which earned rich dividends for many American traders.

In 1837 an Olyphant ship arrived in Canton too late to acquire a cargo for that season, and a member of the Company, Charles W. King, proposed that it be used to send an expedition to Japan. Olyphant welcomed the idea and several American missionaries were enlisted, including S. Wells Williams who was later to accompany Perry. The ship was fittingly named for Robert Morrison, a pioneer British missionary to

China, and Williams stated that the expedition's purpose was
to "cultivate a friendly intercourse with the Japanese, heal
their diseases if they are willing to be operated upon, and
trade a little." The cargo was made up of British and Dutch
goods which were then unsalable in China. It was thought ex-
pedient not to carry any Christian books which might arouse
Japanese suspicions. The intermediaries were to be seven shipwrecked Japanese sailors who had been left stranded at Macao
and whose return, it was hoped, would win the gratitude of
Japanese officialdom.

Avoiding the Dutch at Nagasaki, the unarmed *Morrison*
sailed for the Japanese capital, Tokyo, then called Yedo, and
anchored below the city. Two of the Japanese were landed with
letters to the Japanese officials. While the visitors waited for a
reply, the Japanese hastily erected shore batteries and, in
accordance with the 1825 edict, began cannonading the in-
truder. The *Morrison* fled without injury to its crew and sailed
southward, where another attempt was made on the coast of
Satsuma. Again the exclusion edict was upheld, shots were
fired at the American vessel, and the missionaries returned to
Canton.

This affront to a Christian effort to rescue the Japanese from
their pagan gods aroused the ire of the expedition's leader,
Charles King. In 1839 he appealed to the crusading fervor of
his countrymen with the first American book to be devoted
extensively to Japan, *The Claims of Japan and Malaysia Upon
Christendom.* King called for an official expedition to open
Japan, using force if necessary. The blockade of the Japanese
capital by preventing fishing junks from supplying the city was
one mode of attack, while a secessionist movement was to be
promoted in the Ryukyu Islands by cutting off their line of
communications with Japan. The American government at the
time of publication was occupied with the appeals of the Texas
secessionists for American annexation, and King's proposals
went unheeded. But the cannonading of an unarmed vessel

roused some American tempers. Commodore Perry later charged that the Prince of Satsuma had "decoyed" the *Morrison* into one of his ports in order to fire upon it.

In 1842 the order to fire on all foreign ships was modified and official approval given to a less hostile reception for chance visitors. News had reached Japan of the tremendous military superiority of the westerners, demonstrated in China's crushing defeat by the British in the Opium War. A British naval survey vessel was treated with great courtesy when it entered a Japanese port in 1845. That same year a whaler from Sag Harbor, New York, the *Manhattan*, rescued 22 Japanese sailors from two storm-wrecked junks adrift at sea. Captain Mercator Cooper turned his ship to the nearest Japanese coast and landed some of the castaways to request permission that the rest be repatriated at the Japanese capital. The request was considered by a high court which decided that the sailors could only be returned by the Dutch or Chinese, but the Shogun overruled his advisers and the *Manhattan* was welcomed in the Bay of Yedo. The officers and crew were not permitted ashore, but they received generous gifts of food, while the Japanese carefully studied the construction of the Yankee vessel. Among the *Manhattan*'s crew were eight American Negroes, perhaps the first the Japanese had seen, and these dark skins received special attention from the inquisitive officials who boarded the vessel.

Several groups of Americans landed on Japan's shores in the years following the departure of the *Manhattan* and found themselves treated with friendship or hostility depending upon the circumstances of their arrival and their behavior as guests. In 1848 fifteen deserters—seven Americans and eight Hawaiians—fled to Japan from a New Bedford whaler, *Lagoda*, and claimed to be survivors of a shipwreck. They were a quarrelsome group of rebels and the Japanese, finding them troublesome, treated them roughly. The oriental diet and close confinement led to the death of several of these men before they were repatriated. By contrast, a group of genuine survivors from the wreck of the *Lawrence*, a Poughkeepsie whaler, were well cared for when their ship foundered off the Kurile Islands in 1846. They were repatriated by the Dutch in 1847 and given presents of rice on their departure.

The story of Ranald Macdonald, a daring adventurer who came voluntarily to Japan to take up residence in 1848, illustrates the mixture of suspicion and friendship with which the Japanese received the foreigner. Macdonald was the son of a Hudson's Bay Company official and a Chinook Indian mother. He became an American citizen under the Oregon Treaty of 1845. Raised by a stepmother, Macdonald's mixed origin was concealed from him until a love affair was blighted by the revelation of his Indian blood. Hurt and angry over this reaction of white society, he determined to go to Japan where he believed American Indians had originated. Amongst these people, his ancestors, he hoped to achieve a respected status and spread knowledge of the western world.

Whatever Macdonald's weakness as an anthropologist, his sense of mission remained strong. In 1845 he went to sea from New York to learn navigation. The summer of 1848 found him on a whaler off the coast of Hokkaido. By arrangement with the captain he was set adrift in a small sailboat which he had stocked with an English dictionary, a grammar, and geography and history books. His first encounter was with some Ainu fishermen who at once seemed to confirm his theory by their resemblance to the American Indian of the Northwest. His cordial manner won the friendship of these people who cared for him until Japanese officials had him transported to Nagasaki for repatriation by the Dutch.

Macdonald remained almost a year in Nagasaki, awaiting the arrival of the next chartered vessel. Although closely confined, he was treated with respect and given a number of pupils who had been studying English. While he corrected their pronunciation, he managed also to learn Japanese. Fearing that he might be a missionary, the Japanese forced him to go through a denial of faith by the customary trial, placing his feet upon the Cross. After this he was allowed free use of the Bible, which he had included in his library. The U.S.S. *Preble* repatriated Macdonald in 1849 and he returned to Oregon to write a history of his great adventures.

While adventurous and luckless Americans were landing on Japan's shores, unfortunate Japanese fishermen were finding themselves stranded on the eastern shores of the Pacific. Fishing junks and freighting vessels were limited by Japanese law to a size which discouraged visits to foreign lands, but storms sometimes stripped these tiny boats of their sails and sent them drifting helplessly across thousands of miles of the Pacific. Some crewmen survived the hunger and thirst to be rescued by western ships at sea. A few even lived to land on the North American coast. In 1833 three Japanese landed in British Columbia, the survivors of a crew of 17, after drifting for 17 months across the Pacific. Some shipwrecked Japanese were picked up by homeward bound American ships and carried back to the United States. Some of these men remained for months and years, learning English and successfully adapting themselves to an occidental way of life.

The most famous of these waifs was Manjiro Nakahama, known also as John Mung. He was found in 1841 with four other fishermen stranded on a tiny Pacific islet. A boy of 14, Manjiro was befriended by Captain William Whitfield of the whaler, *John Howland,* who rescued him and took him to his New England home. Manjiro became a part of the family and Captain Whitfield left the local church when the deacon asked that Manjiro, having a pigmented skin, be seated in the Negro section rather than in the Whitfield family pew. Enrolled in school in Fairhaven, Massachusetts, Manjiro proved an apt pupil of both English and navigation. In 1846 he went to sea on a whaler which brought him to California in time to make a small fortune in the gold rush. With this money Manjiro booked passage in 1851 on a merchant ship which passed close to Japanese shores and, like Macdonald, he reached home in a small boat. The Japanese government was initially suspicious of this Americanized homecomer, but in time his worth was recognized and he was given an official post. He not only introduced sponge cake to his country, but translated Bowditch's *Practical Navigator* into Japanese, a valuable contribution to Japan's first naval ventures.

This series of contacts in the pre-Perry years had its effects on both peoples. In the United States Japan became more of a reality, and the accounts of the efforts to establish relations or of the treatment and mistreatment of American sailors stimulated the interests of a westward moving people. In Japan there was an increased awareness and even the accumulation of knowledge by scholars about these English-speaking peoples across the Pacific.

When Captain Kendrick drew Japanese attention to the existence of his nation in 1791, it was known by only a few scholars. A brief description of America was offered in a Japanese geography as early as 1708, but the information about the New World which had reached Japan through the Dutch was scanty. Yankee pride was affronted in 1800 when a visiting seaman was asked by a Japanese whether America was as large as Nagasaki. This seaman, William Cleveland, wrote in his journal that it was "astonishing what a low opinion the Japanese have of America." Great strides were made in the next 50 years, and Perry's crew were equally astonished to have Japanese point out not only New York and Washington on a map of the United States but some western cities as well.

The visits of American ships under Dutch charter led the Japanese government in 1809 to order its interpreters to study English. By 1811 a phrase book had been compiled with such unique pronunciations as "Watto we-doru isu itto?" for "What weather is it?" In response to official Japanese requests in 1809, the Dutch had transmitted an account of the American Revolution and of the establishment of the new nation. By 1847 Japanese scholars were well enough informed to present a detailed description of the United States when they published a world atlas. Included were such items as a short biography of George Washington, a description of the United States Navy, a detailed street plan of Washington, D.C., and a flattering judgment in regard to American politics: "There are no kings or lesser rulers, however, in every state a number of wise men are chosen as government functionaries instead."

Along with the growth of historical and geographical knowledge, increased attention was given to the study of the English language. A lengthy English grammar, based on Dutch studies, was published by Japanese scholars in 1840–1841. The Shogun in 1850, while maintaining the exclusion policy, ordered the compilation of a comprehensive English-Japanese dictionary. Commander Glynn, visiting Japan in 1849, found that the Japanese interpreter "spoke tolerably good English, but understood only as much as he wanted to."

The crowning work of pre-Perry Japanese studies was a five-volume *New Account of America* which was published on the eve of the Perry mission in 1853. Over 50 pages were devoted to maps and drawings of American historical events in which the artist was given unscholarly license. One drawing presented George Washington paying an unexplained visit to Amerigo Vespucci whose death had preceded Washington's birth by 200 years. Attention was drawn to the democratic character of the United States:

> In the New Country, there is no distinction of ruler and subject, only the difference between noble and base, high and low. The heads of the national, state and county governments are different men, but they are all sover-

eigns in their respective positions. Now, their homes, their doings, their food and drink, and their clothing are not different from those of the common people.

The attitude of the Japanese student of the United States was expressed in the preface to a *General Account of America* which appeared in 1854. The author stated that it was the duty of Japanese scholars "to enlighten the people and show them that the barbarians should be respected, but not feared." Within the next few years Japan's experience with the western-ers suggested that they should be both respected *and* feared.

Chapter II

TRADE, RELIGION, AND THE NATIONAL MISSION

WHEN THAT WELL-TRAVELLED Irish bishop, George Berkeley, wrote "Westward the course of empire takes its way" in the 1720's, he might have made the same comment about the eastward movement. Europeans were not only moving across the Atlantic to the New World, but the expanding forces of merchant capitalism were showing a growing interest in the Far East. As the trader sought new worlds, the increasing technical superiority of western weapons and ships made possible a successful assault on the closed markets and riches of India and Asia. The opening of Japan to the trade and culture of the West by American initiative was but a phase of this larger historical movement.

British seamen and merchants took the lead. Portugal, Spain, and the Netherlands had pioneered in penetrating the Far East in the sixteenth and seventeenth centuries, but their total impact was small and their holdings peripheral. The Portuguese and Spanish were expelled from Japan in the early seventeenth century and by the end of the eighteenth century they had declined, like the Netherlands, to the level of minor colonial powers. England, on the other hand, after defeating the Spanish Armada in 1588 advanced in the next two centuries to the mastery of the oceans of the world. With that mastery came access to the shores and hinterland of Asia.

The creation of the British India Company in 1600 was followed by two centuries of conquest during which the subcontinent of India came piecemeal into British control. Madras, Bombay, and Calcutta became in turn the outposts of an expanding empire. By the end of the Napoleonic Wars in 1815 British power was pressing against the gates of China. Through the vision of the energetic Sir Thomas Raffles the Union Jack was raised over Singapore in January of 1819, and a base of growing importance for British power came into being. From the Straits of Malacca British warships could reach the China Seas with little difficulty.

By 1819 Britain's European competitors were weakened to the point at which they could offer no serious rivalry in Asia. Spanish sea power was destroyed with finality at the Battle of Trafalgar in 1805. The French Navy was crippled in the same battle, and the French had failed to secure a base beyond the Indian colony of Pondicherry. Indo-China was yet to fall into French hands. Portugal continued to cling to the port of Macao on the Chinese coast, while the Netherlands retained a series of posts in the East Indies along with the trading concession with Japan. Neither of these countries had the resources with which to oppose Britain and to expand their own holdings. Only Russia was to make great gains, but the Tsarist operations were too far north to give Britain great concern.

"I set no value on objects strange or ingenious and have no use for your country's manufactures," Emperor Ch'ien Lung had told the British envoy in 1793. But Britain's demands for Chinese teas and silks could be best filled by a two-way trade, and a solution was found in the sale of opium. The Chinese found this narcotic, growing in British India, a source of escape from the grimness of life, and the value of its sales soon rose beyond the level of British purchases from China. When imperial edicts banned the importation of the drug, smuggling became an apparent necessity for many British and American merchants. Corrupt Chinese officials were only too willing to co-operate in this profitable but illegal trade. When the Chinese government took drastic action—executing opium dealers before the residences of the foreign traders and seizing large supplies of the drug—relations between British traders and China were disrupted.

The first Anglo-Chinese War began in 1839 with the opium trade as the major issue. Chinese antagonism had also been stirred by the activities of the British missionaries, while the British resented the arrogance with which the Chinese government refused to recognize the foreign barbarians as equals. Britain, with superior technology and organization of power, was an easy victor. The Treaty of Nanking in 1842 not only exacted a $21 million indemnity from the Chinese, but brought under British possession the island of Hong Kong and opened four additional ports to British trade. The Chinese wall was crumbling. Other western nations hastened to use the British victory to their own advantage.

Public sentiment in the United States was critical of Britain's "Opium War" and "imperialist immorality." But the significance of Britain's action for future American interests did not escape astute observers. John Quincy Adams from his seat in Congress defended Britain's action on the grounds that the war was fought for the rights of all nations to be treated as equals by China. Years later, Matthew Perry was to speak of the opening of the Chinese ports by war as "one of the most humane and useful acts" which Britain had ever taken. Perry predicted that it would accomplish more in Christianizing China and elevating social conditions than years of actual missionary work. Although such a viewpoint was in the minority, American traders at Canton lost no time in pressing Washington to seek additional privileges for ships flying the American flag. Appeals to Congress by commercial interests led to the appointment of Caleb Cushing, Massachusetts congressman, as commissioner to China in 1843.

Cushing arrived at Macao on an American warship and found the chastened Chinese government unwilling to recognize another western barbarian at the gates. Firmness and a reminder to the Chinese that refusal to receive envoys was considered by western nations as a just cause of war, coupled with the announcement of the imminent arrival of the American Pacific squadron, brought Cushing success. The Chinese agreed to sign a treaty giving the United States all the privileges accorded the British and more, including extraterritoriality. The latter concession freed smugglers from punishments under Chinese law.

Following the British victory, American tonnage in Chinese ports had doubled between 1842 and 1843. Ratification of the Cushing Treaty in 1845 gave further opportunity for trade, and the total value of cargoes carried under the American flag rose from $9 million in 1845 to over $22 million by 1860. This was still only a tiny percentage of the total foreign trade of the United States, but it brought rich returns to an influential group of American families. For these Americans, predominantly New Englanders, China continued to be the center of dreams which envisioned a great commercial future for their nation.

The growth of the China trade contributed directly to increasing interest in Japan. As the sailing ship began to be replaced by the steamer, coaling stations became of great importance. The crude and inefficient boilers of the early steamers consumed large quantities of coal which in turn cut down on valuable cargo space. The trans-Pacific voyage required refueling and coal dumps were established in the Chinese ports, supplied by colliers from American Atlantic ports or from Britain. When a rumor spread in the 1840's that Japan had large deposits of coal, this appeared to be a boon to American plans for a Pacific steamship line. Secretary of State

Daniel Webster spoke of these coal deposits as "a gift of Providence, deposited by the Creator of all things in the depths of the Japanese Islands, for the benefit of the human family."

The annexation of California in 1848, bringing American harbors thousands of miles nearer to the trade of the Orient, heightened interest in both China and Japan. "Asia has suddenly become our neighbor with a placid, intervening ocean inviting our steamships upon the track of a commerce greater than that of all Europe combined," proclaimed Secretary of the Treasury Robert Walker in 1848. American ships, no longer forced to make the long voyage from the Atlantic around Cape Horn or the Cape of Good Hope, could now cut costs and compete on better terms with their European rivals. The rise of Shanghai, outstripping Canton as a trading port, cut the distances to American harbors by almost another thousand miles. Plans for a transcontinental railroad to carry the goods of the eastern and midwestern states to Pacific ports made the outlook even brighter. "This, sir, is the road to India! This is the great western passage for which contending nations have struggled for centuries," a Pacific railroad enthusiast announced in 1847.

The American whaling industry, driven into the North Pacific by a paucity of whales in other waters, also looked to Japan for convenient harbors in which to provision and refit on the long cruises. This interest won some support from a public which frequently read exaggerated stories of the cruelty inflicted by Japanese on shipwrecked Americans and looked with approval on any measures which could protect these unfortunates. President Millard Fillmore, when he won cabinet approval of the Japan mission, offered the plight of the stranded seamen as a major justification. In the letter which was drafted for the Japanese Emperor by the State Department the Japanese were told, "We are very much in earnest about this." But critics of the Japan expedition, like the editors of the Washington *Union,* claimed that the seaman issue was only "an opening wedge" for more vital commercial considerations. The *Democratic Review* went further in criticizing the proposals made by the Whigs for the trans-Pacific expedition and said that the seaman issue was "a mere flimsy cloak to a matter-of-fact business-like design."

The commercial appeals of a venture which would open trade with Japan were obvious, but some Americans looked to broader and more noble ends. In an age when commerce and civilization were treated as almost synonymous, the beneficial effects of trade with the West on the Orient were seldom questioned. A New Jersey senator, speaking in behalf of government support for a Pacific steamship line, proclaimed that it was "the mission of commerce to civilize the world . . . to carry those principles of liberty and enterprise which have given this country its prominence and its glory throughout the world to the other races and nations of mankind."

Politically the American expedition was seen as a liberating agent. One image of Japan offered frequently in the press was that of a people living restlessly under a harsh, dictatorial regime which crushed their natural instincts for freedom and individuality. The Japanese government, said an American writer in 1830, is an iron despotism, "controlled almost as perfectly as the wheels in a manufactury." Two decades later the *Democratic Review* repeated the image, claiming that the Japanese were "so completely controlled by a despotic system as to be little more than automata in every affair of life." People who could live under these conditions, said the *Whig Review* in 1852, ranked "about on a level with the Feejees of the South Seas or the Esquimeaux." A Boston newspaper concluded that it was "time the Yankee schoolmaster was sent" to peoples who were the victims of this "inveterately vicious absurdity." "We could convert their selfish government into a liberal republic in a short time" argued Commander Glynn after his visit to Japan in 1849.

Religion and morality were further ends to be served by

opening American relations with Japan. In both respects, according to American writers, the Japanese were in a deplorable state. Their religion was "the grossest paganism"; it was "destitute of joy and remarkable only for those austerities which render worship a rarity and a penance." From early youth Japanese "revel in the luxury of suicide." But their greatest vice was incontinence; *DeBow's Review*, noted for its concern for economic statistics, stated that prostitutes were found in Japan "in greater numbers than in any country of Asia except Hindustan." To balance this indictment, the Japanese were told in 1851 by the repatriated John Manjiro that Americans were "lewd by nature, but otherwise well-behaved." This resident of Fairhaven, Massachusetts, seems to have reached his conclusions by observing the character of the American marriage; "Americans merely make a proclamation to the gods" and then they "go on a sight-seeing trip to the mountains."

A few writers were willing to recognize that Japan had long ago had its experience with Christianity only to reject it. The *Democratic Review* gave history a twist by claiming that Japan had once been "a half Christianized nation" only to be "forced back by tyranny and persecution into barbarism and idolatry." Others explained Japan's adverse reaction to sixteenth century Christianity by pointing out that this religion had come from monarchy-ridden Spain and had been Roman Catholicism. The anti-Catholic feelings of mid-century America were appealed to as an additional argument for Protestant missionary work. When the Perry expedition returned, one writer commented that it was "Jesuitical ambition which closed Japan to the world and Protestant energy that has now opened it." Many could agree with the learned Chinese missionary, S. Wells Williams, who concluded that the self-imposed isolation of Japan was "not according to God's plan of mercy to these peoples."

Economics, a sense of national mission, and religion—three of the most powerful forces which move men to action—

combined to support an armed expedition to pry open the doors of Japan. An expansionist-minded naval officer, Captain David Porter, hero of the War of 1812, was the first to propose an official landing operation on the shores of Japan. Writing to President Madison in 1815, Porter argued that the time was favorable and the feat "would be a glory beyond that acquired by any other nation . . . to beat down their rooted prejudices, secure to ourselves a valuable trade, and make that people known to the world." Porter played on the right themes, but he was still too far in advance of his time and his plea went unanswered.

Official support for an expedition was eventually obtained by the work of a few score of Americans vitally interested in the Far East. They set themselves to the task of convincing Congress and the administration that the destiny and duty of their nation pointed at the Land of the Rising Sun. In speeches, in newspaper editorials, and in letters to congressmen and government officials, the case was argued for taking up the task in Asia. Dollars, the Bible, and the American Flag were all waved as incitements to action. In the mood of expansionism which reigned in the 1840's these arguments brought results.

Aaron H. Palmer, a New York commission merchant, was the unofficial leader of this campaign. A vigorous propagandist, he made frequent appeals to Congress and to the Secretary of State, calling for missions to all oriental nations with whom no treaty relationship had been established. On his own initiative Palmer circulated in the Orient thousands of promotional pieces dealing with American manufactures. Beginning in 1842 he was able to send his packets into Japan through the Dutch traders, accompanied by files of New York City newspapers, book catalogues, and the latest almanacs. The information on Japan which Palmer gathered in return was sent to the Department of State. After the conclusion of the Perry mission, Palmer was credited by Secretary of State John M. Clayton with having contributed more to the dispatch of the mission than any other man.

One of the first fruits of Palmer's work was a resolution offered in the House of Representatives in 1845 asking for the establishment of commercial treaties with Japan and Korea. The resolution was tabled, but action soon followed. Alexander H. Everett, the first Commissioner sent to China under the Cushing Treaty, left for his post in June of 1845 with authority to carry on treaty negotiations with Japan. Everett fell ill en route and his mission was postponed. His escort, Commodore James Biddle of the 90-gun U.S.S. *Columbus*, decided to go to Japan alone. Biddle and the U.S.S. *Columbus* reached Tokyo Bay in July of 1846, but a stay of ten days netted him little. Without an interpreter who could speak Japanese, Biddle was handicapped in making proposals and his orders were to avoid exciting "a hostile feeling, or a distrust of the government of the United States." Unable to even set foot on shore without forcing his way, Biddle sailed away.

At the end of the Mexican War another official expedition visited Japan, but it originated in Asia rather than in Washington. An American whaler was wrecked on the Japanese coast, and word reached Canton that the survivors as well as the deserters from another whale ship were being held in Japan. At the request of the American commissioner to China, the U.S.S. *Preble* under Commander James Glynn was sent to repatriate the American citizens. Glynn reached Tokyo Bay in April of 1849, determined to take a much firmer position than had Biddle three years earlier.

When the Japanese dallied in returning the seamen, Glynn gave them an impressive picture of the strength of the American Navy and set a deadline on the negotiations. The time limit was honored and the men returned. When the seamen reached the United States, they received wide publicity for their tales of extreme maltreatment, saying nothing of their own obstreperous behavior. Their accounts, exaggerated or not, added to the argument for a large naval expedition to settle the matter of hospitality for shipwrecked Americans.

Commander Glynn pressed the proposal on President Fillmore as well as upon American businessmen interested in a trans-Pacific steamship line. He was certain that Japan would open its ports "if the business was properly managed" so that American right and might countered Japanese "imbecility and injustice." Aaron Palmer supported Glynn; instead of negotiations he proposed an ultimatum to be enforced by a blockade of Japan's major ports. Victory would be a certainty since Japan had no warships of its own.

Senator Hannibal Hamlin of Maine, later Lincoln's vice president, became a recruit in Palmer's cause in 1850. As chairman of the Senate Committee on Commerce, he pushed through two resolutions which called on the Secretary of State to report on the maltreatment of American seamen in Japan and on the prospects of American trade in Asia. Palmer was employed by the Department of State to prepare a trade report and used his position to submit a plan for opening relations directly to President Fillmore in January of 1851. A few months later Fillmore announced that his administration had approved the formation of a naval expedition to visit Japan.

Expansionist-minded Americans acclaimed the news. The continent had been "finished up," there was nothing to hope for in Europe, but Asia and the Pacific beckoned. "Hurray for the Universal Yankee Nation, Commodore Perry and the new prospective State of Japan" said the *Daily Alta Californian.* American Pacific expansion will be "but an extension of popular virtue, republican simplicity and world-teaching example" cheered a Pennsylvania congressman, Joseph R. Chandler. The rich gains of the Mexican War checked the opposition of most of the critics of military expansionism.

The command of the naval forces was initially given in May of 1851 to Commodore John Aulick, who sailed for the Far East the next month with the East India squadron at his command, a steam frigate, the U.S.S. *Susquehanna,* and two sloops-of-war. Over a dozen shipwrecked Japanese had been collected in San Francisco and shipped on to meet Aulick in Hong Kong as entry tickets to Japan. These men pleaded, however, that if they were returned to their homeland on a western warship rather than on an unarmed Chinese or Dutch ship that they and their families would be severely punished. Three of the men preferred to return to California. Before Aulick could settle the fate of the remaining Japanese, he received orders from the Secretary of Navy, dismissing him from his command and ordering him to await a replacement. Charges had been made against Aulick's conduct during his voyage and although they were subsequently dismissed, they lost him the opportunity to go to Japan. The Secretary of Navy and the Secretary of State agreed on the appointment of Commodore Matthew Calbraith Perry in his stead.

Perry was a member of a distinguished naval family, brother of Oliver Hazard Perry, and a veteran of 40 years of naval service. His major command had been in the Mexican War, when he was in charge of the largest task force that had ever been assembled under the American flag and which he led in the attack on Vera Cruz. Perry was known as a strict and harsh disciplinarian who spurned the cat-o-nine-tails as effeminate and preferred regular lashings with the butt end of a stout rope. On occasion he had been known to knock down his men with his own fists for infractions of the ship's rules. In 1852 Perry had coveted the Mediterranean Squadron command and was initially disappointed over his Asian assignment. But in the official *Narrative* of the expedition, Perry claimed to have been urging a move on Japan before the Fillmore administration acted.

The new commander attacked his problems with great vigor. He conferred with Aaron Palmer and others who knew something of Japan and, according to his own account, "mastered all that he could derive from books." Perry did not need to be convinced of the rightness and desirability of his mission. Aside from his condemnation of the treatment of American Indians, there is no evidence that he entertained any strong doubts about the expansionist urges of his time. American expansion was to Perry, as to many of his contemporaries, inevitable and equivalent to the progress of mankind. "Our people must naturally be drawn into the contest for empire, whether for good or for evil, and it will be wise to anticipate and prepare for events inevitable in themselves," he wrote in the spring of 1852.

Entrusted with writing his own instructions, Perry noted that every nation had "undoubtedly the right to determine for itself the extent to which it will hold intercourse with other nations." But every nation, he believed, had a duty to provide hospitable care for shipwrecked individuals upon her shores. Failure to carry out that duty, as in the case of Japan, meant for Perry that such a nation might "justly be considered as the common enemy of mankind." By conferring this status upon Japan, Perry deprived the Japanese of the right of self-determination.

That Japan was beyond the pale and had no right to expect the treatment normally given civilized nations was the conclusion reached by a number of other Americans. The reasons offered for Japan's excommunication varied. Commander Glynn believed that refusal to permit foreign trade was in itself justification for using force against Japan. Secretary of Navy John P. Kennedy put another burden on Japan when he wrote in 1852 that its government must recognize "its *Christian* obligation to join the family of Christendom." A California newspaper, *The Pacific,* demanded even more:

> Japan must be compelled to contribute her share into the great treasury of knowledge. She must give something more than her meagre mite of lacquered ware, elaborately carved images and similar specimens of curious manufacture.

But this attitude toward Japan was not exclusively American. A British writer of the same period, Charles MacFarlane, argued that "the instincts of nature" and "the natural law" impelled mankind to invade Japan and end its exclusion. Or, as a New Orleans paper put it bluntly, "The world cannot stand still to accommodate a nation in night caps."

Perry also expressed a common attitude which assumed that since the Japanese were racially and culturally different from the western peoples they must be inferior peoples. He wrote of the Japanese as "a weak and semi-barbarous people," a people "vindictive in character," and a "deceitful people" with whom the pursuance of the ordinary rules of diplomacy would not have the least effect. Therefore "extraordinary" diplomacy was in order. Senator Willie Mangum of North Carolina in supporting the Perry mission in a Senate debate proclaimed that "You have to deal with barbarians as barbarians."

The differences between the culture of Japan and the United States in 1853 was actually more profound than Perry realized. The American way of thinking, based on Greco-Roman concepts, Christian ethics, and Anglo-Saxon political institutions, had little in common with that of the Japanese. To Americans with a strong faith in equality, the Japanese concepts of hierarchy and station in life were almost totally incomprehensible. For the Japanese the western concept of law and legal "fact" were also difficult to grasp, since in Japan law was a transitory expression of opinion, subordinate to the individuals who made it. A fact, in the western sense of an unchanging reality, had no place in an oriental universe of thought where permanence was found only in the relationship of man to man and of man to his gods. Projected into international relations, these cultural differences were to breed major misunderstandings.

These philosophic subtleties were of no concern to Matthew Perry who, faced with an attitude which was largely incomprehensible, placed his faith in a universal instrument, force. In his instructions the Commodore wrote that from past experience it was apparent that arguments or persuasion would be unavailing with the Japanese unless they were seconded with "some imposing manifestation of power." There were some fears in Washington that Perry would be too quick to turn his guns on the Japanese; Secretary of the Navy James C. Dobbin wrote to Perry in November of 1853 to remind him that his mission was one of peaceful negotiations, "Congress alone has the power to declare war, too much prudence can not be exercized even in the great work in which you are engaged." Others expected that a conflict would result. The *New York Times,* in commenting on the congressional debate on the Japan mission, summarized the issue as a question of whether or not Congress had lost the constitutional power over war, since Congress had not been asked to approve of the venture. The *New York Herald* went further and reminded its readers of the good effects of Britain's Opium War on China and called the Perry mission a filibustering venture, "tantamount to a declaration of war."

Although Perry called for the largest squadron possible with the maximum of firing power, he did not devote his attention to his guns alone. With the co-operation of American manufacturers, he collected a great many products intended to impress the Japanese with Yankee ingenuity. Among these items were a quarter size steam locomotive, railroad cars and a half-mile of track, a telegraph set with 15 miles of wiring, telescopes, clocks, and a thousand dollars worth of small arms, provided by Samuel Colt with an eye to future business. In another category were eight gift baskets of Irish potatoes. History has failed to record their fate among a rice-eating people. There is evidence, however, that the generous quantities of whisky, champagne, and wines taken abroad had little difficulty in competing against the national drink of *saki* for Japanese favor.

The Navy was slow to fill Perry's demands for the size

squadron he considered necessary, in part because the new steam warships were in early stages of development and subject to frequent breakdowns. Rather than delay his departure, the Commodore finally sailed from Norfolk on November 24, 1852, with only one steam frigate, the U.S.S. *Mississippi,* hoping that others would soon follow. On board were only regular naval personnel, since Perry rejected Aaron Palmer's suggestion that a number of civilian specialists be included to gather information about Japan. The objectives of the expedition were stated in the final orders as three: to make some permanent arrangement for the protection of shipwrecked seamen and their property, to open one or more Japanese ports for use as coal depots and sources of provisions, and to open one or more ports for the disposal of goods by American merchant ships.

Perry was determined to control the news given to the world of the course of his squadron. Once the *Mississippi* left the South Atlantic for the Pacific by rounding the tip of South Africa, the Commodore forbade all correspondence by the crew which mentioned the ships' movements. Private notes or journals kept by crew members were declared the property of the Navy Department, and no accounts were to be permitted to compete with the official narrative of the expedition. Fortunately for the historian, several members of the expedition evaded these restrictions and a number of unofficial reports eventually reached the public.

The *Mississippi* arrived at Hong Kong in early April of 1853 and was soon joined by other ships of the squadron. Perry transferred his flag to the U.S.S. *Susquehanna,* a larger steam frigate than the *Mississippi,* and broke his ruling by taking on board two civilians. One of these was Wells Williams, a missionary and a veteran of the *Morrison* expedition of 1837, who claimed some rudimentary knowledge of the Japanese language. The other was Bayard Taylor, a well-known newspaperman and correspondent for the *New York Tribune,* who signed up as a master's mate and agreed to submit all his dispatches to the Commodore for clearance.

Perry had decided during the voyage to establish one or more bases in islands south of Japan. If the Japanese used force and succeeded in driving away their visitors, the expedition would have a retreat for reorganization of their strength. The bases might also have use in the future for other American ships. For this purpose Perry selected first one of the Ryukyu or Luchu Islands, a chain extending southwest from Japan almost to Formosa, and it was on the largest island of this chain, Okinawa, that the expedition landed in late May. The people and the governor were, however, reluctant to co-operate with the Americans, since they too were governed by the exclusion orders of Japan.

The Commodore made his first use of threat, landing two field pieces and an imposing escort of marines and marching on the capital of Naha. The Okinawans, unarmed, bowed to the inevitable. Hospitality was provided and a base established. Perry wrote to the Secretary of the Navy that if it were not for their fears of Japan, the Okinawans would have been "delighted at our coming" and he felt it his duty to protect them against their "unnatural rulers," the Japanese. Wells Williams saw Perry's action in a different light; "A more high-handed piece of aggression has not been committed by anyone," he confided to his journal.

On June 9, 1853, Perry left for his second base in the Bonins, a small island group 600 miles south of Tokyo, which had potential use as coal depots for a Pacific steamship line. Peel Island in this group had a good anchorage and was populated by a small group of Americans and Hawaiians who traded with visiting whalers. A British claim had been made for these islands, but Perry was contemptuous of "the annexing government" of Britain. He wrote Washington that "as a measure of positive necessity" he was establishing a foothold for the

United States. A piece of land was purchased and a plan forwarded to the Navy Department for further colonization.

After a short return visit to the Ryukyus, the expedition left on July 2 for Japan. The Commodore considered his squadron —the U.S.S. *Susquehanna,* the U.S.S. *Mississippi* and two sloops, the *Saratoga* and *Plymouth*—to be a poor show in contrast to the 12 vessels he had asked for. Nevertheless, he prepared to do his best with what he had. The crews were well drilled as military units, the marine and howitzer groups had practiced landing operations, and the squadron was prepared to land with 17 small boats, five of which carried small cannon. On July 8 the expedition sailed boldly into Tokyo Bay. Some 60 years of infrequent contacts between the two nations were ended, and a new era of relationships was to begin.

Chapter III

JAPAN'S WALL CRUMBLES

PERRY CAME to Japan self-assured and defiant. His squadron pushed past the fleet of small Japanese boats sent out to intercept him and into Tokyo Bay, where he anchored a mile closer to the capital than any foreign ship before him. His decks were cleared for action, the guns manned and ready to repel any attack. When the guard boats closed in and tried to secure their lines to the American ships, the lines were cast off and the boats ordered to disperse before they were fired upon.

Japanese officials of apparent high rank finally appeared, and the Americans consented to their approaching close enough for conversations. Wells Williams' grasp of the Japanese language proved insufficient for the task of communicating with the officials, and an impasse threatened. But the Japanese brought along an interpreter skilled in Dutch; Perry had also acquired a Dutchman who spoke English, and Japanese-American communication began through the medium of a third language. The Japanese were told that a high American official had come to their shores, bearing a letter which he would deliver to their Emperor in person.

The Japanese officials urged the Americans to take their communication to Nagasaki where the Dutch could serve as intermediaries. But Perry firmly rejected this suggestion and threatened to sail directly to Tokyo if necessary, to carry out his mission. His only concession was to agree to deliver a duplicate copy of the letter to a suitably high personage who would arrange for the delivery of the original. Since Tokyo was undefended and had already been thrown into a panic by the arrival of foreign warships so close to the sacred capital, the Japanese agreed to arrange a landing in the vicinity at which a representative of the Emperor would be present.

Perry remained in seclusion throughout the preliminary talks in an effort to impress the Japanese with the greatness of their visitor. He insisted that he be referred to as an "Admiral." The Japanese in turn deceived the Americans by giving false titles to their negotiators. Unwilling to submit any high officials to the humiliation of dealing with the foreigners, they gave the titles of "governor" and "vice-governor" to the prefect of police and his assistant from the small town of Uraga where Perry was to land. It was these two lowly officials, prompted by representatives of the Shogun who remained in the background, who met Perry when he finally set foot on the sacred soil of Japan.

The delivery of the letter to the "governor" took place on July 14, six days after the American squadron anchored in the closed waters. Both sides used their resources to provide an impressive pageant. Perry landed to the music of two bands, accompanied by over a hundred marines in full uniform, and with a personal escort of two tall, muscular Negroes, armed to the teeth. Offshore the American squadron swung at anchor, guns primed and aimed, ready for any treachery. The Japanese erected a special building for the ceremony and provided it with several arm chairs for Perry and his aides. The leaders of the Japanese delegation sat on camp stools, while the rest of the delegation sat on mats in oriental fashion. Around the building were several thousand Japanese soldiers, armed with swords, spears, and brass-mounted muskets, and each of their units flying the flag of their feudal prince. At a respectful distance was a large gathering of civilians, curious and anxious to see the behavior of the foreign intruders.

The ceremonies were completed in half an hour. Perry was introduced to an official who was called the "First Councilor of the Empire," actually a provincial governor who had documents authorizing him to receive the American letter in behalf of the Emperor. Perry delivered both the original and duplicate of the message which President Fillmore addressed to his "Great and Good Friend," the Japanese Emperor. The "Admiral" then re-embarked, warning that he would return the following spring with an even larger naval squadron to receive the reply to the President's request. It was to be some years before American knowledge of the Japanese political system revealed the misconceptions on which the appeal to the Emperor was based. Actual political power was held by an oligarchic group of feudal lords, headed by a shogun whom the Americans called "tycoon" of the House of Tokugawa. The Emperor was a figurehead, not even to be consulted about the policy crisis which the American expedition provoked.

Perry was asked to leave Japanese shores at once when the ceremonies were over, but the Commodore was curious and believed that further defiance of the exclusion laws was important. After permitting several Japanese on board the *Susquehanna* to observe its engines, he steamed into the inner bay of Tokyo and came almost within sight of the capital itself. Anchoring, he launched a number of small boats to survey the bay and even sent one some distance up one of the Japanese rivers. When he had gathered his information and was satisfied that he had impressed the authorities with his determination to travel where he pleased, Perry left Japan for Okinawa with the major part of his squadron. The *Saratoga* was sent back to Shanghai to prepare for the return of the expedition.

In Okinawa Perry was so encouraged by his preliminary success with the Japanese that he requested land from the Okinawans for the establishment of a coal depot at the harbor. He also demanded that his men be left free to travel and trade among the Okinawans without official surveillance. The Regent of Naha in a delaying action offered a number of reasons why it was impossible for him to make these concessions. Perry responded with an ultimatum. If his demands were not met by noon on the next day, he would land a force of 200 men and take over the Regent's palace until his needs were satisfied. The threat worked, and it gave added assurance to Perry of the effectiveness of the fear of force in dealing with oriental peoples.

Back in the United States the new Democratic administration of President Franklin Pierce was receiving the news of the success of Perry's first effort. The expedition had been initiated by the Whigs, and the Democrats had denounced it in the 1852 election campaign as an effort to gather in the votes of American expansionists. But expansionist-minded Democrats were not ready to disavow a venture which might well bring further glory to the flag. Secretary of Navy Dobbin sent Perry word of the President's gratification with the progress of his efforts. But Perry was also warned of the President's conviction that the end should be attained "not only with credit to the United States, but without wrong to Japan." The Pierce administration strongly rejected Perry's aspirations to annex the Ryukyu and Bonin Islands. The tremendous gains of the Mexican annexations of 1848, to be followed late in 1854 by the Gadsden Purchase, satisfied for the time being the land hunger of many expansionists. Perry was informed that President Pierce was "disinclined" to retain possession of distant islands whose defense would be "inconvenient and expensive."

The general public reaction to the news of Perry's first visit was very favorable. Wells Williams, the missionary-interpreter, was one of the rare few to sound a sour note in regard to the

historic significance of this contact between Japan and the
United States. Writing to his brother, Williams said that the
event was:

> . . . the meeting of the East and West, the circling of
> the world's intercourse, the beginning of American inter-
> ference in Asia, the putting of the key in the door of
> Japanese seclusion, the violation of the sanctity of Japa-
> nese soil, and to me alone, a full revenge for the un-
> provoked firing on the defenseless *Morrison* . . .

But Wells' taste for revenge did not quiet his concern about
the goals of Perry's effort. Its "real reasons," he wrote, are
"glorification of the Yankee nation and food for praising ourselves."

Back in Japan the members of the Shogunate, the Shogun's
Council, were facing a harsh dilemma. The policy of seclusion
had been initiated for the defense of Japan and had the sanction of over 200 years of ancestral law. But for some decades
before the arrival of Perry, Japanese leaders had been debating
the adequacy of the exclusion policy as a means of continuing
to defend the interests and security of the nation. From the
north Russia was advancing and establishing trading posts in
the Kurile Islands; from the south the British, having defeated
the Chinese, were pushing their commercial and whaling
operations closer to Japan's shores. The Opium War had demonstrated clearly that any military opposition to the European
advance would require great efforts and great sacrifices.

Two general schools of thought developed. The advocates
of *joi*, "expel the barbarians," favored a policy of all-out resistance. They recognized that Japan had much to learn from
the West in military matters, and some favored the introduction through the Dutch of the weapons and skills which would
remove some of the inequalities. But these Japanese patriots
believed that their nation must fight, if necessary, rather than
be humbled by the foreign demands. The other school, *kaikoku*,
"open the country," was pessimistic about the possibilities of

military success, and favored temporary concessions to the westerners. At the same time this group favored using the opened ports to westernize rapidly Japan's military force by introducing foreign instructors and sending students abroad. Both schools agreed that the western powers represented a threat to Japan's independence and that western military techniques must be imported to meet that threat. Their differences centered on the tactics to be used in meeting the immediate threat.

Faced with this division of opinion, the head of the Shogunate's Council of State circulated copies of Perry's letter among all the feudal lords of his domain and solicited their views about the policy to be followed in dealing with Perry when he returned. There was no unanimity in the replies. One strong minority favored total rejection of the American overture and preparation for the defense of Japan. Others accepted what appeared to them to be the inevitability of trade and the curtailment of the exclusion policy. A third group urged a policy of delay and conciliation of the foreigners, while preparing militarily for the day when Japan could deal with the westerners as equals.

It was the latter view which provided the basis for the Shogunate's policy. A realistic appraisal was made of Japan's technological inferiority in the art of war, and the patriotic dream that the two-sworded samurai could easily drive the foreigners into the sea was dismissed. One opinion of ignorant people even held that foreign feet had no heels, since western shoes all had leather heels to prop up their wearer. From this it was concluded that it would be a simple matter to tip over the invaders and leave them helpless on their backs. But on the level of the Shogunate, it was realized that Perry's cannon could vent great destruction on Japan's coastal cities, while the ancient cannons of the defenders would drop their shots far short of the targets. "Despise not the lessons of the Chinese opium war," Lord Mito warned the Shogun.

Some of the Shogunate's advisers even urged an alliance with Russia as the least aggressive of the western nations, in the hope of effective Russian aid against the Americans, British, or French. In the fall of 1853, a few months after Perry's departure, a Russian squadron under Admiral Evfimii Putiatin arrived at Nagasaki. Secretary of Navy Dobbin had informed Perry of the dispatch of a Russian naval expedition to the Far East, "probably in the laudable pursuit in which the squadron under your command is now engaged." But Perry was anxious to maintain a monopoly of this "laudable pursuit," and had tried to block the Russians by buying up all the coal in Shanghai, knowing that they needed to refuel in order to reach the Japanese coasts. The American in charge of the naval stores proved susceptible to Russian entreaties, however, and when Admiral Putiatin begged for the loan of 20 tons, it was given. Perry was furious when he learned of this aid, but the Russians did not beat him in getting a treaty. The Japanese told the Russians that the Shogun had died, and that they would be unable to transact any business for a year. With this news the Russian expedition returned to Shanghai, where it sought the loan of more American coal as well as permission to join forces with the Perry mission.

From his public statements Perry seems to have been a convinced Russophobe, believing in the eventual struggle of "the Saxon and the Cossack" for the domination of the shores of eastern Asia. "The antagonistic opponents of freedom and absolutism," he argued in 1856, would fight a mighty battle and "on its issue will depend the freedom or slavery of the world—despotism or rational liberty must be the fate of civilized man." He was, therefore, unwilling to do anything which would give the Russians the slightest encouragement, and he strongly rejected their overtures. The outbreak of the Crimean War early in 1854, making Russia the enemy of Britain and France, was a further setback for the Tsar's expedition.

The Japanese had informed Perry through the Dutch of the

death of the Shogun and of the suspension of public business during the period of mourning, but the Commodore was determined to avoid any further delay. On February 12, 1854, the American expedition returned to Tokyo Bay. The squadron was now at full strength with nine ships, including three steam frigates. The Japanese received their returned guests politely, but remained as firm as ever in trying to limit the American area of operations. More than two weeks were consumed in negotiating over the location at which Perry was to receive the answer to President Fillmore's letter. According to Japanese sources, Perry repeatedly threatened to use force, warning that he would return with an even larger squadron if the answer was unsatisfactory and boasting of the American military power in the defeat of Mexico. A site was finally agreed upon near Yokohama and considerably closer to Tokyo than the first point on which the Americans had landed. On March 8, 1854, Perry again stepped on shore, this time to reach a definite agreement about future Japanese-American relations.

After serving the Americans tea, the Japanese presented Perry with a long scroll on which the Shogun's answer was written. Two of the American requests were granted. Hospitality was henceforth to be offered to ships and their crews in distress; one harbor, Nagasaki, was to be opened to enable American ships to secure coal, wood, water, and provisions. But Perry was quite dissatisfied with the reply, and refused the offer of Nagasaki because of the Dutch tradition of subservience in that port. Wells Williams commented critically on the subsequent negotiations:

> The letter last year asked for one port; now Perry wants five. . . . What an inconsistency is here exhibited, and what conclusions can they draw from it except that we have come on a predatory excursion.

The Commodore went further and pressed the Japanese to sign a commercial treaty modeled on that made with China shortly after the conclusion of the Opium War. The Japanese

were firm in rejecting the opening of trade relations, and
pleaded that the Americans must accept gradual change; it was
impossible, they said, to discard the laws and customs of three
centuries at once. Perry accepted this point with reluctance
and instead secured the opening of two ports for the provision-
ing of American ships, with the further proviso that an American consul would become a resident of one of the treaty ports.
The negotiators affixed their signatures to a treaty on March
31, 1854, and Perry's mission was formally concluded.

The negotiations were accompanied and perhaps even facilitated by a great deal of feasting and drinking; the Japanese
exhibited a fondness for the American liquors and the Americans developed some facility with chopsticks. There was also
an exchange of presents. The American gift which most delighted the Japanese was a quarter-sized railroad which was
operated in a loop of over a hundred yards. The Americans
in mock fashion pretended to sell tickets to the major Japanese cities and ports, while the Japanese crowded on top of the
cars and were whirled around at a speed of 15 miles an hour.
In addition the Japanese were presented with a telegraph, a
number of mechanical devices, and copies of G. W. Kendall's
The War Between the United States and Mexico and R. S.
Ripley's *War with Mexico* with grim, grisly illustrations which
impressed the Japanese with the realities of western warfare.
Several members of the expedition believed that the Colt
revolvers were the individual gifts most coveted by the Japanese.

The presents of Japan to the Americans marked the differences of the cultures, consisting mainly of artistic products
such as lacquer ware, porcelains, and fine cloth. Some of
Perry's men felt that the gifts the expedition received were a
poor exchange in terms of the monetary value of the American
manufactures given Japan. The Japanese in turn were to learn
quickly that western nations placed far greater value on
Samuel Colt's products than on artistic creations. The Ameri-

cans admired the Japanese muskets for their fine handwork but laughed at their firing power. Once they grasped the value of weapons, the Japanese became so bold as to ask Perry for four howitzers from his ships' armament. The Commodore was at first indignant, but finally gave the Japanese a single howitzer and forwarded the request for more to Washington.

The new treaty was sent off to Washington on the *Saratoga* on April 4. It was given Senate approval in July and signed by President Pierce on August 7, 1854. Perry remained at his anchorage for several weeks; before leaving he took his ships close enough to Tokyo to assure himself that the city could be destroyed by a few heavily armed, shallow-draft steamers. Then he set off to inspect the new treaty ports of Shimoda and Hakodate.

The Japanese negotiators had made greater concessions than the Shogunate had expected would be necessary to avoid war with the Americans. When the news of the treaty spread to the feudal lords, it aroused strong opposition among those who believed that the end of exclusion jeopardized Japan's sovereignty. Perry's visit to the treaty ports created additional hostility and provided a sample of the type of friction which was to characterize Japanese-American relations for several decades. The Japanese, from their point of view, found many of the Americans to be unpleasant guests. The sailors complained about the Japanese prices and the drunkards among them rowed with the local population. One of Perry's chaplains began missionary activities—carefully avoided before the treaty was signed—by leaving Christian tracts in a Japanese temple. The Americans, in turn, complained that the Japanese officials continued to spy on them when they travelled on shore and put many obstacles in the way of what were considered normal Yankee business transactions. There was also some shocked reaction to what appeared to be Japanese immorality; mixed nude public bathing, display of phallic symbols, and an open interest in sex.

While these initial problems of the new relationship were disturbing the Japanese, Washington was expressing its elation over the news of Perry's success. The text of the treaty was to be a secret until signed by the President, but it was reproduced in the *New York Times* two days after it received Senate approval in executive session. When charged with releasing official secrets, the *Times* claimed the existence of a correspondent in Japan, allegedly the favorite of the Emperor, who had rushed a translation of the Japanese version to New York. But this was a minor incident amid the general rejoicing in which the limits of Perry's treaty were commonly overlooked. The *Times* Washington correspondent went so far as to claim that "the hand and blessing of God can be seen in the degree and privileges and freedom which has been obtained." Praise for the Japanese was widely accorded. The *New York Herald* which had spoken with some contempt of this oriental people now characterized them as "enlightened, free and tolerant."

American evaluations of the significance of the treaty expressed the viewpoint of a nation with unlimited optimism and faith in its destiny. Trade with the Far East was expected to skyrocket. The treaty, according to the *Daily Alta California,* was "the entering wedge that will, ere long, open to us the interior wealth of these unknown lands, which shall pour their riches in our lap." On the other side of the continent, the Baltimore *Sun* reported rumors of the impending purchase of Alaska and the Russian lands across the Bering Sea to give the United States a predominantly land route to Japan, China, and India which would "knock the Isthmus of Suez into a cocked hat." Secretary of Navy Dobbins, in presenting the treaty to the President, stated his faith that it would "advance the cause of civilization, liberty and religion."

The editors of the *North American Review* were almost alone among Americans in voicing some fears as to the future of Japan after the western impact. "We trust," they said, "Japan may acquire that skill in the use of European arms which shall protect her seaports from the insults of lawless seamen, and her territory from the covetousness of any foreign power." An Irish editorialist, thinking of the fate of his own nation, suggested in the Dublin *Nation* that the American expedition might be for the Japanese "the fatal parent of their subjugation and destruction." And Perry's British counterpart, Lord Elgin, after negotiating the Anglo-Japanese treaty, expressed his fears to his journal, "God grant that in opening their country to the West, we may not be bringing upon them misery and ruin."

While Perry was being feted in the United States and granted a $20,000 bonus voted by Congress, the new treaty was being put to the test by the early birds among the American traders. In May of 1854, before the treaty was even ratified, an American clipper, the *Lady Pierce*, entered Tokyo Bay. Fitted out as a pleasure craft by its owner, Silas Burrows, the *Lady Pierce* came from San Francisco, and carried on board a shipwrecked Japanese who had drifted across the Pacific. The reception given to Burrows was very cordial. As a Japanese official told him, "Commodore Perry brought with him too many large guns and fighting men to be pleasing to us; but you have come in your beautiful ship to visit us without any hostile weapons." In return the Americans opened the ship to hundreds of curious Japanese who were permitted to make careful drawings of the clipper which were later used to produce two Japanese duplicates. When Burrows inquired about the possibilities of trade, he was referred to the treaty port of Shimoda.

American commercial interests were prone to equate the end of exclusion with the opening of trade and to ignore the strict limitations of the treaty. Burrows found the prospects of trade at Shimoda disappointing, but the *Lady Pierce* was succeeded in Shimoda by another trading ship, the *Caroline E. Foote*. This latter ship brought home to the Japanese the elastic interpretation which some Americans were prepared to give the shipwreck convention. On board were a number of Americans with their wives and children, prepared to establish residence at Shimoda and to open a ships' chandlery. Another ship arrived shortly after with two more American entrepreneurs who planned to open a grog shop to cater to the whaling ships' crews. More than 40 American whalers were expected to visit Shimoda in 1855. Unprepared for this rapid expansion of foreign enterprise, the Japanese officials ordered the Americans to leave, claiming with some justification that such activities were not contemplated by the treaty with Perry. Article VIII, referring to the procurement of provisions and goods by the American ships, stipulated that these should be handled by Japanese officers appointed for that purpose and in no other manner. The Americans argued in reply that "when a treaty gives a thing, it gives everything which is necessary to the enjoyment of the thing given."

At this point in the dispute another American naval squadron arrived in Japanese waters, the Ringgold-Rodgers expedition. Authorized by Congress shortly before Perry left on his mission, this expedition was ordered to survey and chart Far Eastern waters for future steamship routes as well as to test the treaty which Perry was expected to negotiate. The expedition's commander in Japanese waters, Lieutenant John Rodgers, was a worthy successor of Perry in ability and aggressiveness. Rodgers visited the Okinawan port of Naha in November of 1854 and found the Okinawans unwilling to meet his demands for food, pleading the meagerness of their resources. Repeating Perry's methods, Rodgers issued an ultimatum, landed a force of 100 men with a cannon, and marched on the capital. The Okinawans granted all that was demanded.

Rodgers then sailed for Shimoda, where he arrived at the high point of contention between the Japanese officials and the American ship chandlers and groghouse keepers. After hearing the arguments, Rodgers decided that the Japanese were unwilling to honor the Perry treaty. He wrote Washington that

Japan's acceptance of Perry's proposals seemed to have been "dictated by apprehension of some greater evil." Only a repetition of Perry's methods would be effective, since "words without authority of many cannon will avail little" in Japan. But Rodgers had no authorization to use force, and restricted himself to verbal protests in behalf of the ship chandlers. For the purveyors of alcohol he had little sympathy, since they contributed to the drunkenness of his own crew and had no proof of American citizenship.

The disappointed traders left Japan after threatening to return with a filibustering expedition. When they reached California, they organized the first anti-Japanese lobby. Claims were filed against the Japanese government in federal courts for business losses, and a protest sent to the Secretary of State. The California press took up their cause, and responded with a number of anti-Japanese editorials. One newspaper denounced the Perry treaty as "a miserable abortion," while another called for the bombardment of Japan's coastal towns as proper punishment for the perfidious Orientals. In the east, James Gordon Bennett's belligerent *New York Herald* took up the cause of the businessmen and demanded action from the Pierce administration.

The departure of the Rodgers expedition in June of 1855 gave Japan a year's respite from the visits of American warships and a brief breathing space in which to review their relations with the western intruders. Despite their continued exchanges with the Dutch, the Japanese were commercially naïve. The Shogunate's original proposals to Perry had been to supply American ships with such things as food, wood, water, and coal free of charge for a trial period of three to five years. The Commodore had insisted that the Americans could not accept goods without payment, and article VII provided that the Americans could exchange gold and silver coins or other articles for the provisions which they received. This was undoubtedly an opening wedge for trade. A hundred years later, on the anniversary of the Perry treaty, a Moscow radio commentator was to denounce the Commodore as having come to Japan as "a colonialist to build a bridgehead with the gun and bayonet so that the American capitalist could convert Japan into an American colony." Perry's imperialist visions fell far short of the Russian charges, but he had won concessions which were to press Japan into coping not only with the technology of the West but its economy as well.

Chapter IV

WARSHIP DIPLOMACY AND "CURIOS"

WHEN GENERAL U. S. GRANT visited Japan in 1879, he was shocked by what had happened in the quarter century following the Perry visit. "I have seen things that made my blood boil in the way the European powers attempt to degrade the Asiatic nations," he told Japan's emperor. Believing themselves incapable of effective resistance to the demands of the western naval squadrons which followed in Perry's wake, the Japanese made concession upon concession. Rights which "no European nation, no matter how small, would surrender," Grant complained, were denied to Japan and China. The former President, like other American observers, feared that Japan, like China, was to be carved up as the victim of European imperialism.

The British were first in line after Perry, a fitting order since it was Britain's coercion of China which had softened up Japan for the Americans. The news of the dispatch of an American mission to Japan had been welcomed in London. Foreign Secretary Lord Malmesbury said that it was "better to leave it to the Government of the United States to make that experiment; and if that experiment is successful, Her Majesty's Government can take advantage of its success." Less than three months after Perry's departure, Sir James Stirling, Commander-in-Chief of Britain's China squadron, arrived at Nagasaki with four warships. After weeks of negotiation, Stirling secured a convention which opened Nagasaki and Hakodate to British ships for repairs and supplies. The convention also included a most-favored-nation clause, granting to Britain any privileges henceforth granted to other nations. This device, subsequently written into other western treaties, extended each concession squeezed from Japan to all other treaty powers.

Like Perry, Stirling threatened to sail to Tokyo when the Japanese stalled on signing his treaty. When the British admiral returned to secure ratification of the treaty, he again followed Perry's example and to impress the Japanese increased the size of his squadron to 11 vessels. The Russians followed the British and gained a treaty which expanded relations further by entitling them to pay for their ships' supplies in either goods or cash. Russian citizens also secured freedom of action in the ports of Shimoda and Hakodate. France and Holland followed the Russians. France obtained its first treaty, and Holland expanded upon the existing treaty relationship.

The arrival of Townsend Harris, the first American consul, at Shimoda on the U.S.S. *San Jacinto* in August of 1856 was to be followed by an even greater widening of Japan's contacts with the West. A prominent New York merchant, Harris was appointed by President Pierce with the recommendation of Commodore Perry and given authority to negotiate a commercial treaty. Persistent, righteous, and unyielding, Harris overcame all Japanese objections to further negotiations and in 1857 won an expansion of the Perry treaty and a broad commercial treaty in 1858. A leading scholar of American diplomacy in the Far East, Tyler Dennett, called Harris' feat "the most brilliant diplomatic achievement of the United States in Asia for the entire century."

Before coming to Japan, Harris travelled in Asia and shared

with other Americans the moral indignation aroused by European treatment of China. But he was not opposed in practice to using warship diplomacy. In Siam Harris made a treaty which permitted American merchants to bring opium into Siamese ports duty free and which granted American missionaries freedom to seek converts. These major concessions were the product of long and tedious bargaining. By the time the Siamese treaty was concluded, Harris confided to his journal that the dispatch of two or three men-of-war was the "proper" way to negotiate with these "false, base and cowardly people."

At Shimoda Harris threatened to sail to Tokyo when the governor failed to receive him, and again the technique worked. A temple was set aside for his residence, and Harris raised the first consular flag to fly in Japan. A persistent Japanese legend links Harris with the "Madame Butterfly" story of a geisha who entered his household as a lady attendant and who later committed suicide when she was ostracized by the local population. Harris' journal contains no hint of such a romantic interlude and instead is marked by his complaints against the inadequacy of the local diet, his frequent illnesses, and the harassments of the local officials who made life unpleasant for their unwelcome visitor. Less than a year after his arrival, however, Harris obtained from the Japanese the right to use Nagasaki as a port of supply, permanent residence rights for Americans at Shimoda and Hakodate, and the grant of extraterritoriality, making American violators of Japanese laws subject only to their own consular courts.

With no American warships in the harbor during his negotiations, Harris had to rely largely on persuasion, helped on one occasion by threat of future action. Difficulties developed over the rate of exchange between Japanese and American coinage. Perry, in his ignorance of Japanese coinage, had accepted equal exchange with a silver coin which contained only one-third the silver of its American equivalent. Harris proposed that coins be exchanged, gold and silver, weight for weight. The Japanese were agreeable but wanted to discount the American coins by 25 percent, the amount they claimed it would cost them to melt and remint the foreign coins. Harris stood firm on 5 percent discount. When the Japanese were slow to compromise, Harris asked that the conference room be cleared of all but the most important officials. According to his journal, he then read a paragraph from his instructions saying that if the Japanese did not meet "reasonable expectations" his country was ready to use arguments of the sort that Japan could not resist. Harris recorded the results of his remarks: "the fluttering was fearful—the effect strong." The Japanese settled for a 6 percent discount.

After negotiating his first commercial convention, Harris broke precedent by securing an audience at the Shogun's court in Tokyo and asking for a comprehensive commercial treaty. In September of 1857 he wrote to Secretary of State Lewis Cass to inform him that a display of American naval force would secure his new treaty at once, but that he also recognized that another humiliation of the proud Japanese would not fail to leave "a sore feeling in their minds." Lacking warships to back his demands, Harris argued that the Japanese should make a model treaty with the Americans which could then be given to the concession-hungry European powers. When he played upon the rumors of the impending arrival of new British and French squadrons from China, the Japanese complied and gave Harris his commercial pact.

Four additional ports were opened for trade and the tariff set low enough to favor American imports. American residents were permitted the free exercise of their religion, but pledged not to excite religious animosity. In turn Japan was promised that the President of the United States would act as "a friendly mediator" on request in any differences arising between Japan and the European powers. Provision was made for Japanese purchase in the United States of warships, cannons, and munitions as well as for the hiring of scientists, naval, and military men for Japanese service. There was no reluctance about aiding the Japanese to arm; already in October of 1856 an American merchant ship had tried to dispose of a cargo of ammunition in Japan, but it turned out to be too old to be salable.

Less than two weeks after the Japanese signed Harris' treaty, a British naval squadron arrived to seek more commercial concessions. Japan agreed to a treaty which followed closely the American model, except that the British secured a cut on the textile tariff from 20 to 5 percent to favor their exporters. Russia, France, and the Netherlands again followed on Britain's heels and by the end of 1858 were enjoying similar advantages. The Japanese capital was now opened to foreign representatives, and in the summer of 1859 Harris moved from Shimoda to take up residence at the court of the Shogun with the ministers of the other treaty powers.

The new network of treaties which Harris had initiated was revolutionary in its impact upon Japan. An influx of foreigners where for centuries no alien had intruded and the resulting destruction of traditional patterns was a shock to Japan's institutions. The Japanese officials were unable to foresee the changes which the foreigners would introduce. The American commercial agent at Hakodate wrote Harris that the American sailors demanded that they be supplied with rum and women or they would seize the port. Harris in turn pressed the demands upon the Japanese officials who agreed to make these provisions as "a health measure." Seamen brawls with the local populace created other difficulties. One of the officers of the Ringgold-Rodgers expedition boasted in his memoirs that on several occasions he and his fellows turned on the samurai and kicked them when they were unable to dissuade the Japanese from watching their activities. This same officer complained after a stay in Japan that "natural depravity and impurity of taste is perceptible at almost every turn." But to the popular Japanese mind the foreigner was looked upon as a desecrator of Japan's sacred soil and blamed for an extraordinary succession of earthquakes, floods, fires, and storms. With more reason foreigners could be viewed as the source of new diseases which spread quickly among a people long isolated and without the normal immunities.

Japan's economy was also greatly disrupted. Japanese gold coins were exchanged for the silver coins at a rate of 3 to 1 rather than at the world rate of 16 to 1. Foreigners were quick to take advantage of this situation and to make large profits by exchanging foreign silver for Japanese gold coins at the 3 to 1 ratio and then shipping the gold to China where it commanded its full value on the world market. Harris profited by this device and saved $6,000 out of his first year's salary of $5,000, as well as making an additional $2,500 by taking foreign gold coins from the Japanese at one-third their market value. Within a year Japan's gold supply was seriously depleted, the cost of living rose rapidly and brought economic distress to many Japanese.

The anti-foreign leaders among Japan's feudal lords began to concentrate their strength at the Imperial Court at Kyoto. Here the Mikado lived with only nominal political power, while the Shogun ruled. This Imperial Court began to grow in strength while the Shogunate was weakened by its policy of conceding to foreigners. The Emperor refused to give his sanction to the 1858 series of treaties and in 1859 took the initiative in asking the Shogun to revert to the policy of exclusion as soon as possible. The Harris treaty, said the Imperial Edict, was "a blemish on our Empire and a stain on our divine land." There was recognition, however, by both the Imperial Court and the Shogunate that action could only be taken after Japan had advanced technically to the point of being able to match the military power of the westerners. In the meantime the policy of procrastination and hedging was the only means of checking the extension of foreign influence.

The officials who negotiated with Harris appealed frequently for delay and caution in expanding the areas of contact between the Japanese people and foreigners. Harris dismissed their pleas as an effort to evade responsibility. When he was warned of the existence of dangerous groups of *ronin* pledged to strike down the intruders, he assured the Japanese that their fears were exaggerated. Harris was personally, however, far more judicious in his public appearances than many of his fellow Americans and other westerners. Many of the traders came to Japan from China, where they had habitually been contemptuous of the Oriental and his customs, and these men saw no need to change their behavior patterns in Japan.

In the summer of 1859 attacks began on foreigners as well as on Japanese who worked for foreigners. Three Russian sailors were the first to be assaulted, followed by employees of the French, British, and Dutch ministers. The Shogunate made some effort to provide protection, but the police system was inadequate. Among the assassins were samurai retained by powerful lords of the "Expel the barbarians" faction, and these attackers were protected by their employers. The anti-foreign outburst was a part of the general turbulence produced by the rapid economic changes in which violence was used by peasants and samurai against Japanese leaders as well. The price of rice rose more than tenfold between 1860 and 1867, and some other necessities of life became increasingly scarce.

In January of 1861 the Dutch interpreter who had served Harris since 1856 was assassinated. The murderer was not apprehended, although Harris was convinced that the police were searching diligently. In May of 1861 Secretary of State William Seward, despite the more immediate concern of war with the southern states, proposed a joint naval demonstration in Japanese waters to suppress anti-foreign activities. The proposal was strongly opposed by Harris who did not believe that with the best of intentions the Japanese could secure prompt administration of justice with the existing police system. He was disturbed by the inability of the western governments to understand the situation and wrote to his British colleague, Sir Rutherford Alcock:

> I had hoped that the page of future history might record the great fact that in one spot in the Eastern world the advent of Christian civilization did not bring with it its usual attendants of rapine and bloodshed; this fond hope, I fear, is to be disappointed. I would sooner see all the Treaties with this country torn up, and Japan return to its old state of isolation, than witness the horrors of war inflicted on this peaceful people and happy land.

When the other western ministers withdrew to Yokohama for the protection of their naval forces, Harris remained unmolested, the lone foreign representative in the Japanese capital. Anti-foreign feeling was not all-pervading, since an American vessel, the *Cheralie,* wrecked on the Japanese coast in 1862, demonstrated that hospitality was still freely offered. The American consul who reached the stranded crew reported that the local population, the local officials, and the officials sent from Tokyo all vied in administering to the needs of the shipwrecked men.

The years 1863 and 1864 saw the most extreme use of western warship diplomacy. An attack on the British legation in 1862 and the subsequent murder of a British subject who had crossed a travelling procession of a high Japanese official led London to lay plans for a new naval demonstration in 1863. In the spring of that year a Japanese Imperial Edict proclaimed that intercourse with the West would end the following June. The Shogunate notified the powers that the termination of exclusion had been only an experiment; it had failed and treaty privileges were therefore being withdrawn. The reaction of the powers, led by Britain, was to insist on the maintenance of the rights they had acquired. As Sir Rutherford Alcock, the British minister, stated bluntly:

> All treaties made with Japan have been forced upon it; and it is in vain to expect that Treaties so entered into

can be maintained by a religious abstinence from the use of force as a means. All diplomacy in these regions which does not rest on a solid substratum of force must of necessity fail in its object.

For the United States the showdown came at a most inauspicious time, since the nation was torn in two by the Civil War and there was little naval power available for warship diplomacy in Asian waters. But circumstances led the United States into firing the first shots. In June of 1863 an American merchant ship, the *Pembroke*, en route from Yokohama to Nagasaki and Shanghai was fired upon in passing through the Strait of Shimonoseki which led out of Japan's Inland Sea. One side of the Strait was held by the Lord of Chōshu who took the initiative in trying to enforce the edict to rid Japan of the foreigner. The American ship escaped unharmed, but within a month damage was inflicted on French and Dutch vessels using the Strait. When the news of the first attack reached Tokyo, a six-gun American sloop, the *Wyoming*, was anchored in the harbor of Yokohama. Robert Pruyn, Townsend Harris' successor as American minister, had been given discretionary power in the use of naval forces by Secretary of State Seward and ordered the *Wyoming* to take punitive action against the Chōshu lord. While losing six men as a result of shots from the shore batteries, Commander McDougal of the *Wyoming* succeeded in sinking two of the Chōshu ships. In Tokyo Minister Pruyn presented the Japanese government with a claim for $10,000 to compensate the crew and owners of the *Pembroke* for the dangers they had faced and the losses occasioned by delaying their voyage.

A month after the American punitive expedition, a seven-ship British squadron attacked the city of Kagoshima, the seat of power of the Lord of Satsuma, whose clan had been responsible for the killing of the British subject in 1862. When their demand for an indemnity of over a hundred thousand dollars was refused, the British destroyed the city's forts and reduced the city itself to ashes. The Satsuma leaders then paid the indemnity and began negotiations for the purchase of a modern warship from Britain.

In September of 1864 the treaty powers combined on a new attack on the Chōshu lord who was attempting to close the Strait of Shimonoseki. Although no British ship had been attacked, Britain took the lead and furnished nine ships, while France and the Netherlands supplied a smaller naval contingent. The only American naval vessel in Japanese waters was a sailing ship, the *Jamestown*, which would have hampered the movement of the steamers. The British were anxious to secure American participation and offered to tow the ship to the conflict. A solution was found when the Americans rented a small, unarmed steamer and transferred a gun and crew from the sailing ship to carry the United States flag into battle. The joint expedition successfully destroyed the forts of Shimonoseki and opened the Strait to western traffic again.

The ministers of the western powers then decided to impose a heavy indemnity on the Shogunate with the proviso that it would be remitted if another port was opened to foreign trade. The Japanese economy was already under some financial strain, and Robert Pruyn had only collected the $10,000 asked for the *Pembroke* after he brought a token force of some 60 seamen and marines from the *Jamestown* to Tokyo to impress the Japanese. A figure of approximately $2 million was first set as the cost of the joint punitive expedition, but the French minister persuaded his colleagues to raise it to $3 million to make it even more likely that the Shogunate would take the alternative of opening another port. The money was paid, nevertheless, and the United States received $785,000 as its share of the indemnity. When the State Department Examiner of Claims pronounced the whole affair an act of extortion, Secretary of State Seward put the money aside in a frozen fund.

The Shimonoseki expedition and the indemnity contributed to the weakening of the power of the Shogun who had failed to carry out the exclusion policy. Political factions turned to the support of the Emperor, and the military efforts of the Shogun, begun in 1866, to maintain power were unsuccessful. In 1868 the Emperor was restored to his ancient position as the sole source of power. Although many of the supporters of the new government, the Meiji Restoration, favored the expulsion of the westerners, they knew that Japan was far too impotent to carry out this action. Only through westernization of the military forces could such an end be achieved.

In 1866 the western powers, with the help of a strong naval demonstration, collectively negotiated a new set of commercial treaties which fastened additional bonds on Japan. Import and export taxes were set at a maximum of 5 percent of the value of the goods and many items placed on a free list, preventing Japan from regulating foreign trade and increasing its revenue through tariffs. The 1866 pact was "one of the most thoroughly un-American treaties ever ratified by the American government," Professor Tyler Dennett concluded in his review of American diplomacy in Asia. Unable to meet its revenue needs from the tariff, Japan turned to oppressively high taxes on land as a source of capital to be used in westernizing the nation.

While American policy was following a course which closely paralleled that of the often condemned European "imperialism," the American image of Japan was becoming an increasingly favorable one. Many Americans had their first opportunity to view these mysterious island people in 1860. In that year Japan sent its first embassy to the United States to exchange ratifications of the Harris treaty. A party of 77 individuals headed by two ambassadors travelled on board a vessel provided by the American Navy, the U.S.S. *Powhatan*. The Japanese sent along as an escort a war vessel which became the first to carry the flag of the Rising Sun across the Pacific.

The party landed at San Francisco in the spring of 1860, where they were treated to the first of an intensive series of receptions and entertainments which characterized American hospitality. After a tour of the city which gave the curious the opportunity to see the oriental guests and comment on their dress and appearance, they were feted at a large banquet held at Job's Saloon where they met more than a hundred of San Francisco's leading citizens. After a week in the California city they went south by steamer, crossed the Isthmus of Panama by railroad, and were conveyed by American naval vessels to Washington.

The arrival of the oriental guests via the Potomac drew huge crowds, and even the roofs were jammed as they were driven up Pennsylvania Avenue from the Navy Yard and lodged at the Hotel Willard. For the next three weeks there was an almost steady round of receptions in which they visited the White House and Congress and were entertained by the leading citizens. Crowds of curious gathered at times outside of their hotel and even jammed the corridors. Hundreds of children gathered outside of their windows and chanted, "Jappy-knee! Jappyknee! Give me a fan, won't you; give me a pipe; give me a cent, etc." The obliging guests tossed coins to the children and obliged hundreds of collectors, young and old, by writing something for them in Japanese.

From Washington the party travelled by train to New York, visiting Baltimore and Philadelphia en route. The same curiosity that moved Washingtonians brought out large crowds in the other cities, some crude individuals even leaping on to the party's carriages to peer inside at these strange creatures from another world. The guests took this behavior without complaint and often equalled the Americans in curiosity over some of the sights. So different were Yankee customs that the Japanese often laughed at what they saw and their hosts took this as evidence of good spirits. In their first view of the United States, the embassy was shocked at the social equality granted women and refused to permit them to visit their ship while in San Francisco harbor. But in time they came to accept the presence of women at receptions, shook hands with them heartily, and one New York matron even claimed that a Japanese had kissed her hand at a reception given by General Lewis Cass, President Buchanan's Secretary of State.

The press reception to the Japanese visitors was overwhelmingly favorable. Their activities were given full treatment in newspapers and magazines. Those Americans who did not see the embassy in person could see sketches of the visitors in the illustrated magazines. Observers commented on the ease and dignity with which the Japanese conducted themselves in the many situations which were so alien to their experience. That they remained courteous and affable even when besieged by curiosity seekers was also noted in their favor. The Japanese civilization was obviously not the crude and unsophisticated one which had often been presented in American writings about Japan in the previous decades. Japan possesses "a higher degree of culture and organization than prevails in any other of the Asiatic races," *Frank Leslie's Illustrated Newspaper* told its readers in reporting on the embassy. They should not be confounded with the Chinese, so "degraded a race as the birds-nest and puppy-dog eaters," said the same magazine. The Japanese are "the British of Asia," said *Harper's Weekly*, "civilized as we boast of being, we can learn much of the Japanese." Comments were also made on Japanese generosity in leaving behind $20,000 to be distributed in tips to those who had served them in the various hotels in which they had resided.

The American image of Japan was also changed by the slow growth of the appreciation of Japanese art and architecture. The lacquered boxes and other Japanese products introduced by traders were looked upon at first as mere curios, but soon observant American eyes began to see in them unique aesthetic qualities. When the embassy visited President Buchanan in the White House, they noted that the wares given to Commodore Perry as presents to the American President were "tastefully displayed" in the President's home. Americans also began to appreciate Japanese prints, although recognition of the quality of this art reached the United States largely through Europe. A French artist, Felix Bracquemond, in 1856 discovered the great Japanese artist, Hokusai, by means of some prints used as wrapping paper in packing oriental china. Bracquemond's excitement over this art form spread and by 1862 a shop for the sale of "japonaiseries" had opened in Paris. The American artist, James Whistler, who had come to Paris to study became an enthusiastic collector of Japanese art. Whistler brought his enthusiasm to London and to Dante Gabriel Rossetti, who became a leading collector. The 1860's saw the beginnings of a cult of British admirers of Japanese prints, screens, fans, and other artistic objects. Some of the qualities of Japanese painting were introduced to the United States through Whistler's own painting, and slowly through those circles of artists and art lovers who learned of British and French enthusiasm.

A display of Japanese "curios" at the Philadelphia Exhibition in 1876 aroused so much interest that the following year Tiffany & Company offered Americans a large selection of articles purchased for this new market. Also in 1877 a Japanese company devoted to the encouragement of native arts opened a branch office in New York to cater to the American connoisseurs who had developed a taste for Japanese creations.

In 1878 a Harvard-trained scholar, Ernest Fenollosa, was appointed to a chair in political economy and philosophy at the University of Tokyo. Fenollosa, who came initially to teach English, became interested in Japanese art at a time when the Japanese were indulging in an orgy of "foreignism" in which some extremists went so far in their acceptance of western aesthetic cultural standards as to discard their fine collections of Japanese art. The American professor fought this uncritical westernization; he organized Japanese groups to encourage the indigenous art forms and helped to organize a National Art Museum. In 1887 he was given official support by the Japanese government and headed a commission of specialists in making an inventory and registry of Japan's art treasures. Fenollosa himself acquired a fine collection which he sold in 1886 to the Boston Museum of Fine Arts. This became the first major collection of Japanese art in the United States, and Fenollosa returned to Boston in 1890 to be the curator of the Museum's Department of Oriental Art. Before his departure his contribution to the preservation of Japanese art forms was recognized by an Imperial decoration and an audience with the Emperor. In the United States he lectured from coast to coast on Japanese art. Some Americans now recognized that Japan's civilization stood with those long respected in the West as achieving the highest levels in sensitivity to beauty and artistic creativity.

Japanese architecture also began to receive some attention in the United States by the end of the nineteenth century. Japan was the only oriental nation to participate in the Philadelphia Centennial Exhibition in 1876, and the Japanese pavilion drew more visitors than any other national exhibit. Much attention was given to the display of bronzes, porcelains, lacquer ware, and screens, but there was also great interest in the building itself. Shipped across the Pacific and by train from California, the Japanese pavilion was a two-story U-shaped building, largely of cedar, which introduced a number of novel features to American attention. Four years later an American architectural magazine pictured a small summer house built in Maine under clearly discernible Japanese influence. In 1886 Edward S. Morse published a comprehensive volume, *Japanese Houses And Their Surroundings,* with copious illustrations and detailed technical data for the use of American architects. Interest in this volume led to the issuance of a second edition in 1889. A Japanese pavilion was also constructed for the World Columbian Exposition in Chicago in 1893, a building which remained on display until it burned in 1943. The Chicago pavilion influenced a great many Amercan architects, including Frank Lloyd Wright who built an American home on Japanese lines shortly after seeing the exhibit. In San Francisco the Japanese went further for the International Exposition of 1894 and built a Japanese village which created a sensation. Some of the buildings in this village remained permanently on display, providing ideas for many architects.

American respect for Japan also grew as Americans watched with amazement the speed with which Japan was able to adopt and refine western technology. Already in 1861 the *American Annual Cyclopaedia* wrote of Japanese attainments in the "useful arts" as "extraordinary, surpassing in some particulars those of the nations of the West. . . . They imitate perfectly our manufactures." The same publication noted that the Japanese were Mongols, but possessed "greater mental activity and capacity for the acquisition of knowledge than any other nations belonging to that race." In the annual edition for 1869 the *Cyclopaedia* concluded that the Japanese "have already far outstripped the Chinese in progress toward Western civilization." Two years later this American review reported that the transformation of Japan into a "thoroughly-civilized country" was progressing with "a rapidity which challenges universal admiration." By 1871 approximately 500 Japanese students had been sent to the United States to complete their studies and further the westernization process. That same year Americans could congratulate the Japanese on the great changes in their attitudes toward women when 21 young ladies from the Japanese aristocracy were sent to the United States to be educated.

The rise in Japan's status in the eyes of many Americans was accompanied by and probably encouraged the changes in attitude with which the United States dealt with Japan in diplomacy. Co-operation with the European powers in militantly upholding the one-sided treaty provisions began to weaken in the 1870's. In 1875 Secretary of State Hamilton Fish made it clear that Americans on Japanese soil were required to observe and obey the laws of that empire, with the United States retaining only the power of "trying and punishing." By contrast

Sir Harry Parkes, the British minister, denied the binding effect of Japanese law on British citizens and even claimed the right to be consulted before any laws were enacted by Japan which would affect foreigners. An American adviser to the Japanese Foreign Office, Eli T. Sheppard, pointed out that the British minister was "assuming the right to control the law-making power of this Empire." When Japan in 1878 passed laws requiring all vessels to pass through quarantine to avoid the introduction of diseases, Parkes asserted that this legislation would not be observed by British ships. In 1879 a German ship, coming from a port in which cholera was raging, followed the British example and refused to pass through the Japanese quarantine. Ex-President U. S. Grant, then visiting Japan, believed the Japanese government would have been legally justified in sinking the offending vessel.

American sympathies and encouragement were also given to Japanese efforts to secure a revision of the unequal treaties. The second article of the 1866 treaty stated that it was "subject to revision on the first day of July 1872." Guido Verbeck, an American missionary who advised the Japanese government, suggested in 1869 that they anticipate this date and send a mission abroad to begin discussions on the revision. Because of the growing friendliness of the United States this was the first country selected for the mission. The Japanese Minister to Washington, Arinori Mori, wrote in 1871 that "while the British government may deem it wise to use force in its dealings with the eastern nations, the American policy appears to adhere resolutely to the principles of peace, justice and equal rights to all." The only exception the Japanese Minister noted was the "unwarrantable operations" which the American Navy was conducting that year off the closed coast of Korea in a poorly prepared effort to "Perryize" that country.

In December of 1871 a diplomatic mission, headed by Prince Tomomi Iwakura, Minister of Foreign Affairs, left Japan to sound out the treaty powers on revision of the 1866 treaty. The mission came first to the United States, crossing the continent from San Francisco by the new transcontinental railroad, and stopping in Chicago where a gift of $5,000 was given to the mayor to aid in the relief of the many victims of the great Chicago fire. Congress appropriated $50,000 for the entertainment of the visitors; like the 1860 mission, they were received with great cordiality. The American Board of Commissioners for Foreign Missions, anxious to improve relations with Japan and to extend its religious work, presented a memorial to President Grant, urging a favorable revision of the treaties. This seems to have been the first of a long series of efforts by religious lobbies to influence American policy toward Japan.

Secretary of State Fish showed his willingness to negotiate with the mission, but found that it lacked authority to conclude a new treaty. Fish urged prompt action before the next Congress convened, and one of the Japanese was hurriedly sent back to Japan to secure fuller powers. Negotiations moved on in the meantime, and the United States proposed a relinquishment of extraterritoriality in exchange for a satisfactory Japanese legal code and a system of courts. Tariff revision was also discussed favorably, provided Japan opened up all of its ports and the interior to foreigners. But when the envoy returned from Japan he brought orders that no revisions should be concluded outside of a general conference to be held with the other treaty powers in Europe. The Japanese were afraid that separate negotiations would weaken their position, since any individual concessions would have to be extended to all because of the most-favored-nation clause. On the other hand, Secretary Fish did not feel that it comported with the dignity of the United States to send a delegation to carry on negotiations in Europe after receiving the Japanese mission in Washington.

The Iwakura mission left for London in mid-summer of 1872, where they learned to their disappointment that the British Foreign Office was unwilling to revise the 1866 treaty if it meant giving up any advantages. The other European treaty powers took a similarly discouraging position. Disappointed, the Japanese returned home in 1873, having received one more lesson in western diplomacy. Work was begun on revising Japan's penal code to bring it closer to western standards, in order to remove one major objection to the relinquishment of extraterritoriality.

A number of Americans continued to be concerned about the injustices involved in the western treaties and to agitate for their revisions. An American newspaperman wrote to Townsend Harris in 1875 to solicit his views on the treaty structure which he had himself inaugurated. Harris replied that he had expected that the treaties would be revised as soon as the Japanese had enough experience to suggest changes. "I never for a moment claimed a *right* which purely belonged to the municipal affairs of a nation. Such interference is the result of absolute conquest and not of any international right. The provision of the Treaty giving the right of extra-territoriality was against my conscience," said Harris. Judge John Bingham, American minister to Tokyo, 1873–1885, opposed the discriminatory practices of the other treaty powers at many points and in 1878 negotiated a treaty with Japan which restored tariff autonomy. But to prevent American traders from being placed at a disadvantage in competition with other western nations the treaty contained a "joker clause," postponing implementation until all other western treaty powers would similarly restore the tariff-making power to Japan. Even so, the British strongly criticized the Americans for breaking with the cooperative policy by which the western powers stood united in fighting for their privileges. When it was known that both Italy and Russia also looked with favor on treaty revision, Britain made an agreement with Germany to block any general revision.

The United States made other moves to demonstrate a friendship for Japan based on the principle of equality. In

1889 a convention was negotiated by the outgoing administration of Grover Cleveland and Secretary of State Bayard which placed Americans under the jurisdiction of Japanese courts when they were travelling outside of the treaty ports. President Harrison's Secretary of State, James Blaine, failed, however, to present the treaty to the Senate for ratification. Of far greater significance was the action of the United States in remitting the Shimonoseki indemnity. The final Japanese payment on the $785,000 was made in 1874, at which time President Grant asked permission of Congress to use the money to finance a student exchange with Japan. Grant's request was the work of an organized campaign begun in 1870 and led by Professor Joseph Henry of the Smithsonian Museum and Professor David Murray of Rutgers University. Some 400 American college presidents, faculty, and school superintendents petitioned Congress in 1872 to return the money to Japan without qualification. A number of Chambers of Commerce with interest in Japanese trade joined in the campaign. Bills were introduced and passed one house of Congress on several occasions, but it was not until 1883 that the legislation finally reached the White House. In view of the injustice which seemed to have been done Japan in collecting the money, it was decided that the United States had no claim to it and could not stipulate its use. On receiving the money, the Japanese government decided to make some long needed improvements to the harbor of Yokohama in order to facilitate foreign trade.

None of the other recipients of the Shimonoseki money restored the funds to Japan. Sir Harry Parkes, the British minister who had sponsored the punitive expedition, expressed his contempt of the American concern for returning the money. Parkes was also the chief opponent of treaty revision in the 1880's, when a series of efforts were made by the Japanese government. Some Japanese also opposed revision in view of the price which would likely have to be paid for the concessions from the western nations. As Viscount Tateki Tani, Minister of Commerce and Agriculture, stated the case in 1887, it would be better for Japan to "wait for the time of confusion in Europe" when Japan's rapidly growing navy and army might hold the balance of power in the Far East. Then, by throwing its weight toward one side or the other, Japan could unburden itself of the treaty restrictions without supplication and additional concessions.

Recognition of Japan's growing power as well as the commercial importance of her good will finally led Britain in 1894 to negotiate a revised treaty, granting Japan limited tariff autonomy and ending the consular courts. The treaty was to go into effect by 1899. By that date Japan had demonstrated her rank as a naval and military power by a decisive defeat of China in 1895, an event which hastened the treaty revision process. Some Japanese noted with some touches of bitterness that an impressive array of force was the most effective way of securing concessions from the West as it had been in securing concessions from Japan. This lesson was not forgotten in subsequent Japanese diplomacy. Baron Kentaro Kaneko summarized this Japanese point of view for Americans in 1904:

> In the region of world diplomacy, where reason fails, there is but one course left. That course Japan was compelled and determined to follow by devoting herself to the completion of her compulsory educational system, to the fostering of her industry, and to the reorganization of her army and navy by modern scientific methods. At last came the event [The Sino-Japanese War] in consequence of which Japan was no longer compelled to beg for a revision of the extra-territorial treaty, but could force upon the Western nations a recognition of her competence to abolish that treaty.

Chapter V

ARMING WITH AMERICAN AID

MANY JAPANESE leaders drew one major lesson from their experience with the West. To end the bombardments, the payment of indemnities, and the chain of concessions, they must build their own counter-power. To equal or surpass the might of the foreigner they must adopt western technology. Only when Japan could meet the westerners on their own terms would Japan once more be the master of its own house. To the men of the Meiji Restoration this meant not only adopting the weapons of the West, but a major reorganization and westernization of Japan's political and economic life. This task had to be accomplished quickly if Japan was not to collapse under the combined pressures of the western trader and diplomat, of the missionary and merchant. "They had to build with sword in one hand and trowel in the other," wrote E. H. Norman in his description of the almost miraculous feats accomplished by the Meiji pioneers.

Since the threat to national integrity came from across the seas, it was naval power which had priority in building Japan's defense. For some 200 years prior to Perry's arrival the Japanese had been forbidden to venture on the high seas. Ships were limited to one mast and to a size which made ocean navigation hazardous. But the nautical skills were not lost;

coastal shipping continued throughout the period of isolation. Japanese fisherman were able mariners and the ancient naval tradition was quickly revived.

A few farsighted feudal lords and their advisers had seen the need for a Japanese navy even before the arrival of Perry. When in 1850 Dutch traders brought news of expeditions preparing to end Japan's exclusion, the Lord of Satsuma petitioned the Shogun for permission to construct a warship. But fear of a hostile invasion did not shake the ancient ban and the request was denied. Only after Perry's visit in 1853 was the ban lifted.

The Shogunate turned first to the Dutch for help in building a modern navy. With no knowledge of costs, the Japanese talked at first of the purchase of 50 or 60 warships in Europe. When the Dutch pointed out the vast amount of money required, the order was scaled down to two ships. The outbreak of the Crimean War in 1854, making naval vessels a commodity in great demand, made it impossible for the Netherlands to act on even this small commission. To retain Japan's favor, the Dutch sent one of their own paddle-wheel steamers, the *Soembing,* to train some Japanese naval officers in steam operation. In 1855 it was decided to present this ship to the Shogun as a gift. Armed with six guns and renamed the *Kanko,* the Dutch ship became the first vessel in the new Japanese Navy.

Other western nations were quick to follow the Dutch in helping Japan build a naval force. The Japanese, in turn, showed remarkable aptitude in quickly learning how to operate these instruments of power. The British minister, Sir Rutherford Alcock, recorded his fears in 1863 that Japan's aspiration for naval power boded ill for the West, but Alcock's was a unique warning voice. Westerners knew that the effectiveness of their diplomacy was due to Japan's weakness, but at the same time they competed in their eagerness to contribute to the new might.

The Russians, who in 1904–1905 were to see their naval forces smashed by Japan, were a half century earlier supplying their future enemy with naval ordnance. A Russian frigate, the *Diana*, was wrecked on the Japanese coast, but her batteries were salvaged and the 56 cannon presented to the Shogun by the Russian commander in 1856. Japanese carpenters were employed under Russian direction to build ships to return the shipwrecked crew to their homeland. When the job was finished, the workmen began to build the same type ships for Japan.

The British were also influential in making contributions to Japan's power. At the suggestion of Rear Admiral James Stirling, £10,000 was voted by Parliament for a ship to be given Japan. The presentation of a four-gun steamer was made in 1857 in the name of Queen Victoria, and the new vessel was commissioned as the *Hanriu*. In the same year the two steamers purchased from the Dutch arrived, creating a squadron of four steamers. The naval training school, opened in 1855 with Dutch instructors, supplied many of the officers.

Americans who commented on these naval developments viewed them favorably. The first contributions to Japan's rearmament had been the variety of weapons presented to the Emperor by Commodore Perry. The American commander had demurred when the treaty commissioners asked that he give each of them a launch equipped with a brass howitzer, but only because he considered the boats and guns as essential to his squadron. He finally made a gift of one launch and howitzer from the *Saratoga* and recommended to the Navy Department that they send out two more. These gifts, Perry wrote, would be "returned a hundred-fold" on some future occasion. A young Japanese officer had asked members of the Perry expedition for the "recipe for percussion caps." The editors of an influential journal, *The North American Review*, urged officials to meet all such requests, since they saw no reason for the United States ever going to war with Japan while the Japanese needed western arms to protect themselves against European imperialism.

American anti-imperialist sentiments and the fear that Japan, like China, would be exploited by the European nations to the disadvantage of American commercial interests provided the major justification for aid to Japan. Yankee pride was also flattered when Americans rather than Europeans were chosen to play the role of teachers in bringing skills. And for many Americans the opportunity to work in Japan was a lucrative venture in an exotic land which has ever exercised its fascination for westerners.

The dispatch of an embassy across the Pacific to San Francisco and Washington in 1860 was an opportunity to help the young Japanese Navy. An American naval vessel was delegated to carry the members of the embassy, but Japan decided to send one of its own ships, the Dutch-built *Kanrin Maru,* across the Pacific as an escort. This was to be the first long training cruise for the men who only six years before were barred from travelling the high seas. Japanese navigators had as their guide Nathaniel Bowditch's *Practical Navigator,* the American classic which Nakahama Manjiro had introduced into Japan before Perry's arrival. For this pioneering voyage, however, the Japanese government requested some American aid. An American lieutenant, John M. Brooke, stranded in Japan by the loss of his own ship, was assigned to the *Kanrin Maru* along with an American engineer, a surgeon, and four or five sailors who were to instruct the Japanese seamen. With this help a stormy voyage to San Francisco was accomplished without serious difficulties. Brooke and his fellows received official commendation from the Japanese government, the first Americans to serve under the Japanese flag. Brooke later made more history during the American Civil War by joining the Confederate government as Chief of the Bureau of Ordnance and preparing plans for the redesign of the *Merrimac* as a pioneering ironclad.

Members of the Japanese embassy gathered a great deal of information in the United States for use in their naval establishment. They studied the operations of the Navy Yard and the casting of cannon in Washington. They made careful sketches and recorded the operational procedures of all the American ships which furnished them transportation. In Washington they presented their hosts with a beautiful rifle, constructed by Japanese craftsmen in the pattern of the Sharpe rifles brought by Perry, but now improved by Japanese invention which made it possible to cock, prime, and cut the cartridge in one operation. To Japan went gifts from the War and Navy Departments; a hundred muskets, four howitzers, shells, and machines for filling shells and making bullets. American officers were sent to teach the Japanese the uses of these gifts, but the skills were quickly learned and their services dispensed with. According to Townsend Harris, the Shogunate thought it unwise to employ foreigners who might learn too much about the weak state of Japan's defenses.

American ships were purchased to join those of Dutch and British construction under Japan's flag. The 1858 treaty with the United States provided for the right of purchase of warships, munitions, and arms of all kinds as well as for the engagement of American military and naval experts. In 1861 a Connecticut entrepreneur, Captain Elbert Stannard, sold his merchant ship and cargo to the Lord of Chōshu to be converted into a warship. But it was the fate of this vessel, the *Daniel Webster*, to be sunk in 1863 by another American vessel, the *Wyoming*, during Commander McDougal's reprisal raid for the Japanese effort to close the Strait of Shimonoseki to the *Pembroke*. In 1862 the Shogunate requested the American minister, Robert Pruyn, to act as purchasing agent to procure three steam warships, a field battery, and a quantity of small arms and naval equipment. Pruyn placed the orders with friends in the United States, earning himself the wrath of a number of congressmen. The Secretary of War barred the arms sale as interfering with the Union war effort, but the Secretary of Navy approved the sale of three ships to Japan for a total of $860,000.

The first ship to be constructed was the *Fujiyama,* a steam corvette with twice the power of any ship then under Japanese command. The ship was finished in December 1864, but President Lincoln stopped delivery when news reached Washington of the Chōshu attack on the *Pembroke.* The American Minister cabled from Tokyo to ask the immediate release of the *Fujiyama.* Pruyn reported that the British were doing a lively and lucrative business in ships and arms, but Washington refused to lift the restraining order. It was not until after Lincoln's death that the *Fujiyama* was released in June of 1865 and delivered to the Shogun in January of 1866.

The Japanese still had a large credit, having paid Pruyn an advance of $600,000, and he suggested that they use the money to purchase captured Confederate ships rather than await new construction. The battle between the *Monitor* and the *Merrimac* had dramatized the role of ironclads and it was not to Japan's interest to purchase additional wooden vessels. So a purchasing mission was sent to Washington in 1867. After being presented to President Johnson and given a state dinner by Secretary of State William Seward, they were escorted to the Navy Yard where their eyes fell upon the *Stonewall.* An ironclad ram built in France for the Confederacy, this ship reached American waters only after the Union victory and was taken over by the federal government. One hundred and seventy-two feet in length compared to the *Fujiyama's* 180 feet, the *Stonewall* had a 500 horsepower engine of the latest design. The Japanese bought the ship for $400,000 and asked the American captain who pointed it out to them to take it to Japan. With the remaining money in their account they purchased naval ordnance and equipment for their expanding squadron.

When the *Stonewall* reached Tokyo in April of 1868, the civil conflict between the forces of the Shogunate and the

Emperor was at a crucial stage. Remaining neutral, the American commander refused to deliver the ship to the government of the Shogun, an act which in effect favored the forces of the Emperor. The Shogun's forces were finally badly defeated on land, but led by a daring naval officer, Kamajiro Enomoto, a group of officers stole a major part of the Japanese fleet under cover of night and sailed northward. On the island of Hokkaido they captured and established their base at one of the early treaty ports, Hakodate. With the American-built *Fujiyama* in the possession of the enemy, the Imperial forces badly needed the *Stonewall* to put an end to the rebellion. After receiving many protests over the delay, the new American minister, General Robert B. Van Valkenburgh, delivered the *Stonewall* in January of 1869. As the *Azuma* the ship was commissioned and inspected personally by the Emperor, the first time Japan's sacred ruler had set foot on shipboard.

The *Azuma* led the Imperial forces northward to crush the last forces of the Shogunate. While anchored in a harbor en route, the pride of the Imperial forces was suddenly attacked by Admiral Enomoto who tried to sink the new vessel by ramming, only to find her construction so stout that the ramming vessel was more damaged than the *Azuma*. On reaching Hakodate the enemy ships were destroyed, and the land fortifications leveled by the guns of the *Azuma*. The last rebels surrendered and the Meiji regime triumphed, with the former Confederate vessel a significant factor in the victory.

The new government looked at its young navy with some sense of security and pride. Before the year of victory was over Secretary of State Hamilton Fish was warned by the American Minister that such was the growth of confidence that the Japanese "perhaps entertained the conceit that they were strong enough to defy our government." The Japanese Navy, reported Charles E. DeLong, the fourth American minister, "has been rapidly increased into quite a large and serviceable one, while our own is in fact unrepresented here with anything that could for a moment live in a conflict with such a vessel as the *Stone-wall*. . . ." Minister DeLong's fears were premature by many decades, but it was obvious that the days when Japan could be easily coerced by a foreign naval demonstration were over. Japan's neighbors, China and Korea, began to look upon the island kingdom with respect and even fear when their relations with the Meiji government were strained in the 1870's. A Britisher employed as a spy by Japan reported in 1874 that the possession of the former *Stonewall* alone made the Japanese a formidable opponent in the eyes of the Chinese. He claimed that Chinese sailors had deserted rather than face possible battle with the ironclad, since the Chinese government was unwilling to send its navy to sea while the *Azuma* cruised the coast.

The sale of the *Stonewall* was the last direct contribution by the United States to the Japanese fleet for some years. In 1875 the first modern warship was built in national shipyards, and from that date increased emphasis was placed on meeting the Navy's needs with Japan's own skills. Britain was the chief source of foreign-built ships. When in 1893 the Japanese Imperial Navy reported 28 ships in commission, ten were listed as having been built in British shipyards, while 10 were of Japanese construction.

The United States did play a leading role in Japan's develop-ment of a submarine fleet. When the John Holland submarine was demonstrated for the American Navy in 1900, a Japanese officer was among the observers. Although the United States government was reluctant to invest in the new underseas craft, Japan ordered five submarines for their own forces. Pre-fabricated in Massachusetts, these vessels were shipped to Japan and reassembled there by American workmen. Com-pleted and tested in the summer of 1905, the boats went to sea on a long cruise without a mishap and without a single Ameri-can on board, again demonstrating Japan's remarkable ability at quick assimilation of western technical skills. Within a year the Japanese Navy had built two submarines of its own and was on its way to the formation of an undersea fleet.

The United States was selected by Japan as the center in which to train its naval officers in the techniques and traditions of foreign navies. But when the request was made in 1861 the Naval Academy at Annapolis was closed by the exigencies of the Civil War and Japanese students were sent to Holland instead. At the end of the war the request was renewed. Congress by joint resolution in 1868 authorized the admission of Japanese students to the Naval Academy at no expense to the United States. The first student, Jenno Matsumura, arrived the next year to face the hurdles of the English language and a formidable academic program. Two more students arrived the following year, 1870. The three first entrants found that their English was inadequate to complete the program, and the sending of students was suspended for several years while provisions were made in Japan to see that applicants received a more intensive language training.

The first Japanese ensigns to graduate from Annapolis were two members of the class of 1877. Although there were more than a dozen enrollments, only six survived the difficulties of adjustment to the life of an American midshipman to graduate. The outstanding Naval Academy contribution to the Imperial Navy was Sotokichi Uriu of the class of 1881, who rose to the rank of rear-admiral and whose brilliant performance in the Russo-Japanese War was surpassed only by the British-trained Admiral Heihachiro Togo. Uriu studied in New Haven for two years before entering the Academy and while in Connecticut became a Christian. After the Russo-Japanese War he was made a baron and later became a member of the House of Peers.

By 1906 American fears of Japan reached a point at which Congress became concerned with espionage and closed the Naval Academy to Japanese and other foreigners. But to help counter the ill-feeling which this action created, Admiral Uriu was feted officially when he came to the United States in 1909 to attend his class reunion. In Washington the Admiral and his wife, a Vassar graduate who came to the United States at the age of nine, were given a dinner attended by President Taft. At the conclusion of the Admiral's speech, Taft's geniality burst forth and he shouted, "Banzai!" and offered a toast to the Emperor of Japan.

The Naval Academy also made a contribution to Japan's forces through its American graduates who served Japan in a number of capacities. The outstanding member was Henry Walton Grinnell, a New Yorker who attended City College as well as the Naval Academy and had a distinguished record in the Civil War. When he was discharged in 1868, Grinnell took a commission as a captain in the Imperial Japanese Navy and was soon raised to the rank of rear admiral for his services as director of the new naval school at Hiogo, where many of Japan's officers were trained. For more than two decades Grinnell served Japan before concluding his career by again serving in the American Navy during the Spanish-American War.

Although Japan concentrated on the Navy, there was no neglect of the land forces which had long been restricted to ancient weapons and organization. A Nagasaki youth, Shunhan Takashima, had appealed to the government in the 1830's to modernize the national defenses in order to maintain exclusion. When he failed to secure action, he used his own funds to buy guns and military books from the Dutch. He gathered a number of pupils who wanted to learn western military science and by 1840 had trained small infantry and artillery companies in western methods.

In 1842 Takashima was arrested and jailed for casting a cannon with the help of western specifications. After Perry's initial visit, the Shogun released Takashima and he was ordered to aid in the construction of harbor fortifications. By 1855 concern for the production of modern weapons reached a point at which the government ordered the bells of Buddhist monasteries melted and cast into cannon and muskets. Religious opposition forced the abandonment of this emergency measure to collect metals, but the drive for arms manufacture continued. In 1868 an arsenal was established in Tokyo and by 1880 Japan was able to supply most of its infantry with muskets manufactured in its own factories.

The American military experience in the Civil War drew the attention of Japanese; students and official missions carefully collected data on American weapons and tactics. One of the teachers of the first two Japanese college students in the United States, enrolled at Rutgers in 1866, recalls that they told him they had come to learn "how to make big cannon so as not to be conquered by Russia." Appeals were made for the admission of Japanese cadets to the Military Academy at West Point, and a bill authorizing the admission of the first six students was reported out by the Senate Foreign Relations Committee in 1872. In the debate which followed, a number of Senators spoke of the commercial and other advantages which would come from training Japanese youth and indoctrinating them in American sentiments. It was pointed out that there were already more than 300 Japanese students in American schools and only 225 in all of Europe. From this educational relationship it was hoped would come a friendship which would insure Japan's trade for the United States rather than its rivals. Proponents of the bill submitted a letter from the superintendent of the Naval Academy at Annapolis, reporting on the fine character of the Japanese midshipmen in attendance and arguing that "the common cause of Christian civilization" was advanced by the admission of Japanese students to military schools.

The opposition to admitting Japanese cadets was led by Senator Eugene Casserly of California, an Irish immigrant who had graduated from Georgetown College in Washington, a lawyer and a journalist. The Senator favored the opening of American schools to the Japanese, but he drew the line at the military academies with a burst of oratory:

You may impart all other art of your civilization to a foreign Power without injury to yourself; but not your art of war. . . . You may sell to other nations even your arms of precision, your engines of war . . . but you cannot admit any foreign Power into the partnership of the military training of your youth . . . without loss of that power and prestige which are necessary to the maintenance of this country as a great nation upon the earth.

Even though the Californian criticized the *Pembroke* affair and the naval conflict at the Strait of Shimonoseki as examples of the danger of strengthening Japan, the measure was approved.

In the House the Foreign Affairs Committee reported the Senate measure with approval, but opposition developed on the floor. Congressman Pierce Manning Young of Georgia, a West Pointer who had resigned two months before graduation to enter the Confederate Army, made a strong argument that the admission of yellow-skinned cadets was a threat to national security. The bill was tabled by a vote of 78 to 55. Although the measure was again introduced, authorization was never given for Japanese cadets. Some 30 years later, in 1905, Congress opened the Academy to another oriental people, the Chinese, with many supporters of the measure hoping to strengthen China against Japan. Japan had in the meantime turned to other nations, particularly the French for technical advice in modernizing the army. When in the Franco-Prussian War of 1870–1871 the French forces were badly defeated, Japan replaced French advisers with Germans.

The rapid change in Japan's power status was reflected almost immediately in foreign policy and diplomacy. The first end of foreign policy was the restoration of full sovereignty and the termination of the special privileges granted in the years of greatest weakness. While the Iwakura mission went abroad in 1872 to seek a revision of the unequal treaties, a new foreign minister, Taneomi Soeshima, began work at home. Taking advantage of the absence on home leave of the im-

perious British minister, Harry Parkes, Soeshima refused to
confer with any diplomat who insisted on the Japanese stand-
ing while the westerner sat and talked. The Japanese Foreign
Office also began to insist on treatment in all areas in accordance with the standard diplomatic practices of the western
world. International law was studied and western diplomats
began to find their own authorities quoted to them in disputes.
The acquiescence of the ignorant and weak was over.

In informing the Japanese of their legal rights and normal
diplomatic procedures, American advisers played the major
role. Soeshima studied under Guido Verbeck, a man who called
himself an "Americanized Dutchman" and who had studied
engineering and theology in the United States before coming
to Japan in 1859 as a missionary. Verbeck was soon called upon
to teach English in a government college where he used the
United States Constitution as well as the New Testament for
his texts. Many Japanese leaders learned about western law
from Verbeck, and it was he who proposed and helped the
government plan the Iwakura mission in 1872 to secure equal
legal treatment. The college grew in size and by 1871 Verbeck
had over a thousand students. He sent the first Japanese to
study in an American college, Rutgers, in 1866, and in 1870
imported from Rutgers William E. Griffis to teach the physical
sciences at the new Imperial University at Tokyo. Griffis also
had a distinguished career in Japan and became the first American scholar to write extensively in the field of Japanese-American relations. Verbeck became an unofficial attaché to the
Japanese Cabinet and served Japan until 1898.

The Japanese Foreign Office was quick to see the value of
more American specialists in law and diplomacy and applied
to the Department of State for help. Erasmus Peshine Smith,
an examiner of claims for the State Department, was appointed
in 1871 as the first official foreign adviser to the Foreign Office.
Smith had graduated from Columbia College and the Harvard
Law School and had written a textbook on political economy.

He brought to the Japanese a sophisticated approach to international relations and technical knowledge in drafting treaties.
Smith's work was soon supplemented by the appointment of Eli
T. Sheppard, a former American consul in China and a specialist in international law. Sheppard became the opponent of
Britain's Harry Parkes who fought Japan's efforts to attain full
sovereignty, even defying the quarantine laws. One of Sheppard's drafts given to Parkes by the Japanese Foreign Office
stated that the British Minister's claims "tend only to
strengthen the unpleasant conviction that you assume the right
to control the law-making power of this Empire." Smith and
Sheppard were followed in 1880 by the appointment of Henry
W. Denison as Legal Adviser to the Foreign Office. A Vermont
lawyer who served in the United States consulate in Yokohama,
Denison held his post with the Japanese until his death in 1914.
He received high honors for his work in the Sino-Japanese War
of 1894–1895, for his part in the negotiation of the Anglo-
Japanese Treaty of 1902 and the Treaty of Portsmouth in 1905,
and for his role in representing Japan at The Hague Court.

Engineers and agricultural experts, missionaries and edu-
cators poured into Japan from the United States in the last
three decades of the nineteenth century. Some met with resistance and failure, some were incompetents seeking only the
high financial rewards offered by the Japanese government.
Critics of the Grant administration charged that often the men
recommended and sent to Japan by the United States government were chosen for their political loyalties rather than their
abilities. But there were also competent and dedicated individuals who left a permanent mark on the character of Japan's
westernization. Many of their contributions had little to do
with military or naval power and they brought to Japan many
things besides guns and the arts of war. McIntosh apples, Con-
cord grapes, and baseball were all imported to take root in
Japan's soil at the same time that the Japanese were acquiring
the instruments of western power. By 1905 a Japanese baseball

team, coached by a University of Chicago pitcher, made a successful tour of the United States. The Meiji Restoration had launched a new Japan on a broad scale, and in creating this new Japan Americans took a leading part.

Chapter VI

VENTURES IN IMPERIALISM

A S JAPAN STRUGGLED to build militarily and to free
itself from foreign encroachments, national consciousness
grew apace. Loyalty to the new government was stimulated on
all levels of society by the institutions introduced by the Meiji
Restoration. Conscription, introduced in 1873, a national education system, and improved communications and transportation knitted the provinces together. The Sun cult of Shintō
was raised to the level of a state religion and the central government, aided by a growing press, spread the symbols of national allegiance across the land. The youngest school boy in
the remotest province soon learned to raise his loyalties beyond his village and clan.

The elements for the creation of Japanese nationalism had
long existed. Long periods of isolation from other peoples, a
common language, a belief in ethnic unity and widespread
myths about the divine origin of the islands provided a base
upon which to build a vigorous society of patriots. Yet until
1868 Japan was so divided geographically into fiefs governed
almost as sovereign states by the heads of the hereditary clans
and so stratified socially that nationalism as known in the West
was almost non-existent.

Japanese nationalism was in large part the outgrowth of westernization. At the close of the eighteenth century and in the early nineteenth when the exploratory activities of Russia, England, and France created a threat of domination by foreign barbarians, national consciousness began to rise. Fear proved to be a unifying emotion, a fear marked by hostility toward intruders. But even by the middle of the nineteenth century these fears and their effects were still confined largely to the ruling classes, the clan leaders, and the samurai. The common people in their contacts with foreigners frequently displayed a friendly curiosity which contradicted the stereotyped view of a natural oriental antagonism toward westerners.

Nationalism in the western world has historically had many forms, perhaps even stages, ranging from relatively harmless glorification of the national culture to the extreme xenophobia which often combines with a sense of mission to produce a drive for the conquest and domination of neighboring lands. Japanese nationalism as it developed during the Meiji Restoration had many potentialities. Anti-foreign feelings declined in the early years of the new regime as the nation reached out to draw upon the intellectual resources of the West in many fields. Westernization for more than a decade became almost a cult. Some Japanese discarded their valuable prints and porcelains for mediocre western art and put aside their comfortable oriental clothes for western garb. But Japan's new leaders seem to have kept always in mind the end of westernization; the creation of the strength necessary to withstand the West and to achieve full sovereignty.

There were in Japan's history the elements with which to create the most disruptive aspect of western nationalism, the aggressive mood which pushes for expansion and the development of empire. There were ancient aspirations for land beyond the sea which were revived with the new national consciousness. Chauvinist writers began to urge that the growing strength of the nation be tested on foreign shores. Shōin Yoshida, a young Chōshu military teacher, was already preaching expansion at the time of Perry's arrival. He believed that expansion was the health of the state and called for a course of conquest which included not only Korea and Formosa, but the Philippines and Manchuria as well. Since western knowledge was essential to build a force capable of imperialist successes, Yoshida tried himself to reach the outer world by hiding aboard one of Perry's ships. The Americans refused to abet an evasion of Japanese law prohibiting foreign travel, and Yoshida and a companion were turned over to the authorities and jailed. But a decade later the writings of this pioneer expansionist began to appeal to a wide audience.

Japanese expansionism focused first on Formosa and Korea. The most dynamic and colorful of the many Americans to visit Japan, Charles LeGendre, gave the expansionists hearty support. Born in France, LeGendre migrated to the United States and made a distinguished record in the American Civil War, reaching the rank of Brigadier General and sacrificing an eye to the Union cause while serving under General Grant in the Battle of the Wilderness. A born adventurer, he sought an overseas post at the end of the war and was rewarded in 1866 with an appointment to the post of consul at Amoy, a treaty port on the South China coast opposite Formosa.

In March of 1867 the bark, *Rover,* out of New York, was wrecked on the Formosan coast and its captain, his wife, and crew murdered by primitive tribesmen. The news reached LeGendre who protested to the Chinese government. The ferocity of these aborigines was well known to the Chinese and, although they claimed a sovereignty over the island, they refused to send a punitive expedition. Commodore H. H. Bell in command of the China squadron then sent a force of almost 200 seamen and marines on the U.S.S. *Hartford* and *Wyoming* to capture the murderers. The expedition landed on the Formosan coast in June of 1867, but when they pushed into aboriginal territory they were ambushed and forced to retreat after losing one of their commanders.

LeGendre, whose jurisdiction extended to Formosa, took the rebuff of the naval expedition as an opportunity to act on his own. With the co-operation of the Chinese authorities he secured a military force and sailed for Formosa in a Chinese gunboat flying the Stars and Stripes. Some friendly tribes were enlisted to join the Chinese ranks and to march into the territory held by the guilty natives. Their leaders were impressed by the size of the invading force and agreed to meet with LeGendre on a peaceful basis. The murders were defended as reprisals for the many injustices done the tribesmen by white men, but promises were made that in the future protection would be given to all castaways. With this assurance and after collecting the effects of the dead seamen, LeGendre returned to Amoy.

LeGendre's feat brought him a commendation from the British government and stirred his interest in Formosa. He visited the island again in 1868 and 1869 to collect materials on the history and culture of the primitive peoples who inhabited the interior. China's failure to deal with this area also led him to write a pamphlet in 1869, *Is Aboriginal Formosa a Part of the Chinese Empire?* But the consulship was too small a post for the ambitious military man, and in 1872 he received an appointment from President Grant as Minister to Argentina. Then the chairman of the Senate Foreign Relations Committee refused to recommend a confirmation of the appointment because of LeGendre's French birth.

Disappointed, LeGendre decided to return to Washington on leave. After first re-visiting Formosa, he reached Japan en route home in October of 1872. It was an appropriate time since the Japanese government was at this moment discussing sending its own expedition to Formosa. A number of shipwrecked sailors from the Ryukyu Islands had been killed in Formosa and some

Japanese officials not only wanted to demonstrate their protectorate over the Ryukyu peoples but also to test China's claims to Formosa. The American Minister to Japan, Charles DeLong, introduced LeGendre to Foreign Minister Taneomi Soeshima, as a man who knew something of Formosa. The Japanese were impressed by the swaggering and energetic general and particularly by the fact that he had not only maps and charts of Formosa, but an intimate knowledge of the aborigines. After some negotiations in which the American minister gave his support, LeGendre was hired by the Foreign Office as an officer of second rank with a salary equal to that of the American minister, $12,000 yearly. He resigned his post as consul with a promise of a general's commission in the Japanese Army if the Formosan venture led to war with China.

In a pamphlet published in 1871, *How to Deal with China,* Japan's new foreign adviser had hoped to provide western nations with a guide. He was a believer in the efficacy of force in achieving diplomatic goals: "I hold that *lex talionis* adapts better than any other to an Eastern race." In his new position LeGendre was given the responsibility of guiding the Japanese government in dealing with China and sent to Peking as adviser to the Japanese Foreign Minister. The ostensible purpose of the mission was to exchange treaty ratifications, but Japan was also determined to secure a clarification from China as to its claims to Formosa and Korea. A secondary issue was the question of securing an audience with the Chinese Emperor, a privilege denied to all treaty powers. LeGendre had recommended in his pamphlet that the western powers insist on this Chinese concession. His career as an American diplomat blocked by the Senate, the proud and ambitious general was determined to prove his brilliance in the service of Japan.

When the embassy left Japan in March of 1873, its strategy was well worked out. The Chinese must be impressed with the fact that they were no longer dealing with the old Japan, content to accept a secondary place in the shadow of the Celestial Kingdom. They must be shown the new, westernized Japan, capable and ready to use western techniques to back its diplomacy. Two warships, one of them the former *Stonewall*, accompanied LeGendre and Foreign Minister Soeshima, to implement Japan's first venture in gunboat diplomacy.

Anxious to check the quest for an audience at Peking, the Chinese met the mission at Shanghai to present the treaty ratifications. The first surprise came when the embassy rejected the oriental residence provided them and instead rented a western-style house which they furnished with western-style furniture. When the Chinese viceroy, Li Hung-chang, visited the mission, he complained not only of the presence of a western adviser, hitherto unnecessary in the dealings of Asians with Asians, but also he spoke with contempt of the other forms of westernization. To LeGendre he said, "This house is well calculated to answer *your* purpose, but I cannot see how it can be comfortable for a *Japanese* ambassador." Soeshima was quick to point out that some of the fine lacquered chairs made in western style had come from his own home. And when the viceroy complained of the ugliness of the western clothes the Japanese Foreign Minister, as LeGendre recalled, made the perfect pointed reply:

> If, Your Excellency, the dress of foreigners is not beautiful, it is quite useful, especially on board our men of war which are also of foreign style. With our ancient costume our men could not have thought of working in the rigging or at the guns. But since we have changed our dress, we get along very well, so well, in fact, that in the ironclad and corvette which we brought with us to China there is not a single foreigner.

The Chinese had a glimpse of the New Japan in this statement and put no barrier in the way of the embassy's visit to Peking. But when the question of the audience was raised, they used the same delaying tactics which the Japanese had attempted to use in dealing with the West. Foreign Minister Soeshima replied by threatening to leave Peking and hinting at the dire consequences which would follow. The audience was then granted to Japan as well as to the representatives of the western powers who were also threatening. The Japanese minister further broke Chinese tradition by wearing his sword in the presence of the Emperor and refusing to kneel in homage. LeGendre wrote triumphantly to friends in Washington of the success of the embassy and claimed credit for the Perry-like firmness which he had urged on Soeshima.

The Japanese mission returned home from Peking, claiming to have received verbal approval for the dispatch of a punitive expedition to Formosa in behalf of the murdered Ryukyu islanders. LeGendre was transferred to the Department of Colonization which was to operate the expedition and he took a leading part in its organization. A number of other adventurous Americans were recruited as military and naval assistants. Lieutenant Commander Douglas Cassel secured a year's detachment from the U.S.S. *Ashelot* to join the Japanese Navy and Major James R. Wasson, a West Point graduate who had resigned from service, was recruited to act as the expedition's military engineer. All three Americans were honored by an audience with the Emperor. The steamship *New York* was chartered from the Pacific Mail Steamship Company to transport the expedition, and LeGendre hired a former British naval officer to keep Japan informed of China's reaction to this military venture.

Before the Formosan expedition sailed, the Chinese government rejected Japan's claim to having Chinese approval for their punitive measures. Any Japanese military action in Formosa, said the Chinese, would be an act of war against China. Since LeGendre was viewed by the Chinese as being the evil genius behind Japan's plans, an effort was made to buy him off. He was offered a post in the Chinese customs service for ten years at the generous salary of $20,000 yearly. LeGendre refused the offer and the Chinese then appealed to American officials in China.

This approach was effective. When LeGendre visited Amoy in connection with preparations for the expedition, he was arrested and held at the orders of the American Consul-General for China, George Seward. Since diplomatic status with associated immunities had been given to LeGendre, a Japanese naval commander in Amoy offered to land marines and free him. The offer was rejected and the former consul was taken to Shanghai, charged with having violated American neutrality laws. The indictment was so weak, however, that it was dropped when LeGendre landed and he was freed. Seward's action had the support of some other members of the American diplomatic service in China and in particular Perry's translator, S. Wells Williams, but it was without the approval of Washington. When the news of Seward's action reached the Secretary of State, he reprimanded him for his zeal in behalf of China and pointed out that neutrality laws could not be violated before a state of belligerency existed. Americans, said Hamilton Fish, were as free to hold military posts under Japan as those who then held posts in the service of China.

Seward's action, taken with the interests of China as one of its ends, illustrated a point of view which was to be held by many Americans in the following decades. Other Americans held equally strongly to a contradictory viewpoint. Should American policy in Asia play favorites and support China against Japan or was it to be a policy of no favorites? Or did American national interests call for a policy friendlier to Japan than China? Affirmative views on all three questions were held by influential State Department officials and segments of American opinion down to the 1930's, often producing a vacillating and indecisive policy.

In Tokyo the new American Minister, John A. Bingham, was also converted to action in defense of China. He succeeded in forcing the cancellation of the charter of the American steamship, but the Americans in the service of Japan refused his requests to resign. Without LeGendre, but with his plans and advice, the expedition sailed under a Japanese commander. In Formosa the friendly tribal leaders known to LeGendre were used to recruit native fighting men to supplement the Japanese forces. War was then waged on the barbaric Botan tribe guilty of the massacre.

One of the Americans who accompanied the expedition was a newspaperman and close friend of LeGendre, E. H. House, whose dispatches were carried in the *New York Herald*. House reported that despite the vaunted samurai tradition the new Japanese Army was an undisciplined and unskilled fighting force. They were unprepared for jungle fighting and the casualties inflicted by surprise attacks, by heat, and disease were high. But at the cost of over 500 lives Japan was victorious and the offending Botan tribesmen were beaten.

While the fighting was in progress, LeGendre was sent to Peking as a special commissioner along with the Japanese Home Minister to reopen the negotiations over Formosa. The Chinese insisted on their ownership of the island and the Japanese insisted on compensation for the lives of the murdered Okinawans as well as payment for the costs of the punitive expedition. LeGendre was urging war if the Chinese refused to meet the Japanese position. But even S. Wells Williams, while denouncing LeGendre as "an evil counselor," urged the Chinese to make concessions.

After some delay, China agreed to the financial claims and when the final payments were made in December of 1874 the Japanese forces left Formosa. The two chief military advisers, Cassel and Wasson, were highly commended for their services by the Japanese commander and rewarded with a bonus at the termination of their contract. When Cassel died in Pennsylvania a year later from a tropical disease contracted in Formosa, the Japanese government sent an additional payment to his heirs.

The significance of Japan's first military adventure overseas was not lost on some western observers. Consul-General Seward in Shanghai wrote Washington that Japan "has been to all appearance the winner. This has happened because she has been the bolder and more active." For some Americans in the Far East the Japanese victory was a tribute and gain for the West. As one Shanghai merchant wrote LeGendre when the conflict was in progress, "If Japan cuts the Chinese Gordian knot, she will have paid the debt of gratitude which she owes to Western Nations for having started her on the path of progress and reform." But the British Ambassador to Japan, Harry Parkes, complained that the Japanese had been "led away by their own conceit and by advice which filled in exactly with that conceit which has been chiefly supplied by that man named LeGendre!" The British-owned *Japan Daily Herald* took the same scolding position and warned the Japanese that while China submitted to Russian encroachments on her western frontiers, "she is scarcely likely to tolerate it from such a petty and feeble power as Japan."

LeGendre resigned from Japanese service in July of 1875 and became the first foreigner to be decorated with the Order of the Rising Sun. Before he resigned he spent two months preparing a lengthy memorandum to guide Japan's future relations with Formosa. During his two years service he also urged other projects upon his employers. One was the sale of Japanese claims to the northern island of Sakhalin to Russia in order to strengthen Japan's international position. In 20 or 30 years, the General argued, Japan could handle Russia, but at present the conflict over Sakhalin weakened the ties with the Tsar. Russian friendship was essential, LeGendre believed, to counter British power in Asia. In the long run, Britain would remain Japan's greatest enemy, not only because Japan would become a rival maritime power, but because in time he predicted that Japan would compete with Britain for the markets of Asia.

Much of Japanese territory was thinly populated and Le-Gendre turned his attention to the colonization of the thinly-settled island of Hokkaido for economic and strategic purposes. In an early memorandum he urged the importation of Chinese as colonists, but later he withdrew this suggestion on the grounds that Chinese made good colonists but poor soldiers. He finally concluded that Japan must import Mormons from the United States where this group was having difficulties over their practice of multiple marriages. By giving approval to polygamy, LeGendre believed that Japan could draw thousands of Mormons who would multiply rapidly to provide good farmers and soldiers for their adopted nation. Hokkaido was subsequently developed with the help of American agricultural advisers, but LeGendre's suggestion in regard to the Mormons was never implemented.

Korea was another area which attracted LeGendre's attention, as he recognized its strategic importance for Japan. In the centuries before Japan turned to self-containment, Korea had played a role in relation to the island kingdom in some respects similar to that of the Low Countries for England. Control of Korea by a strong mainland power was like a loaded pistol, pointed at the heart of Japan, said Japanese nationalists. In 1874 LeGendre urged the dispatch of an expeditionary force to the Korean capital, utilizing the prestige which Japan had gained from its successes at Peking and Formosa, and forestalling any Russian venture. A year earlier military elements had almost succeeded in winning government approval for such an operation, but the peace forces won out. The American general's proposal had, therefore, a sympathetic reception in some circles.

Like pre-Perry Japan, Korea refused to trade with the western world and resisted foreign intrusions. An American trading ship, the *General Sherman,* had disregarded warnings in 1866 and pushed into the interior by means of one of the North Korean rivers. When the ship became stranded on a sandbar, a conflict began with the local Koreans which resulted in the killing of the crew and the burning of the ship. French ships had suffered a similar fate, and the rumor reached Washington that France was contemplating an expedition to occupy Korea. To block exclusive French control, Secretary of State William Seward suggested a joint punitive operation. France decided against such a venture at the moment and American efforts were limited to attempts at securing further information as to the fate of the *General Sherman.*

The Grant administration decided to reconsider the Korean situation in 1871 and to send a joint diplomatic-naval mission to seek treaty guarantees for the protection of American seamen and to open trade. The American Minister to China, Frederick P. Low, and a naval squadron of five ships under the command of Admiral John Rodgers set out from Nagasaki to repeat Perry's feat. While engaged in surveying the Han River before moving up to Seoul, the expedition was "treacherously attacked," President Grant told Congress. The Americans returned the fire and succeeded in silencing the Korean forts. When no apology came for the attack after waiting ten days, Rodgers landed his forces to storm the fortifications. At the cost of three American lives the forts were destroyed and several hundred Koreans killed. But it was still a considerable distance to the Korean capital, and with neither the authorization nor an adequate force, only 1,200 men for such a large scale military operation, the American commander withdrew.

"Our little war with the heathen," as the *New York Herald* called it, ended without producing the desired results. President Grant's message spoke of American action "having thus punished the criminals and having vindicated the honor of the flag," but it was clearly an unsuccessful venture compared to the Perry mission 18 years earlier. "It now becomes the duty of all civilized and Christian governments to carefully consider what their rights are, and their duty to their citizens and subjects" in respect to Korea, Minister Low wrote the Secretary of State. But a major military-naval operation in Korea would have encountered strong political opposition in the American climate of the 1870's. "Probably nothing will be done at present. Our navy is too small to do much so far from home," a confidant of President Grant's wrote LeGendre in Japan.

Japan took up the challenge of a closed Korea a year after LeGendre completed his memorandum. Three missions to Seoul in 1868, 1869, and 1871 had failed to secure recognition from the Korean king. In 1875 a Japanese naval vessel was sent to the Korean coast and was fired upon when it attempted to land boats to secure water and provisions. The fire was returned and a landing party destroyed the fortifications from which the Koreans had attacked.

As in the case of the earlier American expedition, no apology was offered for the attack and the Japanese government decided to send a punitive force in reprisal. A force of two warships and three troop transports carrying 800 men was assembled early in 1876 under the command of Kiyotaka Kuroda, a capable national leader who had visited the United States in 1871 to recruit technical specialists.

Kuroda studied and carefully adapted Perry's tactics in his approach to Korea. He paraded his forces in the most imposing manner, even painting gun ports on his unarmed transports, and finally landing his troops with the maximum of bustle and pageantry, all officers in full dress uniform. The destruction inflicted by the American forces five years earlier led the Koreans to reconsider the utility of resistance and Kuroda's tactics succeeded. The Koreans were given the choice of paying Japan a large indemnity for their previous assault or of signing a commercial treaty. The treaty was accepted without Japan firing a shot. Little more than two decades after Perry's first visit, Japan was successful in "Perryizing" its neighbor Korea.

Japan's treaty with Korea was in western form, opening up three ports and granting Japan extraterritorial privileges. The

United States was the first to follow up Japan's success. Some State Department officials were convinced, as a result of Japan's facility in dealing with Peking and Seoul, that Japan held the key to successful diplomacy in Asia. The American commissioned with the task of establishing treaty relations with Korea, Commodore R. W. Shufeldt, was sent first to Japan in 1880 to enlist official help in his task. But although the Japanese urged the Koreans to deal directly with the Americans, their urgings produced no results.

The American efforts were next transferred to Peking with more success and through Chinese intervention a Korean-American treaty was signed in 1882. The Chinese government still claimed Korea as a vassal in the old Confucian hierarchy of relations. The United States was unwilling to recognize a relationship which had no parallel in western law, but accepted a letter from China along with the treaty claiming Korea as a dependency. Other western powers followed the United States. Britain and Germany made treaties with Korea in 1883, Italy and Russia in 1884, each dealing with the Korean monarch as an independent sovereign.

Korea was not the only territory which drew the interest of the growing numbers of Japanese nationalists and expansionists. In 1875 Japan affirmed its claim to the Bonin (Ogasawara) Islands, once claimed by both Perry and the British. Neither western power had supported its claim by action, and Japan by occupying, colonizing, and forbidding the residence of foreigners took complete control. By a treaty with Russia in 1875 the Japanese obtained undisputed possession of the Kurile Islands in return for recognition of Russian claims to southern Sakhalin. And in 1879 Japan formally declared its control of the Ryukyu Islands despite China's protest that the islands were still tributary vassals. The Chinese appealed to former President Grant to intervene in their behalf when he visited the Far East in 1879. The commission he suggested met and reached agreement on division of the area, but China never implemented its claim.

The new overseas responsibilities provided an additional argument for the expansion of Japan's naval and military forces. Naval expenditures more than tripled between 1870 and 1880. Total military expenditures which were still less than a quarter of the national budget in 1880 were over half of the total in 1890, jumping from approximately $9 to $24 million. Naval tonnage almost tripled in the same decade as Japanese-built ships supplemented those purchased from Britain.

Japanese commercial and political interests expanded in Korea in the years following treaty relations. The peninsula was a rice producer with growing potential as a supplier of food for Japan, while iron ore and other minerals offered additional potential value to an industrializing nation. But the introduction of Japanese capital and industry along with western ideas created in some Koreans the same adverse reactions they had produced a few decades earlier in Japan. In 1882 a political uprising was the occasion for anti-foreign elements to vent their resentments on the Japanese, storming and burning the Japanese legation at Seoul, while the Japanese officials fled and fought their way to the seacoast where they were rescued by a British ship.

The Japanese government followed the western pattern in dealing with oriental outbursts of mob violence. They sent their embassy back to the Korean capital, accompanied by some 700 soldiers and with demands for a large indemnity for the outrage. The Chinese government also sent a large military force, claiming still to control Korea's foreign relations. War was averted, but the two nations spent the next decade competing for the control, each supported by one faction of the Koreans.

War broke out in 1894 after Japan secured control of the Korean government and secured its authorization to expel the Chinese troops. By this date China had also made some efforts at modernizing its fighting forces with the help of foreign advisers, and by the purchase of British and German-made warships. An Annapolis graduate, Philo McGiffin, was second in command on a Chinese battleship when the historic battle of the Yalu River took place in September of 1894. But China had not responded as quickly and with thoroughness to westernization, and Japanese forces won smashing victories on sea and land. At the peace conference in 1895 the Chinese negotiators were assisted by John W. Foster, former American Secretary of State, while Henry W. Denison aided the Japanese. The victory was so clear cut that China was forced not only to recognize the independence of Korea, but to accept the demands of Japanese expansionism and cede the island of Formosa and the Liaotung peninsula of southern Manchuria to Japan.

Before the Japanese were able fully to savor the fruits of victory, they were forced to submit to one more act of intimidation by the West. The Russians, supported by France and Germany, were determined not to permit the Japanese to gain a foothold on the continent. Russia's Far Eastern Fleet was alerted and Japan was advised to return the Liaotung peninsula, including Port Arthur, to China. Faced with a new war aganst three strong western nations, Japan was left with no alternative but a humiliating submission. China paid an additional indemnity for Japan's retrocession, but Japan's bitterness was increased when in 1898 Russia intimidated the Chinese into leasing them the southern tip of the Liaotung Peninsula including Port Arthur.

Proponents of a bigger Japanese army and navy had no lack of winning arguments following Russia's action. But they welcomed fresh support from the United States in the form of the writings of Alfred Thayer Mahan. Preaching a doctrine which approved war and expansion as the mark of a healthy nation, Mahan also attacked contentment with the existing frontiers as a sign of national decay. A progressive nation must expand, and a large naval force was an essential factor in expansion. Mahan's first important volume, *The Influence of Sea Power upon History*, published in the United States in

1890, was soon translated into Japanese. By 1897 it had been adopted as a textbook in the Naval and Military College of Japan, and the Japanese government had placed copies in the libraries of all the high schools and normal schools. Mahan had also some popular appeal and several thousand copies were sold in the first two days his book was available. The philosophy of imperialism expressed more than a half century earlier by Shōin Yoshida was available again in a westernized form.

Growing power, diplomatic and military victories, and a spreading pride in the gains of the new, westernized Japan rapidly transformed a national consciousness into a vigorous nationalism. With this nationalism came a new anti-foreignism. By the end of the 1880's a "Japan for Japanese" sentiment had become apparent to western observers. The Japanese were still willing to adopt ideas and techniques from the western world, but at the same time anxious to free themselves from tutelage as rapidly as possible. Japanese students who had studied in the western world replaced foreign specialists in important posts.

Even such a friend of Japan as Charles LeGendre no longer found the atmosphere a sympathetic one. The General had remained in Japan for some years after resigning his position in 1875, and in 1878 had published a volume entitled *Progressive Japan*. In it he discussed Japan's destiny "to form the advanced post of a transformed superior civilization," and spoke glowingly of the island nation's future. From Japan LeGendre drifted to Korea where he was able to obtain high government posts. In 1891 he returned to Japan in the service of Korea in an effort to secure a favorable revision of trading regulations. But he found the Japanese unwilling to make concessions to the weaker nation. In a pique he wrote to a friend, "Japan has become perfectly hateful to me," only to reconsider and scrawl instead, "Japan has ceased to be what it used to be."

If the unpleasant side of Japanese nationalism was becom-

ing apparent to some foreign residents in the decades of the
eighties and nineties, it was slower in changing Washington's
official view of Japan. Reports reaching the State Department
from Tokyo still presented glowing pictures of Japan's economic, military, and political progress. Minister John Bingham, writing in 1880 of the reigning Mikado, said, "seldom,
if ever, in the history of civil administration, has any other
ruler done so much within so brief a period for the reformation
and well-being of a people. . . ." The State Department's instructions to Bingham's successor, Richard Hubbard, in 1885
said that the first principle of American policy was to see that
Japan achieved sovereign equality "in view of her steady
progress toward sound principles of self-government." On retiring from Tokyo after four years' duty, Hubbard assured
Washington in 1889 that he was convinced that Japan's progress "is not a short-lived or experimental thing, nor a thin
veneering of Western civilization . . . but rather a proof of a
solid and permanent triumph over the past of her history. . . ."

The treatment of Japan in the American press and periodicals echoed the admiring note of official evaluations. Japan's
foreign policy gave no cause for alarm nor criticism. Although
diplomatic and territorial gains were for the most part at the
expense of China, there was no large body of Sinophiles sway-
ing American opinion in behalf of that country. A series of
major outrages against Christian missionaries made it difficult
for the American churches interested in China to commend the
cause of the pagan Manchu government. Beginning in the
1870's the rise of hostility toward Chinese immigrants on the
west coast also helped to create an attitude unsympathetic to
China's fate in Asia. Chinese in America were condemned as
immoral heathens, racially inferior and threatening the livelihood of white Americans. Some of this contempt was transferred to China itself.

When the Sino-Japanese War began in 1894, opinion ran
strongly in favor of Japan. Most interested Americans would

probably have accepted the description of the issues as presented by a former American foreign service officer who had served in Peking. Writing in the *North American Review*, Howard Martin stated:

> . . . the success of Japan in Korea means reform and progress—governmental, social and commercial—in that unhappy country. . . . The success of the Chinese means the forcing back of the Koreans to Oriental sluggishness, superstition, ignorance, and anti-foreign sentiment. It is a conflict between modern civilization, as represented by Japan; and barbarism, or a hopelessly antiquated civilization, by China.

An equally one-sided position was taken by the American minister to China, Charles Denby, who had served ten years at Peking. In a report to the Secretary of State, Denby said that Japan "is now doing for China what the United States did for Japan. She has learnt western civilization and she is forcing it on her unwieldy neighbor."

The official American position was one of neutrality, but a benevolent neutrality evidenced by Secretary of State Walter Gresham's firm rejection of all suggestions for American co-operation with the other western powers to discuss joint intervention. The Secretary understood that such an intervention might demand "a settlement not favorable to Japan's future security and well-being." When in November of 1894 the United States extended its good offices to the belligerents, even that move was criticized in the American press as being to the advantage of China since the Japanese had not as yet won complete victory. "Let China herself appeal to Japan for peace," said the *New York Herald*. There seems to have been a conviction that China would be awakened only by utter defeat. It is "to the interest of the world at large," said a Philadelphia editorialist, "that the war shall not cease until Japan has inflicted a decisive and destructive blow and brought the Chinese Government to confess its helplessness."

Japan's smashing naval victories increased American admiration for the former pupil and testimonials were offered by many prominent Americans. "Japan has leaped, almost at one bound, to a place among the great nations of the earth," said Hilary A. Herbert, Secretary of the Navy. Rear Admiral Stephen B. Luce, founder of the Naval War College, praised the quality of Japan's naval strategy and tactics, and Charles Cramp, a leading American ship builder, concluded that Japan was exceeded only by Britain in the quality of its naval construction.

The American press reported on the tremendous upsurge of nationalist fervor which the war and final victory brought Japan. To the American correspondents in Japan it was a matter of some concern. Even as sympathetic a resident as Lafcadio Hearn described these developments with some alarm. Popular histories uncritically lauding Japan's victories were poured out to the reading public, while even the illiterate Japanese could catch the chauvinist spirit through the fanciful color prints depicting the feats of the military and naval heroes. War plays filled the theaters, while a wide variety of articles ranging from textiles to note paper were imprinted with war scenes. One ingenious Japanese merchant produced chop sticks, each inscribed with a poem recalling a specific defeat of the Chinese.

A few Americans saw danger signs. Senator Henry Cabot Lodge warned his colleagues in Congress after Japan signed the peace that they "have just whipped somebody and they are in a state of mind when they think they can whip anybody." Secretary of the Navy Herbert emphasized the potential threat of rising Japanese naval power and urged more money for American construction. But these were the voices of a small minority. Japan's first ventures in imperialism did little to change the image of a progressive, democratizing nation, following in the footsteps of the nation which first opened Japan's ports to the western world.

Chapter VII

THE FIRST ABRASIONS

W HAT IS THE OCCASION for all this militant insanity we do not know," complained the New York *Journal of Commerce* in 1895. "This rage of displaying the flag in season and out of season, this remarkable fashion of hanging the flag over every schoolhouse and of giving boys military drill, and this passion for tracing one's ancestry to somebody who fought in the Revolutionary War or the War of 1812, or at least against the French and Indians, all help to create a false spirit of militarism." The editors of this New York journal were describing with some accuracy the mood of the decade. The United States in the 1890's was experiencing the extreme manifestations of full-blown nationalism.

Like that of Japan, American nationalism as a widely disseminated sentiment was a recent historical development. The colonial period had seen the growth of a national consciousness which became a vigorous nationalist spirit in the struggle with Britain for independence. But even after the ratification of the Federal Constitution this emotion and its accompanying ideology characterized a minority of Americans. Many residents of the United States still felt closer to their states than to the new national government. Wars have been noted for their effect in creating national unity, but neither the War of 1812 nor the Mexican War were fought by a united people. A large minority, if not a majority of Americans, viewed these conflicts with indifference or actively opposed the policies of the national administration. The tremendous territorial gains of the Mexican War, won at small cost, did much to stir patriotic enthusiasm and to set on foot ventures for further national expansion. But again the sectional conflict of 1861–1865 demonstrated the dominance of regional and state loyalties in the hearts of many Americans.

It was the decade of the 1890's which saw the expression of a vigorous nationalism which now extended to all sections of the nation and to all strata. Great stress was placed on the symbols of patriotism. Historians have noted the rapid rise in the number of patriotic societies in this decade, the growing concern for the "Americanization" of immigrants, and the passage of state laws requiring for patriotic purposes the teaching of American history in the schools. As in Japan, the improvement of transportation through the railroad, the decline in illiteracy through better schooling, and the expansion of the popular press made possible the dissemination of nationalism to the prairie farmer as well as to the factory worker of the cities.

When the nationalist spirit creates a mood of self-confidence touching on arrogance, when new lands and markets seem available for the strong, and when troublesome domestic problems harass those who restrict their vision to the homeland, a milieu is formed in which expansionist ideas can flourish and in which dynamic expansionist leaders can gain political strength. In the United States in the last decade of the nineteenth century, as in some degree in Japan, these conditions prevailed. The destiny of America, the dreams long blurred by the sectional strife of the Civil War and the decades of reconstruction, once more became clear. In 1895 the *American Magazine of Civics* asked a group of distinguished Americans the question, "Ought we to annex Cuba?" Ethan Allen, a New York lawyer, expressed the expansionist spirit in full measure:

> Of course Cuba should be annexed as a part of the United States. Geographically she belongs to us. . . . Canada will come in time; Mexico will follow Texas and California, and drop into her niche under the Stars and Stripes when we are ready. But we want Cuba now. . . . The great spirits which gave us this Republic, and who now watch impatiently that it shall not fail in any step that advances its destiny, beckon to us.

It was only a few years later that a young Kansas editor, William Allen White, proclaimed that it was the Anglo-Saxon's "manifest destiny to go forth as a world conqueror. He will take possession of all the islands of the sea."

This expansionist spirit with its catch phrases to describe America's mission to civilize and Christianize was not new. Much that was said echoed the mood of confidence of the 1840's and early 1850's. But what was new was the widespread support which it gained at the end of the century. The little band of expansionists who retained their dreams through the Civil War found themselves for decades working against strong public apathy. When Secretary of State Seward purchased Alaska from the Russians in 1867, proponents of annexation hailed his action as giving the United States the key to the possession of the Pacific and the control of trade with China. But these bold claims brought no enthusiastic response in Congress. It was only Seward's skillful lobbying coupled with bribery that secured the ratification of the annexation treaty and squeezed the money out of Congress to pay for the purchase. Seward also negotiated a treaty with Hawaii in 1867 which he hoped would be a preliminary to annexation. He then had to wait three years for Senate action, only to have the treaty rejected in 1870.

In examining the "artificial patriotism" of the nineties, the *Journal of Commerce* concluded that "undoubtedly the recon-

struction of the Navy has done much in this direction." The
change in attitude toward the Navy took place in the 1880's.
The Republicans took the initiative in 1884 with a plank in
their national platform which demanded the restoration of the
United States Navy to "its old-time strength and efficiency." The
same year the Democrats condemned the Republicans for
squandering money on the decrepit fleet. But the Democrats
were soon converted to the new outlook and in 1889, at the
close of Grover Cleveland's presidency, this party took credit
for having "set on foot the reconstruction of the American
Navy."

In little more than a decade congressional appropriations
changed the Navy from a collection of rotting hulks to a
modern fighting force capable of supporting a more dynamic
foreign policy. Wooden vessels were scrapped as their repair
costs mounted, and beginning in 1883 Congress authorized the
construction of four steel vessels. Three of these were protected cruisers, later to provide the basis for the famous White
Squadron. By 1890 Congress had authorized some 25 modern
vessels, including fast cruisers which were still called "coast-
wise vessels" with a stipulated limit on their cruising range
in order to secure the votes of the anti-expansionists.

The growth of the Navy provided an audience for the writings of Alfred Thayer Mahan who in turn reached through his
books and articles a wider circle of Americans who became
enthusiastic for a bolder foreign policy. Mahan's *The Influence
of Sea Power Upon History* made this naval officer a national
figure whose doctrines were widely publicized. He attacked
the "coast defense" and "commerce destruction" concepts of
naval strategy which had limited the range of American warships and concentrated naval strength in home waters. The
new Navy was to be freed of its traditional tasks of coastal
protection and instead range the high seas, attacking the
enemy and protecting trade routes.

Mahan offered more than a strategy, he gave aggressive

expansionists a theory to support their demands. He saw "no aggressive action in our pious souls," but he urged Americans at the same time to fix their energies on areas where youthful vigor would find an outlet in conquest and exploitation. Naval growth and commercial expansion would go hand in hand. The alternative was national decay.

Mahan looked westward to Hawaii as a starting point. From there American naval power would move on to the western Pacific to defend Anglo-Saxon supremacy. Absorbing the current ideas of racial conflict, Mahan argued that the only alternative to the conquest of the West by Oriental peoples was American assimilation of India, China, and Japan. But in his early writings there was a tendency to show special favor to Japan. Even after Japan had shown its strength in the defeat of China in 1895, Mahan wrote in praise of the Japanese as "willing converts" to western civilization. According to his predictions, Japan as an island sea power would follow a line of co-operation with the other two great sea powers, Britain and the United States, and even join with them in an alliance against the major land powers.

Mahan's arguments were supplemented by other pleas for an expansionist policy. "We must have a market or we shall have revolution," a Maine senator warned in 1898, putting in concise form the economic justification for the extension of American power. The theme of markets and profits was strongly stressed in regard to the Far East, and there were some genuine fears that the expanding American economy would soon be choked by a surplus. But an economic interpretation falls far short of explaining in full the motives of the men who called for a "larger policy." Leaders like Theodore Roosevelt, Henry Cabot Lodge, Albert J. Beveridge, John Hay, and their associates had succeeded in identifying their own expansive egos with that of the nation and saw the new course of America as the road to personal power. Some were also touched with visions of Destiny and Duty, believing themselves to be chosen men leading a chosen people to world greatness. A previous generation had found satisfaction in building a political empire or one built out of steel, oil, or rails; the dynamic leaders of the nineties hungered for a real empire across the seas. The Hawaiian Islands were proclaimed as the first American stepping stone to Asia and their annexation a strategic necessity. As early as 1872 the Secretary of War had sent a military mission to the islands to survey the capabilities of the various ports for use in the event of war between the United States and "a powerful maritime nation." The mission reported that the harbor of Honolulu would be difficult to defend, but that the Pearl River harbor could be developed into a useful base. In 1884 when renewal of the 1875 treaty with the Hawaiian Kingdom was under consideration, the Senate Foreign Relations Committee added an amendment giving the United States exclusive rights to the use of Pearl Harbor as a repair and coaling station. In January of 1893 a group of white residents, led by American annexationists, overthrew the Hawaiian monarchy and called upon Washington to act.

When news of the revolution reached Tokyo, the British-built cruiser, *Naniwa,* was sent to Hawaii to furnish protection for the more than 20,000 Japanese residents, a colony more than ten times as large as the American settlement. On arrival in February of 1893, the *Naniwa's* commander, Heihachiro Togo, found the harbor of Honolulu already occupied by the Japanese *Kongo,* en route home from San Francisco, a British warship, and the American cruiser, *Boston.* At the request of the American Minister, John L. Stevens, the *Boston* had landed a force of marines to protect American lives and property and, as an official investigation later pointed out, to maintain order in behalf of the pro-American revolutionists.

Japan did not look with favor upon the projected American annexation of the islands, jeopardizing the treaty rights of the oriental residents, and Tokyo withheld recognition from the new republican government. Although cordial visits were exchanged between the officers of the American and Japanese warships, rumors quickly spread among the American residents of impending trouble. The Japanese, it was said, were planning to seize control of Hawaii. The American commander of the Pacific Station reported to Washington the rumor that the *Naniwa* had brought a cargo of arms for the Japanese residents, many of whom were allegedly former members of the Japanese army. An incident then took place. A Japanese convict escaped from a Honolulu penitentiary and swam to the *Naniwa,* asking protection. Since the Japanese government had no treaty relations with the new Hawaiian government and no extradition agreement existed, Captain Togo refused the requests for his return. The *Hawaiian Star* published a report that American forces would be used to support the Hawaiian request and that Togo had boasted of his ability to blow the American ships out of the water if any attempt was made to recapture the convict. The Japanese consul denied the story and arranged the transfer of the convict to the Hawaiian authorities. The ominous incident was over, and the Secretary of the Navy received a dispatch in April of 1893 which reported that the officers of the *Boston* were "on pleasant and visiting terms" with the officers of the *Naniwa.*

The first occasion on which a modern Japanese warship faced an American warship had with historical appropriateness taken place only a few miles from Pearl Harbor. For the next half century Hawaii was to play an important part in Japanese-American relations. President Grover Cleveland blocked the expansionists' plans by withdrawing the treaty of annexation from the Senate, but this was only a temporary setback for the proponents of the new Pacific policy. Theodore Roosevelt in 1897 denounced Cleveland's action as "a colossal crime" and claimed that only by taking the islands promptly could trouble be avoided with Japan. "I am fully alive to the danger from Japan," he wrote his friend, Mahan. Before the year was out, Roosevelt, now Assistant Secretary of the Navy, saw war as an immediate possibility.

In January of 1897 the Japanese consul general in Hawaii announced that the *Naniwa* was again going to call at Honolulu, but that the visit had no relation to the Japanese government's grievances against the Hawaiian government. Nevertheless, shortly after this announcement the cruiser *Philadelphia* was also ordered to Honolulu and Assistant Secretary Roosevelt began to survey the American ships in the Pacific available for emergency dispatch to Hawaii. In March of 1897 a dispute developed between the captain of a Japanese transport and the Hawaiian government over a thousand Japanese laborers who had come to work and were turned back by immigration authorities.

Some American expansionists saw the Japanese-Hawaiian dispute as the occasion for a war involving the United States. Theodore Roosevelt called upon the Naval War College to prepare war plans and agreed with his friend Alfred Mahan that the Hawaiian Islands should be seized and explanations made afterwards. With the Japanese Navy smashed, Roosevelt believed that any Japanese army in Hawaii could then be sent to American prisons.

Fortunately for Japan, Roosevelt was only Assistant Secretary of the Navy and his superior, Secretary John D. Long, was less excitable and not inclined to force an issue, the very existence of which was questionable. But when the *Naniwa* finally passed Diamond Head and anchored in Honolulu harbor in May of 1897, the *Philadelphia* was on hand to greet the new arrival. The anti-Japanese press, as in 1893, printed rumors of a coming battle off Waikiki Beach, but the conduct of the Japanese was in no way threatening. Agreement was reached to arbitrate the dispute over the rejected laborers and the Japanese shipping company involved was eventually indemnified for its losses.

Before the *Naniwa* raised anchor, the news reached Tokyo that a new treaty of annexation had been signed by the white-dominated Hawaiian government. On the grounds that acquisition by the United States of the islands would upset the status quo in the Pacific and endanger the residential and commercial rights of the Japanese residents, a protest was sent to Washington. No threats or hint of force accompanied the protest, but Japan's action was a new cause for alarm in some Washington circles. The Navy Department sent warnings to Pacific commanders to be ready for emergency action. Rear Admiral Lester Beardslee, commander of the *Philadelphia,* was ordered in July to land forces and to assume a provisional protectorate over the islands if Japan used force against the Hawaiian government. The Rear Admiral had already informed Washington that he was "fully persuaded" that no expectation of trouble with Japan existed on the part of the Hawaiian government. But it was not until the *Naniwa* steamed westward for its home port in September of 1897 that all apprehensions ceased.

Although this encounter in Hawaiian waters took place without any scare headlines in the American press, naval circles now looked upon the Japanese Navy in a different light. In the fall of 1897 Captain Albert Barker, commander of the U.S.S. *Oregon* in Pacific waters, prepared a significant intelligence report for the Secretary of the Navy. It was the first of many such reports which were to stress Japanese expansionism and to view the new Oriental Navy as a threat to the United States. "Forty million people cannot be kept within her present limits, she *must* expand," wrote Captain Barker. As long as Russia barred the way to the mainland of Asia, he saw Japan pushing southward and eastward across the Pacific. Mexico was already being infiltrated by Japanese immigrants, Captain Barker reported, and the Japanese were prepared to seize Magdalena Bay in Lower California on the outbreak of war. Unfortified, Puget Sound would quickly fall and from the north and south the Japanese would sweep the Pacific coast, capturing Los Angeles and raiding San Francisco to destroy its naval facilities. If neither Britain nor Russia interfered, the western American states would fall into Japan's hands.

With some variation in detail, this alarming picture of the Japanese conquest of American soil was to become a stock argument in the early twentieth century of those who came to view Japan as the major enemy. Americans were presented this frightening future as propaganda for a variety of ends. It was used initially as an argument for the annexation of Hawaii, in order to prevent the use of the islands as an advance base for the projected invasion. The picture was presented to Congress by the proponents of a larger navy and by the opponents of Japanese immigration. The Japanese threat was also an additional reason for pushing action on the construction of an inter-oceanic canal. Former Secretary of the Navy Herbert, in a magazine article appearing as early as January of 1897, pointed out that the Japanese Navy could reach the Hawaiian Islands from their home waters in two weeks. The American fleet, with full strength in the Atlantic in preparation for the war with Spain, would, without a canal, take three months to come to the defense of the future American islands.

The expanding American Navy—six battleships and one armored cruiser were authorized in the years 1891 to 1898— came out of the Spanish-American War with a tremendous increase in its popular and congressional support. The smashing defeat of the obsolete Spanish forces and the feats of Admiral George Dewey and other heroes created a pride in the American ships which overcame traditional resistance to a large naval force. Congress in 1899 specified that all new construction should have "great radius of action" and the following year the term, "coastline battleship" was dropped. The new Navy was no longer tied to defensive action in American waters, but was to emulate Admiral Dewey and apply the theories of Mahan, carrying the war to the enemy across the seas. The new overseas possessions, Hawaii annexed during the war, and Guam and the Philippines, acquired in the treaty of peace with Spain, had to be defended. The major burden of their defense rested on the American Navy.

The annexation of the Philippines in 1899 created a new source of Japanese-American tension. The expansionists called for the islands' acquisition as stepping stones to the valuable trade of China and sounded the appeals of "manifest destiny" and the duty of carrying Christianity and civilization to the heathen. The anti-imperialists raised the traditional American arguments against the acquisition of an empire, but lost their cause by a narrow margin when the Senate approved the annexation treaty by two votes. Although few naval and military experts believed that the Philippines could be successfully defended against an Asian naval power, the possibility that this area would become a strategic liability received little attention in the debate over the treaty. It was a British admiral, P. H. Colomb, writing in the *North American Review* in 1898, who gave Americans the clearest warning.

> The United States is for the first time giving hostages to fortune, and taking a place in the world that will entail on her sacrifices and difficulties of which she has not yet dreamed. . . . So long as the Empire of the United States was contained in a ring fence of land and sea frontiers, she had in all international disputes the enormous advantage of unattackableness. . . . But with outlying territories, especially islands, a comparatively weak power has facilities for wounding her without being wounded in return.

For a growing Japan the fate of the Philippines was of great importance. If a feeble Spain in Cuba was considered by some Americans to have been a threat to their coast, a vigorous America in the Philippines was easily seen as a threat by Japan. Warnings appeared in the Japanese press that American expansion had upset the balance of power in the Far East and that Formosa, lying close to the northern Philippines, must now be fortified. American efforts at the defense of the Philippines called for a larger naval force in the Pacific. An American force large enough to protect the newly acquired islands was also capable of carrying offensive action into Japan's home waters. A Japanese fleet capable of meeting the new defensive needs of that country was also capable of attacking the Philippines. Naval building on both sides of the Pacific was henceforth caught in this narrow relationship by which defensive naval construction became for the other party a threat calling for counter-construction. By 1907 Theodore Roosevelt had glimpsed something of this new dilemma and wrote of the Philippines as "our heel of Achilles," which cramped any freedom of action in dealing with Japan.

In 1899, the year the Stars and Stripes were raised over the Philippines, a new effort was made to advance American interests in China. John Hay issued the first of his Open Door notes to the powers. Hay announced, in effect, his country's concern for its share in the trade and economic development of the Chinese Empire. Since the first American treaty with China in 1844, the most-favored-nation clause had been used to guarantee equal commercial advantages with the European treaty powers. Any advantages wrung from China and written into a treaty were thus automatically extended to the United States. But by the close of the nineteenth century Russia, Britain, Germany, France, and Japan had all secured leases to sectors of China's coastal territory and had developed spheres of interest in the hinterland. Traditional anti-imperialist sentiment still inhibited American participation in this partitioning process, but, unless something was done, the United States was in danger of being squeezed out of markets.

Under British prompting and with the support of American business interests, Hay sought to commit the imperialist powers to the principle of equal trading opportunities for all within their holdings. The answers to the American note were generally evasive, but Hay pretended to find an agreement with his principle. In 1900 he went further and appealed to the same powers for the preservation of the territorial and administrative integrity of China.

The Open Door notes and particularly that of 1900 were to become of historical importance in later decades. But in their inception they lacked support even within the McKinley and Roosevelt administration. The Navy Department preferred to join Europe in the partitioning process and to secure an American base on the China coast. The General Board of the Navy suggested three sites as possibilities, two on the Fukien coast opposite Japan's new territory of Formosa. Hay accepted the Navy's position and within six months of his appeal in be-half of China's territorial integrity he cabled the American Minister to China to open negotiations to secure an American leasehold. Japan had already concluded an agreement with China, barring any leaseholds on the Fukien coast, so an ap-proach was made to Japan as well. The Japanese government quickly reminded Secretary Hay of his contradictory position, as well as of their non-alienation agreement with China.

Although Hay withdrew his proposal, the Navy Department continued to press for a Chinese base. The Navy's General Board made plans for the seizure of a base on the Fukien coast in the event of a general war. In 1900 the Pacific Mail Steam-ship Company's lease on a coaling depot at Yokohama was taken over by the Navy for the use of the Asiatic squadron. In 1903 a harbor was selected for a base on Kiska Island, where the Aleutians stretch far across the North Pacific. But it was not until 1906, after the destruction of Russia's Far Eastern squad-ron and the withdrawal of the major strength of other western nations to European waters, that the Navy ceased asking for a naval station on the China coast.

More important than naval bases in the expansion of Ameri-can strength in the Pacific was the contribution made by Theo-dore Roosevelt as President to the growth of fighting power. When Roosevelt took office in 1901, the American Navy ranked fifth among the world's fleets. When he left office in 1909, the Navy was outranked only by Great Britain. The Pacific Fleet by that date consisted of eight armored cruisers and seven protected battleships, while 20 battleships and two cruisers operated in the Atlantic. Work had begun on the dredging and fortification of Pearl Harbor and on the strengthening of naval installations in the Philippines.

Japan's sea power also grew during the Roosevelt years. By 1908 the flag of the Rising Sun floated over eight battleships and ten armored cruisers. In the same year Japan's naval spending reached approximately a third that of the United States. An alliance with Great Britain, made in 1902 and renewed in 1905, gave Japan the additional support of the world's greatest fleet in the event of a war with two or more powers. After the Japanese defeated the Russians in 1905, the British reorganized their Far Eastern forces, withdrew their battleships to Europe, and reduced their Pacific squadron to little more than a police patrol. A British observer pointed out that his government by this action "virtually gave its adherence to a Japanese political principle in the Far East equivalent to the Monroe Doctrine of the United States."

With Russia's Far Eastern squadron smashed in the war, the United States was the only potent challenger of Japan. Americans were in the Philippines and American commercial and missionary interests in Asia expanded in the first decade of the twentieth century. But the image of Japan as the enemy was still slow to grow in the minds of responsible American officials and in the press. The possibilities of a future clash were glimpsed on both sides of the Pacific, but, more often than not, pushed aside in the United States by other considerations. The major exception to this generalization was to develop on the west coast of the United States.

Theodore Roosevelt took a major part in shaping the American relationship with Japan. He saw more clearly than most the great growth of Japanese power and its significance for

Asia. As a militarist he admired and respected Japan for its ability to adopt and use effectively western weapons and military techniques. When he was at his cool-headed best he admitted that war with Japan would be an expensive folly; it would mean the loss of the Philippines and even an American victory would not guarantee the national interests in Asia. But on other occasions Roosevelt's personal belligerency and love of battle led him to consider a Pacific war with relish.

Fortunately the President's warlike moods led to only a few dangerous actions in the Pacific. If he had not been forced to carry the heavy burden of the anti-Japanese agitation on the west coast, he might have succeeded in greatly extending the life of Japanese-American friendship. Roosevelt recognized Japan as an important counterweight in Asia, balancing the ambitions of Europe. In this situation the United States could wisely remain little more than a spectator. If the balance was to be tipped, Roosevelt preferred to see it tipped in the direction of Tokyo rather than St. Petersburg or Berlin. Astute diplomacy would see to it that Japan's gains were American gains too. And without the uncritical attachment to China of some of his successors, Roosevelt was not tempted into any quixotic ventures in behalf of that disintegrating empire.

Although not many Americans were as clear in their grasp of the power politics of Asia as Mr. Roosevelt, his concern for the friendship of Japan was typical of his countrymen. The strength of the favorable image of the former pupil was clearly demonstrated during the crucial period of the Russo-Japanese War. From the beginning of this conflict to the signing of the peace at Portsmouth, New Hampshire, in September of 1905, the great preponderance of expressed opinion favored Japan.

The war had its origin in the struggle over the control of Korea where Russia continued to block Japan's efforts to reap the fruits of the 1895 victory over China. When Japan began the fighting with a daring and successful surprise attack on Port Arthur before formally declaring war, the American press treated this act as a brilliant stratagem. A European scholar, lecturing at one of the Ivy League universities, found the academic community delighted at Japan's initiative. As the war moved on from one Japanese victory to another, American cheers for the former pupil were loud and frequent.

Japan benefitted to some extent from the anti-Russian sentiment found in the United States. For decades Americans had read tales of Tsarist brutality, and this checked any sympathy for the Emperor of All the Russias and his officials. The plight of the Russian peasant also marked the country as decadent. "Any country in which a poor man has no chance to become a millionaire is condemned in American opinion," said one foreign commentator. Russian anti-Semitism and pogroms had also aroused the antagonism of many American Jews and some Christians. This Russian bigotry may have been responsible for Kuhn, Loeb & Company, a New York banking house of Jewish partners, taking the initiative and joining British bankers in raising the first of a series of war loans for Japan.

The cause of Japan is "not only her own cause, but the cause of the entire civilized world," wrote Jacob Schiff, president of Kuhn, Loeb & Company, in the war years. "Civilization," "progress," and other glowing generalities were frequently associated with the victory of Japan by many writers. Those who thought more concretely of American economic interests also favored the defeat of Russia. Japan stands as "the champion of commercial rights," said the New York *Journal of Commerce*, while Russia's policy in Asia was one of monopoly and closing the open door. Occasionally a minority view was expressed that Japan's ideal was "Asia for the Asiatics—under Japanese hegemony," but such disturbing thoughts were uncommon. The American cartoonists pictured the Japanese soldier as a heroic figure and there were no traces of the ape-like caricature of the toothy, threatening Japanese so commonly used in the 1930's. Instead Japan was frequently viewed as a noble, samurai warrior, defeating the Russian bear; an underdog winning against odds by virtue of bravery.

Theodore Roosevelt was astute enough to realize that in the flush of victory Japan, as he wrote Henry Cabot Lodge, "will have her head turned to some extent," but he said that the same would be true of the United States if it had accomplished such historic feats. He did not feel that the national interests of the two countries were necessarily incompatible and he was ready to make compromises. In the summer of 1905 through Secretary of War William Howard Taft's exchange with Prime Minister Tarō Katsura, Roosevelt accepted Japan's control of Korea and received a disavowal of Japanese aspirations for the Philippines. Whatever the value of Japan's promise, Roosevelt paid nothing for it. The Korean independence movement was small and helpless, and the President merely recognized a *fait accompli*. Great Britain also accepted Japan's hegemony in Korea.

The American offer of mediation was accepted by both belligerents, and the delegates came to New Hampshire to write a peace. Russia ceded to Japan the southern half of the northern island of Sakhalin, recognized Japan's position in Korea, and turned over the rights and concessions in southern Manchuria. Japan's claims to an indemnity were dropped "with a magnanimity which seems 'Quixotic,'" said the *New York World*. When the Japanese minister to London had been told that the American public expected Japan's demands to be very moderate, he had warned, "The public evidently mistakes the Japanese for angels." It was a surprise to many Americans to find that the peace was bitterly criticized when its terms reached Tokyo, and riots led to the resignation of the Prime Minister.

Theodore Roosevelt not only received the Nobel Peace Prize for his work at Portsmouth, but he bore with the Japanese government some of the bitter resentment expressed by Japanese mobs against all those associated with the peacemaking. The last three years of his administration saw Roosevelt even more deeply involved in relations with Japan. But this was a byproduct of a domestic development as Japanese immigrants in the United States became the victims of racial hostility.

Japanese laborers began slowly to move from Hawaii to California in the 1870's. There were less than 200 in the United States by 1880, but the flow increased in the next two decades, reaching more than a thousand a year in the early 1890's. The shortage of cheap labor, in part the result of the Chinese Exclusion Act of 1882, provided ample opportunities for a hardworking Japanese to make his way in the American West. The success of these immigrants as agriculturalists, the apparent threat which they posed for white labor, and the fact that they had a different culture combined to make them a minority group singled out by racialist elements. Anti-Japanese voices were heard in California as early as 1887, but it was not until 1905 when the Asiatic Exclusion League was organized in San Francisco that the movement wielded political power.

In October of 1906 the San Francisco Board of Education ordered Japanese and Chinese children excluded from the regular schools and sent to segregated classes. The purpose was to relieve crowding and to see that white children would not have "their youthful impressions" affected by association with the Orientals. The first reason given was of dubious validity, since there were less than a hundred Oriental students in the whole school system.

News of the San Francisco action reached Washington by way of Tokyo where the Japanese press received the action as a national insult. A protest was made to Washington, charging violation of the 1894 treaty which guaranteed to Japanese residents of the United States "the same privileges, liberties and rights" accorded to Americans or residents of the most-favored-nation. Japanese newspapers took a critical tone. Cartoonists pictured Lincoln breaking up the Statue of Liberty and American missionaries hurrying home to try to convert their fellow Americans. Extreme nationalist organs took on a belligerent tone.

Both governments were anxious to avoid trouble. The Japanese cancelled the projected visit of a naval training squadron to California ports to avoid incidents. Theodore Roosevelt went to work with vigor, first trying to intimidate and then to persuade the San Francisco School Board to rescind their action. Secretary of State Elihu Root admitted in private that the segregation of Japanese children appeared to be a treaty violation and was therefore unconstitutional. The California Supreme Court justices reportedly held the same views, but legal action would have involved the politically explosive issue of states rights. Roosevelt took the more successful approach of winning concession by removing California's fears of the growing numbers of Japanese immigrants. Japan had already taken some steps to limit migration and accepted in February of 1907 a Gentlemen's Agreement by which the flow of laborers to America would be stopped. The next month the School Board withdrew its order. Feeling against Japanese was still strong and in May of 1907 Washington was further embarrassed by anti-Japanese riots in San Francisco.

Sensation-seeking journalists and anti-Japanese propagandists used the San Francisco difficulties to preach the imminence of a Pacific War. Rumors were spread about an attack to be made on the Philippines. Richmond P. Hobson, a Spanish-American war hero and a favorite of the Hearst press, proclaimed that he had seen an ultimatum sent to Washington from Tokyo and that "Japan could whip us in the Pacific with ease." Fuel was added by reports from the German press where an effort seems to have been made to embarrass Great Britain over the prospect of an attack on the United States by her ally, Japan. But the war-scare mongers were in the minority. The eastern press in particular took a more critical attitude toward California and the *New York World* went so far as to say, "If somebody has to fight Japan, why not let California bear the whole burden of the war?"

The Roosevelt administration was not without its qualms over the situation, although the President himself retained a measured perspective which contrasted with some of his belligerent outbursts on other occasions. Shortly after the first Japanese protest was received in October of 1906, Roosevelt asked the Navy about its preparations for a war with Japan. He was assured that American command of the Pacific would be achieved within 90 days from the time that the fleet left the Atlantic coast. Three months later in January of 1907, the Army and Navy began to undertake joint studies on the conduct of a possible war with Japan. The Navy also decided to turn down the Japanese offer, made six months earlier, to establish closer relations and to exchange information as Japan was doing with its British ally.

Settlement of the school issue did not end American fears. In June of 1907 Roosevelt decided to shift the fleet to the Pacific and again informed himself about the state of the war plans. When news of the fleet move reached the public, it gave proof for some that war was on its way. The Navy tried to convince the country that the move had no international implications, and Admiral Mahan gave his word that the cruise was only a practical training operation. But now even the New York papers, the *Times,* the *Tribune,* and the *Sun,* published articles which assumed that war was impending. Japan, by comparison, remained relatively calm, although Ambassador Luke Wright cabled the Department of State that the fleet move would have an unfavorable effect on the mind of the average Japanese.

The Great White Fleet left Hampton Roads in December of 1907 and its course was reported along with frequent rumors of its impending destruction. Before the fleet sailed, Rear Admiral H. N. Manney predicted to the President that the Japanese fleet would appear in the Atlantic to terrorize the

East coast once the American fleet reached the Pacific. Naval intelligence received a report from Paris that the fleet would be blown up in the harbor of Rio de Janeiro. Rumor also spread that a Japanese destroyer squadron would be waiting to torpedo the American ships when they passed through the narrow Straits of Magellan.

The 16 American battleships weathered all the rumors. When they reached the West coast in the spring of 1908, Roosevelt announced that they would cross the Pacific and continue the voyage on a round-the-world cruise. The President felt that the display of American might would be a deterrent to any Japanese thought of war and accepted the invitation to visit Tokyo en route. The American forces reached Tokyo in October of 1908 and received an enthusiastic welcome from the people of the capital. Special precautions were taken in regard to shore leave for the crews, and the visit was ended without any unpleasant incidents. The occasion was marked with a great deal of oratory about Japanese-American friendship, but the realities could not be ignored by the Japanese. Roosevelt had demonstrated the reach of American power and like Perry had anchored within gunshot of the national capital. For the Australians whose ports were also visited, the presence of the American fleet was "a demonstration of white solidarity against the yellow races," as a government official phrased it. But for the Japanese it was a reminder of the strength of what Japanese journalists were beginning to call "the white peril."

President Roosevelt had remained relatively calm during the early stages of the fleet cruise, but the war rumors seem to have had a cumulative effect upon his equanimity. In April of 1908 while the fleet was still on the West coast, he wrote to his son Kermit that the military party in Japan was "inclined for war with us" and confident that they could land an army in California. The same month he urged the Secretary of the Treasury to move the gold from San Francisco to Denver. His warnings about possible war continued into the summer of

1908 when the ardent Japanophobe and Roosevelt supporter, Richmond Hobson, rose in the Democratic convention to quote the President as saying that war was "probable." Roosevelt denied the statement, but continued to show his concern over the threat of Japan to the close of his administration in 1909. To some extent, he also used the fear of Japan in these months to push his naval building program upon Congress. In 1908 the Navy General Board came out for a two-ocean navy; an Atlantic fleet pointed at what appeared to be the growing threat of Germany and a Pacific fleet to meet Japan.

The return of American naval forces to the Atlantic in the spring of 1909 was accompanied by cries from the West coast about the defenselessness of that shore and pleas for permanent stationing of battleships in the Pacific. A series of books were offered the public in 1909 which set about to change the American image of Japan. The most sensational was *The Valor of Ignorance* by Homer Lea, a Californian who returned from military adventures in China to devote himself to awakening Americans to the Japanese threat. Tramping up and down the California beaches, Lea was convinced by his survey that Japan could effect a successful landing and conquer the entire Pacific coast. The westward movement of the American Army would be hampered by the Great Plains and Rockies, leaving Japan in possession of large parts of the United States. Lea was also a believer in racial theories, arguing that European immigration to the United States had left too few native-born Americans to compose a fighting force valiant enough to expel the Japanese. "A story which every American would do well to ponder," said the *Literary Digest* in its review.

Before going out of print in 1922, Lea's first book sold 18,000 copies, figures which made it a steady seller on the West coast for over a decade. Editions also appeared in Japan, where the militarists found it a useful argument for the success of their cause. After the Pearl Harbor attack in 1941, Lea's book was reissued and he was hailed as a great seer. But little attention was given to his argument that it was the action of his fellow Californians which would bring on the war as a result of treating Japanese immigrants as a "nation of lepers."

Lea's volume was the most popular of a number of books which sought to stir American fears. E. H. Fitzpatrick's *The Coming Conflict of Nations, or the Japanese-American War,* published the same year, was an exciting account of Japan's use of a secret weapon, a smoke screen, to defeat American naval and land forces. Only the intervention of Great Britain saved the United States from complete defeat and brought about an Anglo-American union. Thomas Millard's *America and the Far Eastern Question,* also a 1909 title, claimed that Japan was too weak to attack California, but called for an aggressive American policy in China and Manchuria where the Japanese were allegedly robbing Americans of the rich profits of trade. Like others who looked with fear upon Japan, Millard favored a major expansion of the Pacific naval forces, a rapid completion of a base at Pearl Harbor, and the development of strong bases in the Philippines.

Wallace Irwin whose humorous writings probably created the most widely-held stereotype of the immigrant Japanese also published his first book in 1909. A San Francisco newspaperman, Irwin created a character, Hashimura Togo, a 35-year-old schoolboy who spoke a comic pigeon English and worked for an American family. Togo's comments on life about him so amused Americans that he was hailed as the successor of Peter Finley Dunne's "Mr. Dooley." Togo was pictured as a buck-toothed, ever-smiling, ultra-polite, but crafty "Jap." The stories first appeared in *Colliers* and soon spread to such diverse publications as the *New York Times* and *Good Housekeeping.* The first collection, *Letters of a Japanese Schoolboy,* followed by *Mr. Togo: Maid of All Work* in 1913, and several subsequent volumes, introduced millions of Americans to a face and a type which was to become the standard for American cartoonists for the next generation.

The Japanese-peril books were supplemented in their work by an important segment of the press. Led by William Randolph Hearst, a sensational press treated each Japanese spy rumor as important news and whipped minor incidents into war-scare headlines. Much of this was not journalism based on any real convictions as to the nature of Japanese policy, but went on the assumption that scare stories sold papers. The impact on American opinion was more regional than national, but the journalist's image of a threatening Japan combined with the facts of that nation's rapid rise to power began to corrode the links of friendship. A Harvard scholar with a grasp of realities, Archibald Coolidge, predicted in his *United States as a World Power* (1908) that the two countries would never return to the amicable reciprocity of a decade earlier. The change was a product, he wrote, not only of Japan's maturation and zest for expansion, but of the expansion of American interests in Asia. He believed that the two nations were fated to become active commercial rivals and possibly political enemies.

President William Howard Taft continued Roosevelt's naval building program and the annual naval expenditures of his administration topped those of the previous administration. But Taft and his Secretary of State, Philander Knox, were less cautious in invading areas in which Japan considered its own interests vital. The banker, E. H. Harriman, had a vision of a round-the-world rail system and headed a group of investors interested in building and controlling lines in Manchuria and China as links in this system. The Taft administration had proclaimed its belief in "dollar diplomacy" and the State Department sought to aid the bankers' schemes.

Since Manchuria and its railroads were divided north and south between the Japanese and Russian spheres, Secretary Knox suggested neutralization of these lines as a preliminary to American participation in ownership. Harriman hoped to go further and by buying up the Russian lines to force the Japanese to sell out in the south. Neither Japan nor Russia were willing to admit a new rival in Manchuria and the two nations joined to block American penetration. Instead of dividing his rivals Knox had, in the words of A. Whitney Griswold, "nailed that door closed with himself on the outside." Taft had disregarded the warning Roosevelt had given him in December of 1910 that it was to the interest of the United States "not to take any steps as regards Manchuria which will give Japanese cause to feel, with or without reason, that we are hostile to them, or a menace—in however slight a degree—to their interests." As a result Japan henceforth looked upon any display of American interest in Manchuria as evidence of new plans for winning control for American capitalists.

Although Roosevelt's Gentlemen's Agreement had sharply cut Japanese migration, Taft's administration was marked with continued demonstrations of anti-Japanese hostility on the West coast. The war talk of 1907 and 1908 had left its mark on some Americans who now began to see Japanese plots behind many harmless activities. In 1911 an American company's leasehold on Mexico's Magdalena Bay in Lower California was offered to a group of Japanese fishermen in San Francisco. The Navy, which on occasion used the Bay for target practice, learned of the possibility and passed on the news to the State Department which discouraged the sale. But before any transfer could take place the Hearst press learned of the negotiations and saw the hand of the Japanese government making an effort to secure a naval base in the western hemisphere. Magdalena Bay became by sensational journalism the place from which Japan would invade California and destroy the nearly completed Panama Canal. Senator Henry Cabot Lodge of Massachusetts introduced a resolution in the Senate which stated the grave concern of the United States over the acquisition of any harbor in this hemisphere by a foreign corporation which would give another country practical control. Taft gave the resolution no support, but its passage in August of 1912 was hailed by some as a corollary to the Monroe

Doctrine. Japan had officially disavowed interest in Mexico, but the Magdalena Bay affair established a long-lived myth that the Japanese had plotted to secure a base in North America.

Before President Taft left office, another outbreak of hostility developed in California which introduced his Democratic successor to the relationship between domestic affairs and foreign policy. The California legislature began work early in 1913 on an alien land law to bar Japanese from owning land or leasing it longer than three years. One of the framers of the law stated that its basis was "race undesirability" and its intention was to limit the Japanese in their remarkable success as farmers.

In the 1912 campaign Woodrow Wilson had written to a former mayor of San Francisco that he stood for the policy of excluding Japanese immigrants from the United States because they could not "blend with the Caucasian race." As President he seems to have viewed California's anti-Japanese efforts with sympathy, merely suggesting that the law be so worded as to avoid a direct conflict with the existing treaty protection provided for Japanese aliens.

The Alien Land Act passed the California Assembly on April 16, 1913, setting off belligerent mob reactions in Japan. President Wilson became concerned at this point and made belated efforts to check final passage in the Senate. Secretary of State Bryan was sent to California to speak directly to the legislature and Wilson made a public appeal to the people of the western state to exclude Japanese from land ownership *only* by means which did not raise embarrassing legal questions for the federal government. Neither effort was effectual and on May 9th the California Senate passed the Webb-Heney Alien Land Act.

The Japanese government sent a protest to Washington which Wilson read to the Cabinet on May 13. Their reaction, as noted by Secretary of the Navy Josephus Daniels, was that the protest implied nothing "except a very earnest desire to secure the same rights for the Japanese in California that are given to other aliens." Admiral Bradley Fiske, however, urged that preparations be taken for a possible war and three ships moved from China to the Philippines. Fiske pointed to Japanese population pressures as a cause of a war to acquire Hawaii and the Philippines and warned that Japan "can and does make war effectively without previous warning when she considers that her interests demand it and justify it." Wilson and Secretary Daniels opposed ship movements as inflammatory, and an American naval vessel in Yokohama was ordered to restrict shore leave and to find a plausible excuse for sailing if the situation grew tense.

The Army and Navy Joint Board decided unanimously on May 16 that naval power should be shifted to the Philippines and Hawaii. When the White House vetoed any moves, the Joint Board leaked their recommendations to the press in an effort to force the hand of the new President. Wilson was angry when Daniels brought him the news; "They will be abolished," he said and the Joint Board was officially dissolved.

The news leak set off, nevertheless, a war scare in newspaper headlines. In the Philippines an alert was ordered which kept the gunners of Corregidor at their posts day and night. Manila Bay was mined, and alarmists predicted the arrival of Japanese invaders daily. American newspapers discovered secret Japanese Army activity in Mexico. The Japanese press reported the imminent movement of American troops to Hawaii and the Philippines, along with the assurance of American authorities that such activity was not for "any warlike purposes."

The crisis simmered down by the end of May, but not without some permanent effects. Assistant Secretary of the Navy Franklin D. Roosevelt told the press that war scares like this had value in educating Americans as to their military resources. Secretary of Navy Daniels reviewed Japanese-American relations under Theodore Roosevelt and decided that the Taft administration should have moved the American fleet to the Pacific. Bryan told the Japanese Ambassador that Wilson might recommend to Congress an appropriation to compensate California Japanese for financial losses. But as World War I began in Europe in the fall of 1914, the treatment of Japanese nationals in the United States still remained a major issue between Washington and Tokyo.

Chapter VIII

RELUCTANT ALLIES

WORLD WAR I was European in origin and it was Europe which provided the major battlefields. Despite this geographic focus the conflict had profound repercussions in the Far East. In the beginning of the war the European fleets were withdrawn from the Western Pacific to the Atlantic and Mediterranean. This action destroyed the rough balance of naval power and left the Japanese Navy dominant in the coastal waters of Asia. A major European nation, Germany, was then driven out of Asia by Asians themselves. This Japanese success, like that of 1905, once more demonstrated the weakness of the white man's rule. The dreams of the Asian nationalist for the final expulsion of the western interloper were brought a step closer to reality. At the war's end Japan sat in the councils of Europe as a victor and equal. Asians were no longer the pawns of Europe, but were moving to a new status.

For the United States World War I was as important in relation to the Far East as it was in respect to the American role in Europe. Although the issue which ostensibly drew Americans into the conflict was one of maritime rights in the Atlantic, by the time the peace was signed, the Pacific had replaced the Atlantic as the ocean of greatest strategic concern. The American people, inclined after Versailles to turn their backs on Europe, found their government increasingly involved in the affairs of Asia.

For Japan the European struggle was a grand opportunity. Capable and ambitious leaders had learned that the code of international politics permitted one nation's troubles to be another nation's gain. "When there is a fire in a jewelry shop, the neighbors cannot be expected to refrain from helping themselves," a Japanese diplomat told the American Minister to China. While Europeans killed each other over their differences, Japan's interests could thrive. The engagement of vast armies on the periphery of Germany was an invitation to Japan's soldiers and sailors to hoist the Rising Sun over Germany's holdings in Asia and the Pacific. Russian participation in the Triple Intervention at Shimonoseki in 1895 was avenged in 1904; German participation in that intervention was avenged in 1914.

Few Japanese foresaw in 1914 the extent to which their ambitions would be countered by the expanding interests of the United States. The victory of the Democratic Party and the election of Woodrow Wilson as President in 1912 were interpreted by the Japanese press as a rejection of the vigorous "dollar diplomacy" of the Taft administration. The party of Wilson was believed to be dominated by the agricultural south and not to be the servant of the exporters of American capital and goods. The new President strengthened this belief by publicly repudiating the foreign policy of his predecessor. But the forces which had promoted a bolder Far Eastern policy since the 1890's were not eliminated by the Democratic victory. The continuity between Wilson's evaluation of national interests in Asia and that of his Republican opponents was greater than contemporaries expected.

Asian-minded Americans could cite figures to support their claim that this area had become of far greater importance to their country. American investments in government securities and business in China had grown from approximately $20 million in 1900 to $50 million in 1914. Annual exports to China ranged between $25 and $35 million in the years before the war. Japan had become an even more important market and in 1914 bought $54 million of American goods, almost twice the purchases of China.

The American role in missionary work in Asia had also grown rapidly in the first decades of the twentieth century. The Chinese government had been pressed in 1858 to recognize the principles of Christianity "as teaching men to do good and to do to others as they would have others do to them." The same treaty included Chinese pledges to protect the foreign agents of Christianity and their converts from harassment. British and French missionaries were from the beginning most numerous, but by 1900 there were approximately a thousand Americans working in this field in China. By 1914 their numbers had grown to 2,500, while American mission holdings in property rose to $10 million, double that of 1900.

The number of converts remained small and some, the "rice Christians," were suspected of joining the faith to reap its material benefits. The Chinese Revolution of 1911 and the more favorable attitude taken by the new Chinese government encouraged some American church leaders to believe that a new day was dawning in which the Chinese would turn en masse to Christianity. Sherwood Eddy, a prominent churchman and writer, travelled through China in 1913 and reported unprecedented audiences of more than 2,000 nightly flocking to hear the Christian message. On his return to the United States he presented a hopeful picture of a future Christian China.

American missionaries in Japan were fewer in number than in China, and Japanese resistance to the Gospel checked optimism about immediate gains. "Japan is Christianity's 'Port Arthur' in the Far East," said Sherwood Eddy. "If it cannot win Japan it cannot win and hold China." It was the American businessman who saw the expansionist possibilities in Japan.

Industries were spawned in greater numbers and expanded quickly to open markets for raw materials and machinery. American exports to Japan mounted rapidly, and the textile industry was beginning to consume sizable quantities of American cotton.

As the two major Far Eastern countries grew in importance to the United States, their relative favor in American eyes began to change. When Japan first incurred the hostility of west coast Americans in the first decade of the twentieth century, China did not benefit. The continued evidences of the decadence of the Manchu dynasty and the periodic display of antiforeign feelings, combined with the resistance to western ideas and technology, checked any compensating feelings of friendship for China. A vigorous Chinese boycott of American goods in 1905, partly in retaliation for the ban on migration of Chinese to the United States, became a serious issue between the two nations. By 1906 anti-American manifestations reached the point at which President Roosevelt felt it necessary to order additional troops sent to the Philippines. The boycott ended, but not without some Chinese resentment at what appeared to be an effort at intimidation.

The overthrow of the Manchus and the establishment of the republic in 1911 not only changed the course of Chinese history but began a shift in American opinion in favor of China as against Japan. The American press greeted the revolution with great optimism. The Chinese are "the most democratic people in the world," said the *New York Tribune*. The Washington *Times* claimed that the deliberations of the first legislature "demonstrated a striking aptitude for employing the machinery of parliamentary government." By January of 1912 the *Literary Digest* was predicting that Japan would "no longer be the most Occidental nation in the Orient." The anti-foreign character of Chinese nationalism was generally overlooked in the enthusiasm for the belated awakening of the long-sleeping giant.

The change in American attitudes toward China can be noted in official circles as well as in the press. Changes in personnel in the State Department had already begun to effect a more favorable approach to China before the Revolution. Willard Straight, appointed acting chief of the Division of Far Eastern Affairs in 1908, was a great believer in the economic future of American capital in China. He had served the Chinese government before entering the American diplomatic service and resigned to return to China as the agent of American bankers. Straight had become anti-Japanese while at a post in Korea, and it was he who interested Secretary of State Knox in a venture in dollar diplomacy in Manchuria. Under President Taft, William Rockhill, Roosevelt's Far Eastern adviser, was sent to St. Petersburg, while Edward T. Williams, a former missionary to China who had served the Chinese government, became the assistant chief of the Division of Far Eastern Affairs. More personnel changes took place under the Wilson administration.

President Wilson's views on Asia seem to have been in large part the product of impressions gained from his associations with missionaries from China. As head of Princeton University, the future President had interested himself in his institution's charitable work with the Young Men's Christian Association in Peking, and he brought to his campus some of the Chinese students who were financed by the Boxer Indemnity Fund. He talked with many missionaries and corresponded with a cousin who edited a missionary journal in Shanghai. Shortly after entering the White House, Wilson told his Cabinet that he felt "keenly the desire to help China." He considered the role of Protestant Christianity to be so important in China that he told one applicant for the post, Henry Morgenthau, Sr., that he believed that the American Minister to Peking should be "an evangelical Christian." American interest in China, he explained, was "largely in the form of missionary activities." Wilson was also optimistic about the political developments and commented in 1913 that he saw "the democratic leaven" working in China.

Wilson's first Secretary of State, William Jennings Bryan, was like the President an exponent of what has been aptly called "missionary diplomacy." He believed that America's mission was to carry Christianity and democracy across the seas. In his *Letters to a Chinese Official*, published in 1906, Bryan had written that a man "if he has no mission at all, he is not a man." At the same time the future Secretary of State had praised Japan highly, in contrast to China, for its rapid westernization, reminding the Chinese that they "used to look down upon this little nation with ill-concealed disdain." After the establishment of the Chinese Republic, Bryan's optimism about the spread of Christianity on the Asian mainland was unrestrained.

The new Chinese government was astute enough to realize that the evangelical hopes of the Christian world could be used to their advantage. When in the spring of 1913 the Republic was still unrecognized because of its instability, an official world appeal was sent to Christian churches to dedicate a day of prayer for the welfare of the new government and for its recognition by the powers. American churches responded enthusiastically to what seemed to be a victory for Christianity. A Sunday in April of 1913 was set aside for this act of devotion. President Wilson told his cabinet that he did not know when he had been so deeply stirred as he was by China's call for prayers. When one of the cabinet suggested that it was a play for political support, Wilson rejected the idea. Secretary Bryan said, "It is an extraordinary tribute to Christianity." Whatever the sincerity of the appeal, it brought results. Less than a month after the prayers the United States recognized the new government. The appeals for divine support had also been supplemented by petitions to Wilson from American business interests, chambers of commerce, and many church organizations.

Toward Japan President Wilson never exhibited the same

sympathy and tolerance with which he viewed and treated China. Standards of international morality which he held so highly were often waived in judging China, but applied rigidly and without insight in dealing with Japan. The second Secretary of State, Robert Lansing, and the President's unofficial adviser, Colonel Edward House, were usually more equitable in dealing with the two major oriental nations, but the President's pro-Chinese bias was not easily countered.

The role of the mission boards and their supporting American churches became an increasingly important one in building an American opinion favorable to China. There were about 26 mission boards active by 1913, and through their letters and fund-raising activities many American churchgoers were kept informed, usually in a most hopeful way, of the progress of evangelical work in China. The co-operation which the new Chinese government gave this movement converted it frequently into a most effective lobby in arousing American opinion in behalf of China's cause. The failure of the Chinese people to be converted in large numbers in no way seems to have weakened the strength of this movement's appeal to Americans. When issues developed between China and Japan, most churches could be counted upon to present China's case effectively.

The major effort to develop an equally effective opinion in behalf of Japan was that of the Japan Societies. The first of these organizations was founded in San Francisco in 1905 and was composed largely of businessmen interested in commercial relations with Japan. Similar organizations were formed in other major cities; the most important of which was the Japan Society of New York, founded in 1907. A number of important financial leaders took part in the formation of the New York organization, including Jacob H. Schiff who had played the leading role in raising the American loan to Japan during the Russo-Japanese War. The Societies gave annual dinners and on occasion feted prominent Japanese visitors to the United States.

Encouragement was given to cultural exchange and efforts were made to create a favorable climate for Japan. But membership remained small and without the large constituencies provided by the churches the pro-Japanese lobby never moved any significant segment of American opinion.

A more effective job in putting Japan's case before the American people was done by K. K. Kawakami, an immigrant who came to the United States from Japan in 1901. After graduate work in political science in several American universities, Kawakami turned to a career of journalism in 1905. From that date until the coming of Pearl Harbor, he poured out a steady stream of newspaper and magazine articles as well as books on the major issues of Japanese-American relations. Never completely uncritical of the country of his birth, Kawakami at the same time provided Americans with the viewpoint of the best-informed Japanese leaders. His appeal was, however, to the scholar, the publicist, and to the well-read minority and he probably never succeeded in affecting the stereotypes formed by the popular press.

It was within this framework of conditioning factors that news of Japan's entry into World War I was received in the United States. Japan went to war at the request of its ally, Great Britain, welcoming the opportunity to destroy German power in the Far East. The British urged the Japanese to fight only a limited war, destroying German naval vessels, but taking no action against the German holdings in China. The Japanese rejected this request and agreed to fight only as a full belligerent. An ultimatum was sent to Germany in August of 1914 to withdraw from the Kiaochow leasehold on China's Shantung Peninsula and to disarm or withdraw its forces from the Pacific. When the ultimatum went unanswered, Japan moved. By the end of 1914 with British help the Japanese forces had captured Tsingtao, the chief port of the Kiaochow leasehold, as well as the German-held islands in Micronesia.

The western reaction to Japan's success varied. Britain and

France had a firm grip on their Far Eastern empire and did not consider Japan's expansion as a threat. There were also some Americans who did not see the replacement of Germany in Asia by Japan as a threat to their nation's interests. "There is war in China purely because there has been no Asiatic Monroe Doctrine and because Japan finds the presence of Germany a menace to itself," Theodore Roosevelt wrote a friend in November of 1914. But in Washington circles and particularly within the Navy, Japan's gains were evaluated as a blow to American strength in the Pacific. Admiral Mahan wrote from retirement to a kindred thinker, Assistant Secretary of the Navy Franklin D. Roosevelt, and urged that an appeal be made to Britain to block her ally's gains. "It is one thing," wrote Mahan, to have the Pacific islands "in the hands of a power whose main strength is in Europe, and quite another that they should pass into the hands of one so near as Japan." No American action was taken. Britain had already joined with Japan in an agreement to share the spoils; the German islands below the Equator were marked for British possession. But American concern was shown by the reports of large shipments of ammunition and fuel to American bases in Hawaii and the Philippines, following the news of Japan's victories.

Japan's success in ousting the Germans from Shantung and in establishing what appeared to be a new protectorate brought charges in Congress that this was a violation of the Open Door policy. Even before Japan went to war two resolutions were introduced in the House, warning the Japanese against acquiring any holdings in China as a result of military operations. Both resolutions were tabled but the pro-Chinese sentiments of a small group of Congressmen continued to be heard. In Peking the American Minister, Paul Reinsch, went so far in his opposition to Japan's gains that Acting Secretary Lansing warned him in November of 1914 that to embroil the United States in international difficulties over China's territorial integrity would be "quixotic in the extreme."

In January of 1915 Japan took advantage of the war to communicate the "Twenty-one Demands" to China. Divided into five groups, the first three called for official Chinese sanction for Japanese economic activities in the Shantung Peninsula, southern Manchuria, Inner Mongolia, and in the mining areas of the Yangtse Valley. Japan claimed that this meant for the most part only a formalization of a *de facto* situation. The fourth group called upon China to pledge never to alienate any coastal areas to a third power by cession or lease, giving the Japanese assurance against the return of the German leasehold or the establishment of an American naval base if that proposal was ever renewed. The last group, expressed as "desires," were of a different character in calling for Chinese co-operation in ways which would have extended Japan's political influence over the mainland.

Japan delivered the demands in a peremptory manner, characteristic of European dealings with an inferior oriental state. When the news reached Washington from Peking, there was great alarm on the part of the friends of China. Without waiting for instructions, Reinsch strongly urged the Chinese to make no concessions, implying American support in the event of a showdown. E. T. Williams, Chief of the Division of Far Eastern Affairs, supported Reinsch, but Secretary Bryan was more cautious. An effort was made to secure British action to check her Japanese ally, but other considerations took priority in British policy. Some thought was given by the State Department to seeking a *quid pro quo* from Japan in return for Chinese acceptance of the first four groups of demands. Japan might pledge to refrain from complaints over any future American legislation directed at Japanese immigrants and also reaffirm the principles of the Open Door. But President Wilson was opposed to seeking any compromises and instead two notes were sent to Japan, protesting the demands made on China. The second note, sent after China had agreed to fulfill the first four groups of demands, stated that the United States would never recognize any agreements with China which impaired American treaty rights or violated the Open Door policy.

A policy limited to diplomatic protests was viewed as too passive by some of the pro-Chinese sectors of American opinion. Church bodies were vehement in their denunciations of Japan and called for American intervention. Congressional advocates of naval expansion grasped the opportunity to call for an accelerated program of battleship construction. In the House, Alabama's Congressman, Richmond Hobson, offered a resolution branding Japan's China policy as unfriendly to the United States; in the Naval Affairs Committee, he called for immediate construction of a two-ocean navy.

Japan's action in China was linked with the hostility toward Japanese immigration to promote a new hate-Japan campaign in the press. The Hearst newspapers published a series in 1915 entitled, "Japan's Plans to Invade and Conquer the United States." The articles claimed that Japan had issued a military manual preparing for the attack and pictures were shown of Japanese troops practicing landing operations for a future assault on the California coast. Investigation disclosed that the source of the articles was a distorted version of a cheap Japanese novel, while the illustrations were retouched pictures of the Sino-Japanese War of 1894–1895. Many other journalists joined in exploiting the new source of hostility toward Japan. An article published in the respectable *North American Review* in May of 1916 propagated the myth that Japan had answered the American protests over the Twenty-one Demands by assembling a threatening naval force in Mexican waters. A Japanese naval vessel in pursuit of German ships had grounded on the coast of Lower California in January of 1915 and had landed its guns and ammunition in order to refloat. This incident was quickly used in a variety of forms remote from the facts as proof of Japan's hostile intentions.

American missionary groups with centers in Japan and the

Japan Societies made an effort to counter this new wave of hostility. The Japan Society of New York published volumes of essays in 1914 and 1915 on Japanese-American friendship. Judge Elbert H. Gary, the steel magnate, visited Japan in 1916 and returned to lecture to business leaders on the common economic interests of the two countries and to dispel war rumors. If these efforts won few new friends for Japan, they served to alarm the anti-Japanese forces on the West coast. In 1917, *The Japanese Conquest of American Opinion* by Montaville Flowers attacked as villainous the work of the Japan Society of New York and of the Federal Council of Churches in trying to give the Japanese a good name in the United States.

The files of government intelligence agencies in the early years of the European war reveal the variety of Japanese threats which rumor produced. In May of 1916 the State Department was informed by an allegedly reliable source in Hong Kong that Japan was preparing to declare war on the United States that fall. The same year Army intelligence agents investigated reports of Japanese troop landings in Lower California, and one agent reported that Mexicans had actually seen Japanese landing on remote beaches in military formation. In September of 1918 Naval intelligence reports reached the White House of the landing of several hundred Japanese Army officers in the Philippines, disguised as workmen, to start an uprising which would divert American troops from Siberia. President Wilson found the report "exceedingly disturbing, if true," and asked for a thorough probe.

Fear of Japan joined with the growing concern over German submarine warfare in the Atlantic to support a major naval building program. In October of 1915 the General Board of the Navy made a clean break with the anti-imperialist tradition of a coastal and defensive navy and proposed building a force equal to that of the most powerful navy in the world. The Senate Naval Affairs Committee gave its enthusiastic support and urged that the program be speeded up to reach its goal

in three rather than five years. President Wilson in August of
1916 signed the bill which launched the largest naval construction program undertaken by a nation at peace. The new ships
were ostensibly to meet the threat of war on the Atlantic as a
result of Germany's submarine campaigns, but many of the
men in Congress who voted for the naval bill saw it also as a
counter to the threat of Japan. In Japan the naval propagandists played up the American program as a direct challenge
and claimed that the new United States Navy would be twice
the size of Japan's.

With American entry into World War I in April of 1917,
Japan became in official language an "associated power," and
in effect an ally, in the struggle against Germany. Alignment
against a common enemy did little, however, to ease the rising
tensions. The American declaration of war was received with
some suspicion in Japan. The issue of submarine warfare
seemed insufficient cause for American action and ulterior
motives were sought. Fears were expressed in the Japanese
press that the war would be used to expand American naval
bases in the Philippines. Tokyo hinted to Washington that as-
surances against such developments would be welcome and
that Japan would be willing to buy the islands.

Congressional debate on the question of Philippine independence in 1916 demonstrated that many Democrats saw the
islands as a military liability and an irritant to Japanese-
American relations. Secretary of State Lansing wrote to President Wilson, "If we could only let go, what a blessing it would
be." But neither Wilson nor Congress were willing to go so far
as to favor a transfer to Japan.

Despite his deep concern for what he saw as the vital issues
of the European war, Woodrow Wilson at times seems to have
believed that Asia might have an even higher priority. Two
months before the President asked Congress for a declaration
of war against Germany, he told the cabinet his fears about
Asia. If, he said, neutrality was necessary in order to keep the

white race strong enough to meet the yellow race, he would
keep the United States neutral despite any imputations of
cowardice or weakness made against him. This race threat he
envisioned as coming from Japan, dominating China in alliance
with Russia.

Once the United States was at war with Germany, the President recognized the need for easing tensions and improving
relations with Japan. When an anti-Japanese film was shown
in Washington in 1917, depicting an Oriental military invasion
of the United States, Wilson asked the producers to withdraw
it from circulation as unfair to Japan and calculated to stir up
hostility. Japan was also interested in more cordial relations
with the United States and hinted at willingness to send a high
level diplomatic mission to Washington. Wilson approved of
Secretary Lansing's positive response and in August of 1917
Viscount Kikujiro Ishii arrived to open conversations.

The Lansing-Ishii negotiations which followed were devoted
principally to questions concerning the mainland of Asia.
Japan, in 1912 and again in 1916, had by secret treaty secured
Russian recognition of her special interests in southern Manchuria and eastern Inner Mongolia. Viscount Ishii had been
briefed on American history and hoped now to secure American recognition of Japan's "paramount interests" in China, a
phrase used by Secretaries of State in describing American
interests in Mexico. Wilson and Lansing on the other hand
wanted a new declaration from Japan, pledging respect for the
American concept of the Open Door in China. Neither country
was willing to offer the other anything substantial in the form
of a *quid pro quo* and no substantial ground for agreement was
found. To maintain the appearance of unity in the face of the
Central Powers an ambiguous formula was agreed upon. The
United States recognized that Japan's geographical relationship
to China created "special relations" and "special interests."
Japan, in turn, agreed to a secret protocol in which the two
governments stated their accord in not seeking special rights

or privileges in China abridging the rights of "other friendly states."

Both governments hoped to give to the words of the agreement a content favorable to their own interests. The pro-Chinese elements in the United States were quick to charge the Wilson administration with a "sell-out" to Japan. Unable to quote the secret protocol in its defense, the State Department claimed that it had made no concession to Japan. The United States had only recognized "the self-evident truth of the mutual interest of neighboring nations in the welfare of each other." In the next two years Japan did launch an economic program which made capital available to China and attempted a partnership in Chinese economic development. The program was not generous enough, however, to win full support of the Chinese government and Chinese internal disunity was a further obstacle to its success.

Despite the underlying conflict over China, the United States and Japan were pressed by wartime exigencies into naval co-operation. Both promised to inform the other of their ship movements in the Pacific. In October of 1917 Japan was asked to detail a cruiser to Honolulu to patrol the waters left unguarded by the transfer of American ships to convoy duty in the Atlantic. In May of 1918 Secretary Lansing sounded out the Japanese Ambassador on a further step, the dispatch of two cruisers to patrol the Atlantic coast of the United States. The Navy Department, concerned about possible German attacks on coastal shipping, had asked for four Japanese cruisers. Japan replied that only two of its cruisers had the speed necessary for this patrol duty and one of these was damaged. The Armistice came before any ship transfers were accomplished.

The last months of the war saw no perceptible gains in improved understanding as a result of the *mariage de convenance*. Japan remained wary of growing American power and, when not completely bewildered by Wilson's oratory, Japanese looked for ulterior meanings in his grandiose proclamations.

Even the issuance of the Fourteen Points in January of 1918 was viewed by some Japanese with suspicion, while the proposed League of Nations was denounced by chauvinists as a new device for extending American influence in Asia. Dr. Inazo Nitobe, Japan's leading interpreter of America, wrote many articles which affirmed the friendly intentions of the postwar plans coming from Washington, but Wilson remained an enigmatic figure in Tokyo.

American expectation of future trouble with Japan seems to have been demonstrated in the first weeks following the signing of the Armistice in November of 1918. Secretary of the Navy Josephus Daniels appeared before the House Naval Affairs Committee and asked for a new three-year building program which would add ten battleships, six battle cruisers, and 140 smaller vessels to existing naval strength. President Wilson gave his blanket endorsement to this program in his message to Congress. Daniels explained that the new navy would be a contribution to the new League of Nations as a "tremendous police power of prevention." Unofficially, however, there was considerable discussion of the importance of the new ships in relation to Japan.

The Asian orientation of the naval expansionists was demonstrated early in 1919 when Secretary Daniels announced that the main body of American naval forces would be transferred to the Pacific. When Daniels greeted the fleet off San Diego in August of 1919, he said that he had been acting on a hunch when he ordered the geographical shift. Some naval spokesman explained the move as an attempt to stimulate rivalry within the Navy by building up the Pacific forces to compete with the Atlantic. There were also charges that the Wilson administration had made the decision in order to win Democratic votes in the western states for the 1920 elections. Strategic considerations were doubtless an important factor in the decision whatever the truth of the other reasons offered.

Fourteen of the newest and heaviest battleships were concentrated in the Pacific. The total tonnage of the American Pacific forces was now approximately equal to the entire Japanese Navy, and Japan's unchallenged dominance of Pacific waters during the war years was ended. In 1919 a new dry dock was opened at Pearl Harbor, capable of handling battleships and this Hawaiian naval yard became the major advance base of American power. The Navy Department requested the expansion of Pearl Harbor facilities to handle "any movement, offensive or defensive, across the Pacific." Secretary Daniels also asked Congress—without success—for funds to fortify Guam and expand naval facilities in the Philippines.

The publicity given in Japan to the American moves helped to counter the anti-military spirit which developed after the peace. In July of 1920 the Japanese Diet voted to construct 16 new capital ships, the same number authorized by Congress in 1919, but to be completed in eight years rather than in four as in the American program. Japan's naval expenditures for 1921 were triple those of 1917, but the Admiralty claimed that the new ships would only raise Japanese strength to about half that of the United States. Japan's air enthusiasts also used fear of the United States to promote their demands for expansion. A film sponsored by the Imperial Aviation Association prophetically pictured Tokyo in ashes as a result of an attack from across the ocean.

The burgeoning naval race was accompanied by—and stimulated by—a new series of political conflicts following the collapse of the Central Powers. When the Paris Peace Conference opened in January of 1919, Japanese and American viewpoints clashed almost immediately. Before sailing from New York, President Wilson confided to the Chinese Ambassador that Asia was "the only part of the world" where there was any possibility of future trouble. At Paris the President soon concluded that the integrity of China, the Open Door, and the orderly processes of change in Asia were all threatened by Japan's ambitions. The Japanese delegates also came early to the conviction that the only major obstacle to the achievement of their rightful gains was the American policy of "meddling" in Asia.

The President generally sought little advice from his staff of experts at the peace conference, but when he did his anti-Japanese frame of thought found ample support. E. T. Williams and Stanley K. Hornbeck, the Far Eastern experts, were both determined that the United States should act as China's guardian and their arguments were reinforced by messages from Paul Reinsch in China. Only Colonel Edward House was willing at Paris to suggest areas of compromise with Japan. Two years earlier he had pointed out that politically the United States was unable to meet Japan half-way on the issues of land ownership and immigration. Therefore, "unless we make some concessions in regard to her sphere of influence in the East, trouble is sure sooner or later to come."

Whereas Wilson came to Paris with predominantly negative objectives in regard to Asia, i.e., the blocking of Japan's gains, the Japanese had three clearly defined goals. The first two merely required confirmation by the peace conference of Japan's claims to the German holdings in Shantung and to the former German islands in the Pacific. China had granted Germany in 1898 a 99-year lease to the port of Tsingtao plus several hundred square miles of hinterland with the right to exploit the mines and develop the railroads of the area. In the Pacific, Germany had acquired the Marshall Islands by annexation in 1885 and the Marianas and Carolines by purchase from Spain in 1898. During the war Japan drove the Germans out of all these areas and had no doubts about its right to inherit the rewards of military victory.

Japan's claims had been recognized during the war by a series of notes exchanged with Britain, France, Italy, and Russia, and the British had joined in the program of annexation by taking as a reward the former German islands below the Equator. China had recognized the Japanese claims to Shan-

tung in 1918 and accepted an advance payment of $20 million
in the form of a railway loan to sweeten the agreement. For
Japan the islands offered an outer ring of bases, valuable for
defense or an offense into the South Pacific, while the Shantung
Peninsula could contribute valuable resources to Japan's expanding economy.

The third objective of the peace delegates from Tokyo was
the achievement of an equal social status with other great
powers. This meant the eradication of the white man's open
racial discrimination against the yellow-skinned Oriental. In
the era of mass migration of Europeans to other parts of the
world, Japan found its immigrants barred in most directions by
"whites only" signs. For a nation which had demonstrated twice
its ability to defeat Europeans in military combat, this was an
affront which periodically aroused strong public resentment.
For some, Japanese immigration also offered the best solution
for economic problems. As one member of Japan's House of
Representatives stated the argument:

> Territorial gains may be welcome for the purpose, but as
> territorial aggrandisement can be accomplished only by
> militarism, which is not compatible with the general
> world trend, Japan must avoid following such aggressive
> policies. . . . As an alternative, it becomes imperative
> for Japan to obtain freedom of residence for her people
> in all and any territory in and on the Pacific.

This meant, according to Representative Etsujiro Uyehara, an
"Open Door" principle applied to Japanese immigrants by
Australia, Canada, the Americas, and India. Not all Japanese
were as hopeful about the value of migration, but many felt
that the new world organization to be formed at Paris should
give some recognition to the principle of racial equality. Control of immigration was a matter for domestic legislation, but
an international recognition of racial equality was expected to
discourage inequity in favoring white immigrants over oriental.

President Wilson initially encouraged the Japanese in their

desire for a statement of racial equality in the League Covenant. Colonel House helped the Japanese delegates to draft two resolutions, one asking for a maximum and the other a minimum recognition of the principle of non-discrimination. It was the minimum which was finally offered as an amendment to the Covenant, a general endorsement of the "principle of equality of Nations" and of "just treatment of their nationals." The League of Nations Commission voted 11 to 0 for the amendment, with the United States and British delegations abstaining. But Wilson, as chairman of the meeting, ruled that the amendment had failed for lack of unanimous support. There was some technical argument that could be made for the President's ruling, but Japan was bitter over the negative attitude of the British and Americans.

The strongest opponent to any racial concessions to Japan was Premier William H. Hughes of Australia, whose government held strongly to the "whites only" policy, an approach to immigration which remained a persistent Australian theme. Hughes's threat to reject the League cowed the other British delegates into refraining from voting. Wilson was also afraid of Australia's rejection of the League, but his opposition to the League acceptance of racial equality was supported by other reasons. The President was not himself without racial prejudices, but he also had to consider the possible opposition to the ratification of American membership in the League by race-conscious southern senators and west coast exponents of the Yellow Peril. Whatever the President's reasons, the Japanese delegates had cause to feel betrayed by the man who stood publicly on such a high point of international idealism.

Wilson's decision on the racial amendment followed his fight against Japan's two other objectives. American naval advisers believed that Japan's acquisition of the former German islands would be a threat to the line of communications between Hawaii and the Philippines. They urged internationalizing the island groups and compensating Japan by offering a free hand

in Siberia, where a revolution-weakened Russia could not make
an effective protest. But the President did not want to give
Japan a free hand anywhere and was reluctant to compromise
when he believed principle was involved. Japan's delegates, on
the other hand, claimed that the island groups were far more
than mere souvenirs of the war, but essential to the defense of
their home islands.

Since Japan was already in possession of the islands when
the peace conference met, and since the British and French had
already agreed to their disposition, the American delegation
had to try to undo a *fait accompli*. This proved impossible. The
only compensation offered the United States was to give Japan
the islands as Class C mandates under the League. Although
the mandate system has been aptly called "an elaborate fig leaf
for imperialism," it had some value in prohibiting Japan from
using the islands as military bases by erecting fortifications or
building naval installations.

Japan's claims to the German rights in Shantung aroused
even greater opposition on the part of the American delegation
than the other two issues. To Wilson and some of his advisers
this claim was a step toward a new partition of China. It
brought forth anguished cries from the American missionaries
and their supporters in the United States. The delegations from
China's rival governments, Peking and Canton, had stood with
Japan on the racial equality issue, but appealed for American
support against Japan on Shantung. Wilson was fully in accord
with the Chinese and viewed his position as the protector of
the weak and beyond reproach.

The Japanese delegation also felt strongly about their claims
to Shantung, recalling the territorial gains made by western
powers since the triple intervention of 1895. Japan of 1919 was
a far more powerful nation than it had been in 1895 and was
determined not to be excluded this time from the club of
imperialist nations because of coming late to the penetration
of China. The Peking government had reluctantly given its

legal support to the Shantung cession by treaty in 1918. None of the European powers was in a strong position to oppose Japan in principle, and Japan was determined to push Wilson's obstructions aside. When Italy set a precedent by walking out of the conference because of Wilson's obstinacy, Japan threatened to follow. The President gloomily gave in. Japan gave him a small consolation by promising orally that full sovereignty of the Peninsula would be restored to China and that only economic privileges would be retained.

The pro-Chinese elements in the United States berated Wilson for his final action. He wrote to a missionary friend in response to his complaint:

> What would you propose that we should do? To refuse to concur in the Treaty with Germany would not alter the situation in China's favor, unless it is your idea that we should force Great Britain and France to break their special treaty with Japan, and how would you suggest that we do that? By the exercise of force?

But the defeat was still painful despite its apparent inevitability. House tried to comfort the President by saying that while the Japanese settlement was "all bad," it was still necessary to clean up "a lot of old rubbish with the least friction and let the League of Nations and the new era do the rest." Wilson consoled himself along these lines; he believed that he had gotten the best settlement possible "out of a dirty past."

Several of the strongest of the pro-Chinese advisers in the American delegation resigned in protest. From Peking, Paul Reinsch sent the President a bitter letter and left the American foreign service to take a position with the Chinese government. In the United States, Wilson's political opponents cried "betrayal" as they concluded that the Shantung settlement was the most vulnerable aspect of the Versailles Treaty. American sentiment in behalf of China was played upon by congressional orators whose prime aim was to block American entry into the

League. Ex-President Taft was courageous enough to point out the insincerity of many of these professions of love for China by fellow Republicans. In compromising, Wilson had taken the only "statesmanlike course," said Taft.

Taft's position was not taken by Henry Cabot Lodge, chairman of the Senate Foreign Relations Committee and major critic of the decisions taken at Paris. Lodge not only expressed his ire against Wilson but against Japan as well. He charged the Land of the Rising Sun with having become "the Prussia of the East," and with adopting Prussian culture and ambitions. When his Committee dealt with the Versailles settlement, he amended the treaty text by substituting "China" for "Japan" in the articles dealing with the disposition of German rights in Asia. This crusade against the decisions hammered out at the peace table won him a flood of approving letters from missionaries and church groups. When news of Lodge's action reached Tokyo, it was taken as an affront that the issue should be reopened on the domestic level. Marquis Shigenobu Okuma, former premier, claimed that Senator Lodge was blighting future relations with Japan by his display of spite, while the influential *Osaka Mainichi* assailed Lodge's action as "a provocative act." The Massachusetts senator was able to block American ratification of the Versailles Treaty, but its provisions for the disposal of German holdings remained, of course, in effect.

Wilson's failure to block Japan's gains at Paris was only one aspect of his broader failure to establish a victory without spoils. At one point in his fight with Japan he considered asking all nations to give up their extraterritorial rights and privileges in China. The reaction of London and Paris to such a move would have been similar to that provoked by an Allied request that the United States restore Hawaii to the Hawaiians or Puerto Rico to Spain. German colonies in Africa and Turkey's holdings in the Middle East were all parcelled out among the victors under the mandate system. To expect Japan to renounce the fruits of victory in Asia without other compensations was to expect a miracle.

Before the bitterness created in Japanese-American relations at Paris had time to subside another clash of interests took place in Siberia. The Russian Revolution of November 1917 and the Russo-German peace was followed by a series of Allied interventions in Russia—interventions whose motivations are still a matter of scholarly debate. Britain and France asked the United States to send troops along with Japan into revolution-torn Siberia. Wilson was faced with another challenge to his principles. One of his Fourteen Points had promised Russia "an unhampered and unembarrassed opportunity for the independent determination of her own political development." A military occupation of Siberia was an obvious inconsistency. Yet Wilson feared that Japanese troops acting without partners would establish permanent claims.

In July of 1918 the President overcame his reluctance and ordered a force of approximately 7,000 landed at Vladivostok. An effort was made to bind Japan to the same size force, but the Japanese followed their own course and sent ten times as many men as the Americans. For Japan, Siberia was of strategic importance as a possible outpost of future Russian power on the Pacific and of economic importance for the market it offered Japanese exports. For the United States, Siberia also represented a market, particularly for agricultural equipment, with the International Harvester Company maintaining over 200 Siberian outlets. Both countries were interested in the trans-Siberian railroad which E. H. Harriman had viewed as a vital link in his plans for a round-the-world rail system.

For 17 months American troops remained on Russian soil. When they withdrew in April of 1920, they had failed either to oust the Japanese or to provide permanent safeguards for American economic interests. Japan withdrew some two years later in the face of the advancing Communist Russian state, having also failed to stabilize its economic interests. Both Japan and the United States were henceforth confronted with the Soviet Union as a factor in the affairs of Asia. The joint occupation not only sharpened antagonism toward each other, but added to the hostility of their relations with the new Soviet state.

Woodrow Wilson believed himself a man of peace and an advocate of international understanding. Yet when he left office in March of 1921, his administration had gone beyond that of the belligerent Theodore Roosevelt's in crossing swords with Japan and creating mutual misunderstanding. Japan's view of the United States was expressed in 1920 by a member of the Japanese Diet:

> America appears to think she is divinely appointed to rule the world with a big stick! What is the purpose of her colossal Navy if it is not to make her power supreme in every part of the Pacific? American statesmen profess an undying devotion to peace, and meanwhile they are building warships on a scale unparalleled in history. They preach the doctrine of racial equality and equal opportunity and yet refuse to admit educated Japanese immigrants to American citizenship. They disclaim all intention of meddling with foreign politics, and at the same time continue to bombard us with arrogant notes about our policy in Manchuria, Siberia and Saghalien. In these circumstances America has only herself to blame if sober Japanese are beginning to suspect her of designs upon their country and its most cherished interests.

This Japanese indictment was an extreme one, marked by a nationalistic bias in some respects akin to that which was being indicted. But it was contained more than a little truth.

The Wilson administration had expressed the old faith in America's Manifest Destiny in a new framework. The United States was to lead the world in establishing a new international order, based on the highest morality. Touched with a sense of national omnipotence, the President disregarded the harsh truth that nations and national behavior change but slowly. More than the fiat of the head of one nation was necessary to remake the world on ideal terms in Europe and Asia. As applied to Japan, Wilson's ideals demanded a selflessness of the national leaders not yet found in his own country. A nation which, after defeating Spain, had taken the Philippine colony and crushed its independence movement could hardly proclaim some 20 years later that other nations should not use victory to expand, without being charged with hypocrisy or a short memory. Nor did Wilson's faith that he spoke for world interests alone conceal from others that his goals often coincided with the expanding economic and strategic interests of his own country. Japan, like many other nations, would henceforth assume that professions of idealism coming from Washington were actually a shield to conceal the normal nationalistic ambitions of a growing country. And sometimes this assumption was valid.

Chapter IX

A NEW ASIAN POLICY

ISTORIANS' CLAIMS to the contrary, men often learn more from the present about the past than from the past about the future. Common versions of the recent past have frequently proved deceptive guides to the future. Journalistic seers who wrote about Japanese-American relations in the first years after World War I were prone to predict a Pacific War as "inevitable" within a few years. The conflicting interests of the two nations were clashing at many points. Tensions appeared to be rising to a level at which war would erupt. Technology was making it possible to envision aerial and naval battles across the thousands of miles of Pacific waters.

Apocalyptic books flourished in both countries, picturing the horrors of the imminent conflict. Distinguished naval experts like Hector C. Bywater of Britain and a retired Russian general, Nicolai Golovin, produced lengthy analyses of the strategies which the Japanese and American navies would follow in the great Pacific War. "The only means of averting war with Japan in the twentieth century would be for the United States to evacuate the Philippines and to renounce her interests in Eastern Asia," warned General Golovin, while dismissing as politically impossible any such American retreat. Few writers could counter these prophecies, since there were no discernible "trends" which pointed in directions other than war.

Within American military and naval circles—and possibly in Japan as well—the belief in imminent war was widespread. A secret memorandum was issued by the Office of Naval Intelligence in February of 1920 entitled "Evidence of Japan's Preparation for War." It reported on the problems of Japanese population growth in relation to limited natural resources, and on the conviction of Japanese government officials that expansion on the Asian mainland was the only solution. The United States support of China was viewed as the only major obstacle to this expansion. Three months later another Naval Intelligence report found Chinese officials convinced that the Japanese-American war was "bound to come within five years." A Navy General Board report in September of 1921 concluded pessimistically that American interests in Asia could not be maintained without war.

In Japan a retired general, Kojiro Sato, published a volume in 1920 which quickly ran through three printings, warning his countrymen to prepare for an air attack and invasion by American forces. His vision was not entirely fantasy, since by 1921 the U.S. Army had begun to plan landing operations for the final stages of a future war after Japan's defenses had been destroyed by bombing planes. Landing maneuvers were subsequently held in the Caribbean to prepare for the Pacific eventuality. A Japanese invasion of the United States was also treated as a genuine threat by some Americans. Early in 1920 the Senate Foreign Relations Committee heard sensational testimony in regard to a Japanese-Mexican liaison in which Japan promised support for a Mexican invasion of the United States. The Hearst press headlined the testimony as evidence of the reality of the Japanese threat to national security.

A decade after the close of World War I, the Pacific picture seemed to have changed radically. Japanese-American issues which once appeared crucial had by 1928 melted away. "Ir-reconcilable" conflicts of interest were submerged under pro-fessions of friendship and mutual commitment to the goal of peace. Only a few observers remained skeptical of the prospects of continued Pacific amity. The threat of war, the majority agreed, was in the past rather than in the future.

The optimistic outlook on trans-Pacific relations was the product of events as well as of changes of attitudes and policies in both countries. Although the United States made only minor sacrifices in the European war, peace was followed by a wide-spread popular aversion to war itself. The bitterness which many Americans felt over the realities of the postwar world contributed to the anti-war feeling. President Wilson's idealism and the slogans, "peace without victory," "no annexations," and the faith that this was really "a war to end war" contrasted strongly with the actual settlements hammered out of the nationalistic conflicts by the victors at Paris. The great crusade for which Americans had crossed the Atlantic to fight on Euro-pean soil for the first time in their history began to be viewed as another of the balance of power conflicts in which the United States presumably had no vital interest. This cast of American thought left little reserve of militant idealism on which to draw for a belligerent policy in the Pacific.

Economics also discouraged American militancy. After some initial readjustments, the postwar years brought a new pros-perity to the United States. Getting and spending the wealth produced by greater productivity became almost a national obsession. The business of America was business and not war. Political leaders not only understood this mood but had to work with the demands for budget-cutting and the pressures to shrink the national government to pre-World War I propor-tions. A bold foreign policy could not be maintained in the face of this shrinking process. The military and naval power which survived economy programs was fully involved in defending

American economic interests in Latin America. Developments in the Pacific had to be evaluated in terms of a pacifistic scale of national priorities.

The course of events in Asia did little to disturb and much to reinforce the Far Eastern policies based on the new American mood. Disenchantment with Europe was paralleled by a waning of enthusiasm for the new Chinese Republic. Its government appeared for many years incapable of ruling that vast empire, while *de facto* power was exercised in many areas by predatory war lords. Banditry, nationalist fervor, and Communist intrigue combined to produce assault after assault on western residents and interests. American citizens were killed and kidnapped and American property destroyed. Protests sent to Peking from Washington were seldom answered by effective action. Those Americans who argued for a tougher policy in the Far East were moved to direct their animosity at China rather than Japan.

Japan in the same years experienced internal changes and produced external policies which shaped a more favorable American image of the wartime rival. Some of the idealism expressed by President Wilson had its echoes in Japan and seemed to be evidenced in popular demand for more democratic institutions. In September of 1918 the first commoner was appointed premier, Kei Hara, and in 1925 agitation brought about the introduction of manhood suffrage. A view of Japan's future tinged with a little optimism could easily predict the development of a stable democratic state with which American interests in Asia could co-exist.

The economic dislocations which the aftermath of the war brought to Japan's economy speeded the rise of labor unions and political radicalism. The military cliques became a popular target of the liberal and radical elements. Militarism appeared on the decline. As early as the spring of 1920 an American intelligence report concluded that "the old traditions of duty to the state, loyalty and self-denial are rapidly passing away,

and commercialism and half-baked ideas of Socialism are the
successors." The morale of Japan's armed services was described a year later by American Army intelligence agents as
low and discipline becoming shockingly lax. The lack of military spirit had reached a point where the services had difficulty
in recruiting men for the officers' schools.

The foreign policy of the new Japan reflected some of the
changes which had submerged the former expansionist spirit.
Most important in the eyes of American commentators was the
conciliatory attiude shown toward China even when the excesses of that country's nationalism tried American patience.
Good business relations with China, the Japanese government
believed, could be best secured by non-intervention policies.
With few exceptions this conciliatory policy was maintained
for almost a decade.

This fading of the Japanese "threat," the confused picture
Americans received of Chinese developments, the disturbing
indications that pro-American feelings in China were no longer
universal and the stay-at-home mood of the American people
were the developments with which a new American Far
Eastern policy had to be reconciled. President Harding's Secretary of State, Charles Evans Hughes, set the new course.
Warren Harding had little interest in foreign affairs and was
content to give Hughes a free hand even though the former
Supreme Court Associate Justice had no experience in this field.
But it was not long after Hughes took office in March of 1921
that he began a major reorientation of American policy in Asia.

The situation facing Hughes was not a favorable one for
American interests. Japanese troops still remained in Siberia,
although the American forces had been withdrawn in the
spring of 1920. Shantung still remained in Japanese hands
despite American protests. Japan's insular acquisitions from
Germany included the island of Yap in the Carolines, an important station for trans-Pacific commercial cables. The significance of this control became apparent in 1920. American com-

mercial expansion in Asia, said the *New York Times*, required a line of communication not under the control of "any competing nation." Some business interests took the same position and the new Republican administration could not ignore the Yap issue. The beginning of a naval building race directed at supremacy in the Pacific seemed to foretell an eventual settlement of some of these issues by arms.

The new Secretary of State understood that his country had made a reappraisal of its interests in Asia. His policy accepted that reappraisal. In contrast to the Wilsonian outlook, at times prepared to risk war in the Far East in support of some proclaimed ideal, the new mood was a bluntly economic one. Each policy was measured in terms of the dollars involved and on a balance sheet basis of profits and losses for the American businessman and taxpayer. This outlook was illustrated by Senator Thomas Walsh of Montana who in congressional hearings pressed spokesmen for larger naval appropriations to prepare a balance sheet in which the cost of a future war with Japan could be totalled up against the value of whatever trade that war was intended to protect. Hughes himself said in 1921 that he acted on the assumption that "this country would never go to war over any aggression on the part of Japan in China." The House Military Affairs Committee in 1922 expressed the same outlook when it reported an Army appropriation bill with a proviso that no money could be used for troops stationed in China except in time of emergency, nor could payments be made for more than 5,000 troops stationed in Hawaii. The proviso was removed from the bill on the floor as an unconstitutional restraint upon the President, but it indicated the temper of a substantial number of congressmen.

Secretary Hughes' understanding of the prevailing priority system of national interests led him to respond readily to at least one congressional initiative based on this system. Budget-minded representatives joined with anti-war congressmen in attacking the naval arms race in which the United States was

running against Japan and Britain. Senator William E. Borah
of Idaho assumed congressional leadership of this movement
and in December of 1920 introduced a joint resolution request-
ing the President to open negotiations with these two competing powers to cancel the race. Borah used as one of his
arguments the Japanese view expressed by Count Ishii that his
country was forced to build more ships because of the American naval construction program.

Incoming President Harding resented what appeared to him
to be congressional interference in the management of foreign
affairs, but the Borah resolution passed in the spring of 1921.
Political pressures increased from a well-organized disarmament movement and in July Harding sent an invitation to the
four leading naval powers to meet in Washington to discuss
arms limitation. The British, pressed for funds to keep their
fleet on a par with the United States and seeing the conference
as a possible solution to the problems raised by their alliance
with Japan, accepted the American move. At British suggestion the conference call was broadened to include a general
discussion of Far Eastern questions on the agenda. Invitations were sent to all nations with Pacific interests.

Japan accepted Washington's call reluctantly. The inclusion
of political matters on the agenda suggested to Tokyo a new
western effort to limit Japan's freedom of operation in Asia.
The Japanese press also hinted that the conference might be
used to terminate the British alliance which had been in operation since 1902. Nevertheless the Japanese Cabinet decided to
co-operate and a capable Japanese delegation arrived in Washington in time for the opening meeting of the conference on
November 12, 1921.

Many criticisms have been directed at the achievements of
the conference which was concluded in February of 1922.
Naval expansionists in all the major participants complained
that the limitations placed upon their fleets seriously weakened
their national power. After the Japanese-American War began

in 1941, some American critics even attributed the Pearl Harbor disaster to the debilitating effect on the United States Navy of the treaty limitations which terminated in 1936. Such criticisms are, however, based on hypotheses which can only be upheld by ignoring many of the salient facts. The main American objective at the conference was to check the naval race and to benefit from the by-products of reduced international tensions and lowered naval expenditures. This objective and these benefits were achieved for more than a decade. Without the 1922 agreements it is still unlikely that Congress would have voted money to build beyond the limits set by treaty, while both Japan and Britain would have been unrestrained by other than domestic factors.

The major credit for the achievements of 1921–1922 must go to Secretary of State Hughes. He startled the delegates in his opening speech by claiming that disarmament should be achieved by disarming. He went on to present a bold plan which included a ten-year holiday in the building of battleships and aircraft carriers, fixing Japanese strength in these categories at approximately 60 percent of the tonnage of the United States and Britain. Japan's delegates, like those of Britain, France, and Italy, were stunned at the enormity of the American proposal. When they recovered, a move was made to secure a 70 percent tonnage ceiling, even though chauvinistic Japanese newspapers denounced this level of limitation as a national dishonor. After some concessions on specific ships and weeks of negotiations, Japan accepted the proposed 60 percent tonnage level. France and Italy accepted 35 percent as their capital ship strength.

In addition to limiting total capital ship tonnage, the negotiators agreed to set a limit of 10,000 tons on the size of cruisers and to increase the area of non-competition by a measure of disengagement in the Pacific. The three major Pacific powers pledged to freeze the status quo of their fortifications in a quadrangular area of the Pacific. For the United States, this excluded Hawaii but included Guam, the Aleutians, and the Philippines. Britain excluded Singapore, but included Hong Kong while Japan was barred from further fortification of any but the home islands. The offensive power of all three nations was thus limited by banning the development of well-fortified advance bases.

Some British evaluations of the Washington Conference emphasized its benefits in substituting for the Anglo-Japanese alliance a Four-Power Treaty which pledged consultation by Britain, the United States, Japan, and France over conflicts of interest. Britain had allied with Japan when Russian expansionism seemed about to jeopardize the British position in China, but the Japanese defeat of Russia in 1905 and the hiatus produced by the Soviet revolution and civil war had removed that threat. The termination of the alliance, although a shock to Japan, gave the British greater freedom of action. Termination also gave Japan greater freedom of action by breaking the intimate relationship with the British Foreign Office, a relationship which might have exerted a strong modifying influence on Japanese policy in the difficult decade of the nineteen thirties.

The five major Pacific powers were joined by Portugal, Belgium, and the Netherlands as well as China in signing a Nine-Power Treaty on China. The signatory powers agreed to respect the "sovereignty, the independence, and the territorial and administrative integrity of China" as well as to refrain from seeking special rights or privileges in China. The Chinese delegates in return pledged their government not to lease or alienate territory to any power and to refrain from using the railways of China to discriminate economically in respect to any nation.

Some optimistic Americans hailed the Nine-Power Treaty as "a Magna Charta for China," and as a new international affirmation of the Open Door Notes. But like the earlier statements, the new treaty made no reference to the existing vested interests and leased territories. If a situation arose which seemed to any nation to involve the treaty stipulations, the signatories were only pledged to enter into "full and frank communication" with each other.

An obvious weakness of the Washington Conference was its failure to extend the tonnage limitations to all categories of naval vessels. Due largely to French obduracy, no agreement was possible on total tonnages for cruisers, submarines, and auxiliary craft.

American naval critics were correct in pointing out that tonnage limits along with the check on further fortification of the Philippines did mean effective hegemony for the Japanese Navy in Asian waters north of Singapore. But American acceptance of this hegemony involved no sacrifice for a nation whose system of cost accounting had ruled out a war with Japan over China and rejected any large military expenditures in an effort at defending the Philippine Islands. Independence and freedom of action for these islands was considered to be only a matter of time. The United States was not bereft of all power in dealing with Japan. Some 40 percent of Japan's exports and imports travelled across the North Pacific to Canada and the United States through the zone of American naval hegemony, while another 30 percent travelled southward within striking range of Singapore-based British naval power.

Such arguments for the wisdom of the Washington agreements had little effect on the admirals of the American Navy who saw their forces weakened. Japan remained in their planning the Number One Enemy, a nation some day to be faced in a Pacific showdown. A vigorous campaign was waged by the Navy, supported by naval expansionists in and out of Congress, to counter the public enthusiasm for disarmament. "We are preparing now for the shock of the next Congress and you cannot send too much information about the Japanese Navy," the naval attaché at Tokyo was informed by Washington in the spring of 1923. In addition to the traditional technique of

scaring larger appropriations out of Congress, a public relations program sought to impress the taxpayer with the importance of a strong Navy for national defense. The establishment of Navy Day was the most successful publicity measure;
Theodore Roosevelt's birthday on October 27 was the chosen
date for the first celebration held in 1922. This move, so
shortly after the closing of the Washington Conference,
brought some national criticism, and at least two states, Maine
and Wisconsin, refused to co-operate in celebrating Navy Day.

A professional propagandist, William B. Shearer, was attached to the staff of the Senate Naval Affairs Committee in
1925 by Senator William King of Utah, and Shearer soon became a major source of news stories designed to alert Americans to the Japanese naval threat. After making a personal
"survey" of American naval strength in the Pacific, Shearer released sensational stories on the state of American weakness
which were widely printed by the Hearst and other newspapers sympathetic to Shearer's cause. He found the Panama
Canal defenses "totally inadequate" and the Canal open to
capture from the Pacific. The American air force was rated by
Shearer as only 16 percent of the fighting strength of the Japanese air force, while American battleships in the Pacific were
said to be outranged by Japanese guns by 3,000 yards. Before he was attached to the Senate Committee, Shearer had
gained national publicity by his effort to bring a taxpayer's
suit against Secretary of Navy Wilbur to restrain him from
sinking one of the American battleships decommissioned as a
result of the Washington Treaty.

Japanese patriots who viewed the Washington Conference
with similar hostility to their American counterparts also cam-
paigned against the naval limitations. The ratio of capital ship
tonnage 5-5-3 was charged with stigmatizing Japan as an inferior, and the three figures were chalked on walls and printed
on posters to remind Japanese citizens of their alleged humiliation. The expansionists won the approval of the Diet for ship-

building in the categories not covered by treaty; five cruiser keels were laid down in 1922 and construction begun on another five in 1924. Congress responded in December of 1924 by authorizing the construction of eight new cruisers.

Faced with a new and expensive naval race in the unlimited cruiser category, the same forces which earlier pressed for the Washington Conference urged President Calvin Coolidge to seek a new treaty to eliminate the loopholes left by the 1922 negotiations. The President acted in February of 1927 with invitations to the signatories to meet in Geneva the following summer. France and Italy, both determined to compensate for the inferiority which they felt had been imposed on them in capital ships at Washington, refused to attend. By extensive building in the unlimited categories, their naval leaders hoped to maintain their status and pride as major naval powers.

The other three powers met in 1927 with delegations dominated by strong-minded, high-ranking, naval officers capable of overruling the civilian advisers in decisions affecting what they considered to be national security. The American proposal to extend the Washington Conference tonnage ratios to all categories met with strong objections. The Japanese asked for cruiser stabilization on the basis of existing tonnage, which would have given their Navy approximately 70 percent of American tonnage. The British claimed that the needs of their empire required a minimum of 70 cruisers with a total tonnage of more than twice that proposed by the Americans. The differences were further complicated by British insistence that cruiser tonnage be set in the 7,500 ton class with six-inch guns, while the Americans claimed that only 10,000 ton ships with eight-inch guns filled their needs.

The Geneva Conference foundered on the cruiser issue, despite Japanese efforts to mediate in the British-American conflict. The press of Japan and the United States found some agreement in putting the blame for failure on Britain. The

Stanley Baldwin Cabinet had debated the question of parity in cruisers with the United States, but had finally accepted Winston Churchill's arguments in support of a much larger tonnage. American opinion directed some of the blame for failure on the vested interests of the shipbuilders and steel companies who profited from naval construction. This emphasis was the result of later revelations made by the professional lobbyist, William B. Shearer, who was sent to Geneva on the payroll of several American companies to work against any agreement limiting naval building. Shearer had, in the words of President Hoover, "organized zealous support for increased armament" and worked to "create international distrust and hate." A congressional investigation of Shearer's activities noted that he had worked to stir anti-British feeling as well as anti-Japanese sentiment, and in the tradition of twentieth-century propagandists had accused his opponents of treason, tagging them as "internationalists and communists."

The reaction to the failure of Geneva was strong in Washington, and the Coolidge administration was favorable to carrying on the cruiser building program. As former Assistant Secretary of the Navy Franklin Roosevelt saw the situation in 1928, " 'All right,' we seemed to say, 'If you can't agree to our proposed methods of reducing warship building, we'll show you what we can do. We have all the money and resources in the world. We will build the kind of navy that no other power can equal. . . .' Naval competition today is the result of our bungling diplomacy." Roosevelt's criticism is a partisan oversimplification, but the Coolidge administration did approve a five-year building program in December of 1927 which included the construction of 26 cruisers and three aircraft carriers. Japanese navalists were quick to charge the United States with launching a new arms race, ignoring their own cruiser-building program. Congress, however, was reluctant to support the financial outlay which the construction program called for, and it was legislatively curtailed in 1928 wth the proviso that it would be suspended in the event of a new naval limitations treaty.

When Herbert Hoover assumed the presidency in 1929, he lost little time in making a new effort to extend the Washington Treaty. Britain's new Labor Premier, Ramsay MacDonald, made a visit to the new President, and an invitation was subsequently extended to the naval powers to meet in London early in 1930. Ambassador Hugh Gibson suggested that the Geneva impasse be broken by the use of a "yardstick" by which naval strength could be measured in more inclusive terms than tonnage alone. The age of vessels and their gun caliber were two factors which also affected their battle efficiency. A great deal of enthusiasm was generated among disarmament advocates for this new approach, but it all came to nought when the Navy Department professionals refused to commit themselves to any formula.

The London Conference made some progress using only the tonnage approach. A ceiling was set on cruiser tonnage which assigned Japan 60 percent of American tonnage in heavy cruisers and 70 percent in light cruisers. Japan had already built enough cruisers to reach more than parity with the United States, and the new ratios required additional building by the United States to reach the assigned superiority. Japan was assigned 70 percent of British and American strength in other ship categories with the exception of submarines, where equality was granted with the two rival nations. France and Italy refused to enter the tonnage-fixing treaty and an escalator clause was included to meet their potential rivalry. If either France or Italy expanded its tonnage, Britain was allowed to build beyond treaty limits to meet this challenge, while American and Japanese levels would be permitted to rise accordingly. Since battleship construction was a major financial burden, agreement was reached by the three powers to extend the capital ship building holiday until 1936.

As in 1922 supporters of large navies in all three countries protested the London agreements as endangering their nation's security. In the United States more than 20 naval officers testified before the Senate committee on the dangers of the new ceilings assigned, but the Senate ratified the London treaty with only nine "nays." In Japan a vigorous military-civilian conflict was fought, involving the larger issue of civilian dominance over the Navy and Army General Staffs. The government and Foreign Office triumphed, but it was to be one of the last victories of the liberal Japanese forces over the militarists. The Navy General Staff had to be placated with a major replenishment program within the new tonnage ratios.

London in 1930 saw the last of the naval limitations conferences in which the conferees parted in substantial agreement, and it was the last Japanese-American negotiation to be conducted without mutual recriminations. When the Washington Treaty came up for renewal in 1936, Japan's drive to extend control over Manchuria and American determination to block Japan's expansion by political and economic measures had created tensions too great to tolerate naval limitations. Each power resumed building at a pace and to tonnage levels which national leaders hoped would provide security in a world of competitive rearmament.

The Washington and London treaties did not in themselves fail, but the United States and Japan failed to use the period of reduced naval tension to eliminate latent conflicts of interest. The relaxation of tension may have been responsible for some minor amicable settlements. Japan promised in the course of the Washington negotiations to remove the last of the occupation troops from Siberia and carried out its promise at the end of the conference. As a result of negotiations in which the good offices of Secretary of State Hughes were influential, Japan also agreed with the Chinese government to restore its leasehold at Shantung, acquired from the Germans in 1915. Britain took parallel action in promising to restore its leasehold at Weihaiwei, an action subsequently postponed until 1930.

The Chinese delegates took heart at these promises and asked for the return of all leased territory, but Britain and France were no more willing to return their other leaseholds than Japan was to restore Port Arthur.

Another achievement related to the Washington Conference was the settlement of the Yap Island controversy. The United States compromised to the extent of recognizing the Japanese mandate in return for equal rights on the island for American nationals operating the trans-Pacific marine cables. Japan also granted American missionaries the right to erect religious buildings and schools in other mandated islands acquired from Germany.

Subsequent to the Washington Conference, Hughes succeeded in getting the Japanese to cancel the Lansing-Ishii agreement of 1917. By a series of clever diplomatic maneuvers the Japanese were put in a position of either terminating the 1917 agreement or consenting to the publication of the secret protocol by which they had pledged not to seek special rights or privileges in China. Cancellation strengthened the political position of the Harding administration in dealing with its pro-Chinese critics, but in no way did the elimination of the executive agreement change the relationship of Japan to China.

Hughes' great successes were countered in 1924 by an action which he complained had "undone the work of the Washington Conference and implanted the seeds of an antagonism sure to bear fruit in the future." He was referring to the work of Congress in passing the 1924 Immigration Act with an amendment which unilaterally abrogated the Gentlemen's Agreement of 1907 and banned future Japanese immigration. The quota system applied to European states by the legislation would have legalized less than 150 Japanese admissions yearly.

Under the 1907 arrangement, voluntary exclusion did not apply to the parents, wives, and children of Japanese aliens resident in the United States. About 4,000 individuals were admitted yearly, 1921–1924, under this provision, a number which some West coast racists viewed as a genuine "Yellow Peril." When complete exclusion was called for, the Japanese had few defenders in Congress. Even so, Japan might have been treated as were the European nations but for a blunder which was exploited by the exclusionists.

Secretary Hughes was opposed to an exclusion amendment which he knew would be considered insulting in Japan. In discussing the pending legislation with the Japanese Ambassador, the Secretary encouraged the dispatch of an official note stating how seriously Japan would look upon exclusion. Ambassador Masanao Hanihara delivered such a note, deploring the "grave consequences" which would result in contrast to the present "happy and mutually advantageous relations." The State Department forwarded the note to Congress where it was published in the *Congressional Record*. Leading exclusionists, including Senator Henry Cabot Lodge, used the words "grave consequences" to charge Japan with threatening the legislative body. With nationalist pride aroused the exclusion amendment was voted by both houses with only a small group of dissenters.

President Coolidge asked that the bill be changed by the Conference Committee to postpone exclusion for two years, while he negotiated a treaty with Japan to eliminate the immigrant flow which exclusionists wanted to check by action offensive to Japan. The Committee recommended delay for one year only, but enough southerners joined with the western exclusion bloc to reject delay. President Coolidge then signed the bill, though deploring the exclusion provisions.

The seriousness of congressional action was recognized by Americans who knew of Japanese sensitivity to insult on the racial issue. An American humor magazine caustically awarded each member of Congress voting for exclusion a certificate for service "in furthering the cause of war." The expected reaction took place in Japan where a wave of anti-Americanism rolled across the country. Boycotts were proclaimed against

American manufactures, a patriotic Japanese committed *hari-kari* in front of the American embassy, Viscount Kentarō Kaneko, Harvard '78, resigned as president of the Japanese-American Society, and the hapless ambassador, Hanihara, resigned his post. To add to the resentment, the United States Supreme Court ruled in the spring of 1925 that Japanese who had served in the American Army during World War I were not included under the legislation which granted citizenship to all aliens in service.

Both American and Japanese observers attest to the profound and lasting impact of the exclusion legislation on the relations of the two peoples. An American military attaché, returning to Tokyo in the spring of 1926 after an absence of two years, commented on the disappearance of American prestige, "we have a people grievously hurt and bitterly resentful." "An explosive force has been lodged in the Japanese mind" wrote a Japanese scholar in 1926 while visiting the United States.

Japan's anger created new expressions of hostility in the United States. Secretary of the Navy Curtis D. Wilbur was quoted by newspapers as saying in September of 1924 that there was "nothing so cooling to hot temper as a piece of cold steel," a remark reprinted in Japan where it cooled no tempers. President Coolidge disavowed Wilbur's statement and criticized other belligerent American talk coming from naval circles. Nevertheless the Navy announced in December 1924 that battleship maneuvers would be held in the next year in waters west of Hawaii and culminating in a cruise to Australia. Former Assistant Secretary of the Navy Franklin Roosevelt criticized the "flamboyant public announcement" of the maneuvers as tactless, since both the American and Japanese public could easily draw the wrong conclusions. The sober *Osaka Mainichi*, one of Japan's largest newspapers, feared that the trans-Pacific cruise would make the breaking out of war "inevitable." The Navy did not change its plans, and a war game was conducted between Hawaii and Samoa in July of 1925. It demonstrated that the Hawaiian Islands could be taken by an enemy force willing to take heavy casualties.

The year 1925 was also one in which troubles in China began to overshadow and outweigh Japanese-American conflicts. Both countries were affected unfavorably by China's increasing hostility to foreign residents and interests; their common difficulties soon contributed to more harmonious exchanges.

Chinese nationalism was greatly stimulated as a result of the Shanghai incident of May 30, 1925. When a hostile Chinese mob demonstrated before one of the police stations in the International Settlement, a British officer ordered his men to fire into their midst. A number of Chinese were killed and became martyrs and inspiration for anti-foreign outbreaks in other cities, which resulted in loss of lives and destruction of foreign properties. The privileged position of the white man must be overthrown, the nationalists proclaimed, and the signs which banned dogs and Chinese from European enclaves must be torn down forever.

Even before the Shanghai incident the increase of Chinese militancy and the spread of civil disorders forced some American reappraisals of the traditional relationship with that nation. Ambassador Jacob Schurman, a few months after his arrival in Peking, reported to Secretary Hughes in December of 1921 that "We are universally regarded by the Chinese people as their special friend." But by the spring of 1922, following the outbreak of civil war and increased banditry, Schurman was advising American tourists not to visit China. A year later in the spring of 1923, he was complaining of the "growing disregard" of the Chinese for foreign life and property and urging that the American military garrisons be strengthened to cope with the increased threat. Thomas W. Lamont, the financier, advised Hughes that military intervention was both "necessary and wise" in view of the breakdown of the central government.

Hughes moved cautiously in regard to military involvement, but by 1924 recognized that protection of American nationals in China's interior would soon be impossible without it. Small American armed units were landed on China's coast to defend lives and property more than a half a dozen times between 1922 and 1925.

Hughes' successor, Frank B. Kellogg, had an even more difficult time, as Chinese nationalism was reinforced by Russian Communist advisers and as anti-foreign activities were directed not only at businessmen but at American missionaries as well. "Old China hands" began to press for more militant action. A policy "strong enough to put the fear of America in the heart of every Chinese bandit" was the plea of one China specialist in an appeal to the American public in 1923. By 1927 a widely read American Far Eastern expert, Nathaniel Peffer, concluded that "only a miracle" could prevent the United States from drifting into war with China. Major General William Crozier argued in *Current History* the following year that a few American divisions could effect complete occupation of China and crush all guerrilla warfare. Philosopher John Dewey called the General to task for ignoring the strength of Chinese nationalism, while historian Charles Beard pleaded that before a "new children's crusade" was launched into China some calculation be made of the cost. The advocates of the "hard policy" continued to press for militant action, while the reluctant Coolidge administration used military demonstrations only when they seemed absolutely necessary to protect American lives.

Within Japan there were also advocates of a belligerent response to civil disorders and to Chinese nationalism, but for most of the decade the government maintained a conciliatory policy which included some sympathetic understanding of Chinese resentment of western imperialism. Foreign Minister Kijurō Shidehara who took office in 1924 was a strong believer in Sino-Japanese co-operation as a means of advancing Japan's economic interests on the mainland. On several occasions he refused to join the western powers in naval demonstrations against China. The government of Premier Giichi Tanaka, which took office in the spring of 1927, returned to a more militant defense of Japanese treaty rights in Manchuria and Mongolia, but still tried to preserve the friendly relationship of the Shidehara period. This proved in the end impossible and Japanese military clashes with the Chinese earned them the enmity accorded the European powers.

During the period of Japan's conciliatory policy, Americans who followed Far Eastern developments were able to read in their periodicals favorable reports on Japan, in contrast to the disillusioned and often hostile interpretations of Chinese nationalism. As early as the spring of 1924 the diplomatic historian, A. L. P. Dennis, warned that Japan's friendship for China might mean major trade gains in competition with the United States. By 1926 a well-known Far Eastern specialist, Harold S. Quigley, concluded that Japan had given the world "an amazing proof of her civilization in her temperate conduct. . . . No State today calls Japan enemy, not even China." In 1929, seven years after the close of the Washington Conference, a former attorney general, George Wickersham, expressed his belief that the conference had "ended all question in the minds of any reasonable men of future antagonism between the United States and Japan." During the naval appropriations debate in Congress that year, Britain rather than Japan seemed to be the major rival to be feared. A Foreign Policy Association report by T. A. Bisson as late as October of 1930 concluded that there was "every indication" that Japan's foreign policy of moderation was "solidly established."

Japan was also viewed by American writers as coming closer to the United States in its political institutions. The extension of male suffrage to local elections in 1927 was hailed as "a turning point in Japanese history as great as was the Magna Charta's in England" by a writer in the *Century Maga-*

zine. The question posed by a *Harper's* article in 1929, "Is Japan Going Democratic?" was answered strongly in the affirmative.

There were voices which continued to pose Japanese expansionism as the major threat to American interests in Asia, but they were in the minority and often dismissed as propagandists for race prejudice or expanded naval budgets. Most Americans probably dismissed the Far East completely from their thoughts. As an astute American diplomat, Nelson T. Johnson, wrote to a friend in 1926, the American public was only interested in this area "when it is served up highly spiced with statements concerning future war, the trickiness of the Japanese and the necessity of our being sympathetic toward a suppressed China." Since none of these elements could be easily exploited by the popular press in the face of current Asian developments, only a minority of the public were aware of the new orientation.

A number of minor developments attested to the détente between Washington and Tokyo. In 1924 the first American loan to Japan since the Russo-Japanese War was negotiated by New York bankers, $150 million for a 30 year period. American dollars also flowed to Japan with American tourists who averaged over 5,000 annually and reached peak proportions of over 8,000 in 1929 and 1930.

Peace groups, encouraged by these developments, turned their efforts to cementing Japanese-American friendship. One such effort, sponsored by prominent American women, was the "doll diplomacy" begun in 1927. Dolls were collected in both the United States and Japan and sent across the Pacific to tour schools, giving numerous speakers the opportunity to disseminate platitudes about international friendship. This program continued until 1935, when New York's Mayor La Guardia sent two full-sized dummies as "Mr. and Mrs. America" to Japan. They were returned in due time to the United States, dressed in Japanese clothes, and with this final absurdity the cultural exchange was ended.

The American stock market crash of 1929 and the world economic crisis were not long in making an impact on foreign policies. The effects were different on each side of the Pacific. For Japan the curtailment of silk exports and the drop in silk prices produced unemployment, strikes, and bankruptcies. A restless people found leadership in a young militarist-nationalist elite who were to give Japanese foreign policy a more aggressive character. In the United States the same social unrest led to a questioning of the merits of a capitalist economy and an inward turning of national thought. The priority system of national interests which placed domestic considerations ahead of international seemed likely to be reinforced. The character of American political leadership, however, gave a different turn to American policy.

Chapter X

NON-RECOGNITION AND NAVALISM

ACCORDING TO one view of human history, nations drift unaware and irresistibly down the broad river of their destiny. National leaders may from time to time dip their paddles in this stream, slowing down or speeding up movement, but never overcoming the currents of history. If this is the true story behind the behavior of men's political units, the prophets of an inevitable Japanese-American war were right in the predictions they made in the early 1920's. They merely overestimated the speed of the currents which would sweep the two nations into an unavoidable collision. The efforts of Secretary of State Hughes and Foreign Minister Shidehara were then futile attempts to stop the flow of forces beyond the control of man.

But there is no rational proof that nations have destinies. Men in positions of power can make influential decisions, even if they are sometimes unaware of their full import. Whole peoples can be lead slowly and sometimes painfully to accept new directions and to work toward new goals. The war which erupted at Pearl Harbor in 1941 can be best described as the product of a number of decisions. The most important of these were made in Tokyo and Washington. These decisions were influenced by, and in turn influenced, decisions made in London and in the capitals of China.

Japan began a new course in 1931 with the launching of a war of conquest and pacification in Manchuria. The United States began a new course in 1931–1933 with the refusal to recognize the changes which Japan was making in the status quo of Asia. Vigorous militarists set Japan's new policy, while in the United States the energetic leadership of Henry L. Stimson and Franklin D. Roosevelt was chiefly responsible for the innovations in Far Eastern policy.

The American change of course defied the inclination of a depression-ridden citizenry to concentrate on domestic ills and to dismiss claims for "responsibilities" in other areas of the world. When the major national concern was overwhelmingly economic, a foreign policy was initiated based on legal and moralistic assumptions. It pointed toward eventual military involvement in an area of the world where the United States had only a minor economic stake.

The sources of the new policy are not to be found in the public mood of the 1930's nor in that of the previous decade. The ideas on which the policy was based can be found in the militant idealism of Woodrow Wilson and in the viewpoints of men like Theodore Roosevelt and Henry Cabot Lodge. These men shared the belief that foreign affairs must take precedence over domestic concerns and that for many reasons the United States must play a larger role on the world stage.

The drastic change in Japanese-American relations began in what Arnold Toynbee called the "Annus Terribilis," 1931. Throughout the western world that year men began to doubt that their civilization would survive, since the economic system no longer seemed capable of providing a livelihood for a large segment of the population. The masses were ready for charismic leaders, having lost faith in their old institutions and their defenders. Men looked for new systems and programs which promised to eliminate large scale unemployment and restore faith in human progress. To a substantial degree Japan and the United States shared this predicament.

The American stock market crash in the fall of 1929 had an almost immediate impact upon Japan. As the best customer of the Japanese, the United States was absorbing that year over 40 percent of Japan's exports. By the end of the year the New York silk market collapsed, and the price of Japan's major export, raw silk, dropped by one-half. With one-third of Japan's agricultural households depending upon cocoon raising as a secondary source of income, the farmer's cash returns dwindled. Tenant farmers, unable to meet their rents, were dislodged and joined the discontented unemployed in the cities. As cottons and rayon replaced silk, the important American market seemed lost permanently. The tariff act signed by President Hoover in June of 1930, while keeping raw silk on the free list, made advances of from 5 to 200 percent on other Japanese products and further curtailed exports to the United States.

The economic crisis strengthened the hand of a group of Japanese nationalists and militarists who were allied in a national reconstruction movement. Their goal was the elimination of economic distress and social unrest at home and the re-establishment of Japan's honor overseas. To achieve this end they aimed at the replacement of the civilian government which had curtailed army and navy spending and at the installation of a government dominated by military men. The movement viewed as futile Foreign Minister Shidehara's policy of diplomacy and compromise in coping with rising Chinese nationalism. Japan's Asian destiny was being betrayed by civilian appeasers.

The reconstructionists moved boldly in September of 1931. Members of the Kwantung Army headquarters staff, stationed by treaty along the route of the Japanese-owned South Manchurian Railway, provoked a clash with Chinese troops near Mukden. By pushing forward as the Chinese were driven back, local military commanders succeeded in launching a successful campaign for the conquest of Manchuria. Cabinet members in Tokyo, including the Minister of War, were taken by surprise and failed to bring the Kwantung Army under control. The contributions of Foreign Minister Shidehara to Sino-Japanese friendship were quickly wiped out, while the military victories strengthened the position of the Army in the Japanese government. In September of 1932, a year after the conflict began, the Army pressed the government into recognizing Manchuria as a separate sovereign state under the name of Manchukuo. Recognition was extended despite the objections of the Japanese Foreign Office and the Elder Statesmen who knew that the new state was the puppet of the Kwantung Army.

When Japan began its conquest, the Chinese government appealed to the League of Nations for action under Article XI of the Covenant. That article provided that in case of war or threat of war the League should take "any action that may be deemed wise and effectual to safeguard the peace of nations." One result of the Chinese appeal was the establishment of a Commission of Enquiry composed of a British, French, German, Italian, and American representative. The Commission was headed by Lord Lytton and its findings generally referred to as the Lytton Report.

The Commission's findings were made public in October of 1932 and began with a consideration of general developments in China. The role of Chinese nationalism which intensified bitterness toward foreigners was viewed as important in stimulating Japanese action. Chinese nationalism was said to be "permeated by memories of former greatness, which it desires to revive" and demanding the end of the "unequal treaty privileges" which Chinese public opinion viewed as humiliating. China, an historian might have noted, was beginning to express the same spirit shown by Japanese nationalism more than a half century earlier. The Commission took some note of the rise of Chinese communism, but it was viewed as a menace to the Kuomintang rather than an important threat to the treaty powers.

More than any European nation, Japan was now regarded by the Chinese as the most serious challenge to national aspirations, because of repeated intervention in behalf of Japanese nationals and their property. Chinese nationalist propaganda, the Commission said, was particularly effective in Manchuria where over 200,000 Japanese were living along the South Manchuria Railway and in the Kwantung leased territory.

The Commission recognized the importance of Manchuria to Japan, not only economically, but also as a patriotic symbol of the sacrifice of a hundred thousand Japanese lives in 1904–1905 in checking the encroachments of Russia. For the majority of Japanese, Manchuria was still of great strategic importance in respect to the continued threat of Russia. In view of the economic, strategic, and sentimental interest Japan had in Manchuria, the Commission concluded that it was not unreasonable of Japan to demand the establishment of a stable government in the area, one capable of maintaining the order essential for economic development. But that government must represent the people of Manchuria, said the Commission. Japan was advised, therefore, to seek a new treaty arrangement with China to protect its interests in the area, while China was urged to facilitate the development of a stable government in an autonomous and eventually demilitarized Manchuria.

Whether the Kuomintang was capable of the task of keeping order in Manchuria is a moot point. W. Cameron Forbes, American Ambassador to Japan, reported to Washington in January of 1932 that only the "exceptional exercise of force of some kind" could establish and maintain order in Manchuria. The Japanese government was unwilling to give China the opportunity of acting on the Lytton recommendations by restoring the status quo ante bellum.

The Japanese representatives at the League of Nations argued that the Lytton Report failed to go far enough in recognizing the abnormal conditions in China which because of internal anarchy could not be treated as an "organized State." Too little weight, the Japanese complained, was given to the unique character of their national interests. "Japan's interests in China are vital, British interests in China are substantial, American interests in China are sentimental," said one Japanese diplomat. Skepticism was expressed in regard to the possibility of a strengthened Chinese government; "Japan cannot idly wait for such an uncertain eventuality in order to solve the Manchurian question." The League of Nations failed, therefore, to induce the Japanese to change their position and to return to a policy of diplomacy rather than force to defend its interests.

Viewed with perspective, it is clear that Japan not only violated its commitments to the League of Nations Covenant, but also misjudged the long-range effects of its use of force in China. Manchuria conquered still failed to provide adequately for Japan's excess population and raw material needs, while Manchurian industries drained investment capital and technical personnel, much of which could have been better used in home developments. The military effort stirred Chinese nationalism to even greater intensity and provoked a national resistance which slowly sapped Japan's energies. A program of conquest which had as one of its ends the blocking of Russian influence in Manchuria and North China ended in Communist control of all of China.

Japan's reconstructionists made another blunder in failing to foresee the effect of their military conquests on Britain and the United States. Slowly these two countries realigned their Far Eastern policies as their leaders reached the conviction that Chinese nationalism was a lesser threat to their interests than the new expansionism of Japan. Not all British and American leadership agreed on the wisdom of an Anglo-American front against Japan, and movement in this direction was frequently marked by two steps forward and one step back. In less than a decade, however, Japanese policies turned China's critics into China's allies.

When Anglo-American opposition formed, Japanese nationalists refused to admit error in the choice of their means. An air of injury was added, instead, to a sense of mission. Patriotic leaders became convinced that Japan alone must assume the "responsibility" for peace and order in Eastern Asia. "Japan must act and decide alone what is good for China," said Ambassador Hirosi Saito in Washington in April of 1934. In the United States a similar sense of "responsibility" was developing in regard to Asia. Veteran diplomat Hugh R. Wilson expressed a view common in some circles when he wrote to a friend in 1933, "It so happens that the Lord made the world in such a way that in dealing with the Far East or the American Continents, the voice of the United States must be predominant." These conflicting views were to be tested in a decade; in two decades both were found wanting.

The news of the Mukden affair in September of 1931 was received in Washington with annoyance. Domestic problems were imposing a heavy burden on the Hoover administration, while the State Department was concerned with preparations for the Geneva Disarmament Conference to open in 1932 and with the many ramifications of the international economic collapse. An election campaign was soon to be fought in which the Democrats could be expected to indict the Republicans for failing to check the rising unemployment and bankruptcies. Whatever the Hoover administration did in foreign affairs, there could be little hope that any policy would attract mass political support. Foreign crises have been used for domestic political advantage, but in 1931 to attempt to make the cause of Manchuria, China, or the Kellogg-Briand Pact one over which the average voter could forget his more immediate problems was probably impossible.

Neither Herbert Hoover nor his Secretary of State Henry L. Stimson was capable, however, of viewing the disruptive events in Asia with philosophical detachment while they tackled more manageable problems. Both had what Hoover's fellow Quakers spoke of as a "concern" for the orderly course of international affairs and for the American future in Asia. Hoover had been forced to accept a breakdown of normal standards of international economics, but he was reluctant to watch, without protest, a breakdown in the political realm. Unlike his Secretary of State, Hoover had qualms, nevertheless, about taking any action which might lead to a war and sought to find some way by which "moral pressures" could be enlisted in China's cause.

Henry L. Stimson was a younger member of the generation of Theodore Roosevelt; like that President he generally held the view that any vigorous action was better than no action. At times he seemed convinced that militant action was the only language which could be used with the desired effect in international relations. He had served as Secretary of War under President Taft and commanded troops in World War I. His record had been a good one, and he prided himself on his "combat psychology." Stimson's ideal world was one of ordered and disciplined relations between states according to standards set by a stern Christianity and an Anglo-Saxon sense of proper procedures. He was not a man given to doubts about his understanding of the world. As a result of his service as Governor General of the Philippines he believed that he also comprehended what the westerner calls the "Oriental mind." More than any other peoples, it seemed to him, the Oriental had to be faced with firmness, a show of force and a demonstrable willingness to use it. Recognizing and respecting his superiors, the Oriental would then bow and retreat. This interpretation of the "Oriental mind," regardless of its dubious validity, had a respectable American tradition to support it, stretching back to Commodore Matthew Perry.

Secretary Stimson demonstrated his approach to the Far East a few months after he took office in March of 1929.

Chinese nationalism had led to the seizure of the Russian-operated Chinese Eastern Railway in Manchuria in July of 1929. The Russians retaliated in November by moving in troops and taking control of two Chinese border towns. When Stimson first heard of the Russo-Chinese conflict, he called together the ambassadors of the major powers in Washington and proposed intervention in the form of an international commission to rule on the dispute. The experienced diplomats recognized the unwanted complications in which such an action would involve their respective countries and unanimously rebuffed the Secretary's initiative.

When the news of Russian military occupation of Chinese border towns reached the Department of State, Stimson decided to act unilaterally. Casting about for some legal grounds on which to act, he decided to use the Kellogg-Briand Pact. In 1928 and 1929 most of the governments of the world had signed this agreement which renounced war as an instrument of national policy. To a great extent the signatures represented a gesture for the benefit of the peace movements of the western world which hoped to establish peace by outlawing war. Disclaimers were generally made to provide for the use of war in the defense of vital national interests; provision for enforcement of the vague pledges was carefully excluded.

Stimson knew that the United States had not been appointed guardian of the Kellogg Pact and in a frank moment admitted that it and other European treaties no more fitted the Asian situation than "a stovepipe hat would fit an African savage." He decided, nevertheless, to invoke the Kellogg Pact as a means of calling the Russians to task for military action. Since the United States in 1929 did not recognize the existence of a legal government in Russia, the American note had to be forwarded by France. By the time it arrived at Moscow the Russians and the Chinese had patched up their difficulties. The Soviet Foreign Commissar, Maxim Litvinov, used the occasion to send Stimson a stinging rebuke. The American Secretary of

State was charged with trying to intervene in a non-existent conflict and to reprimand a government which his country did not recognize.

If the Secretary of State was chastened by this venture, he had fully recovered two years later when he confronted the Sino-Japanese conflict in Manchuria. He did for a time accept the counsel of his State Department advisers to be cautious and not play into the hands of the militarists in their struggle with liberal civilian elements. President Hoover was also reluctant to call Japan to task for treaty violations when the American notes could be so easily ignored. The President was willing, however, to accept Stimson's suggestion that an American observer be permitted to sit in on the deliberations of the League of Nations when it considered China's appeal. Stimson, like Hoover, hoped that some sort of expression of "world opinion" as represented in the League would be sufficient to check the Japanese military and strengthen the civil authorities.

As the Japanese continued to advance and by December of 1931 took virtual control of Manchuria, Secretary Stimson grew impatient. Seeking more effective action he began to consider the possibility of joint economic sanctions. The Far Eastern Division chief, Stanley K. Hornbeck, assured the Secretary that Japan would collapse within a few days or at the most weeks after its trade was cut off. The idea of sanctions as a means of enforcing peace had considerable popularity in this period among League supporters in the United States, since it appeared to be a relatively simple way to coerce sovereign states without the use of war. President Hoover, however, was not convinced that sanctions would not involve the nation in dangerous complications; he spoke of it as a policy of "sticking pins in tigers" which could easily lead to war.

Blocked in taking economic measures by the President's attitude, Stimson found in January of 1932 a legalistic device which expressed his lawyer and law-giver outlook. Actually suggested first by Hoover and reinforced by a letter from

Walter Lippmann, Stimson's move was the issuance of the non-recognition doctrine popularly identified with his name. Like Secretary of State Bryan who in 1915 responded to Japanese expansion with a statement refusing to recognize any changes in China construable as treaty violations, Stimson proclaimed a similar statement on January 7, 1932. Notice was sent to Japan and China that the United States would not "admit the legality" nor recognize any treaty which impaired its rights in China or which was brought about by a violation of the Kellogg-Briand Pact.

None of the European powers with interests in China was consulted in the issuance of the non-recognition note and none of them responded to the American action with any enthusiasm. When the Japanese naval attack on Shanghai followed Stimson's warning, Hoover agreed to the transfer of a regiment of Marines from the Philippines to Shanghai to demonstrate some determination as well as to provide protection for American nationals. But Japan's only overt response to the non-recognition doctrine was to dispute its legal basis.

Britain had been a signatory to the Nine Power Washington Treaty of 1922, and Stimson sought to enlist London's cooperation on this basis. Article 7 of the treaty called for "full and frank communication between the Contracting Powers" when a situation involving the sovereignty and territorial integrity of China arose. If Japan refused to take part in such discussions when the Treaty was invoked by Britain and the United States, the Secretary of State hoped for an Anglo-American initiative in launching collective economic sanctions.

Great Britain in 1932 was facing severe economic problems of its own, and the British public was no more willing than that of the United States to become embroiled in a Far Eastern conflict. In large part as a result of Chinese nationalist boycotts, British exports to China had been drastically cut in the previous decade, and the Foreign Office had no sentimental attachment to the Kuomintang government headed by Chiang

Kai-shek. Some British Far Eastern specialists also viewed Japan in China as the chief obstacle to an undesirable spread of Soviet influence and opposed action which might serve Russian ends. Stimson found London, therefore, disappointingly cool to any suggestions for a joint policy in policing Japan. Some American scholarship has blamed Sir John Simon, the British Foreign Secretary, in particular for refusing to stand up to Japan at the side of the United States. Such charges must be balanced, however, with the recognition that Stimson, as London understood, was unable to move beyond further note-writing, due to the attitudes of President Hoover.

In the face of the timidity, as Stimson saw it, of London and the White House, he was still determined he said to "put the situation morally in its right place." The Secretary of State decided to state the American position in the form of an open letter which would receive wide publicity and yet avoid what he called "yellow-bellied responses" from other powers. The letter was addressed to Senator William E. Borah, chairman of the Senate Foreign Relations Committee, and dated February 23, 1932. The text of the letter reviewed the importance of the Open Door policy, the Nine Power Treaty of 1922, and the Kellogg-Briand Pact and without naming Japan specifically it made clear that these principles of American policy were being violated. An appeal was made to other nations to follow the non-recognition doctrine and thus place a "caveat" on Japan's gains which would effectively bar the legality of any titles or rights acquired. Further American action was hinted at in the suggestion of reconsideration of the 1922 limitations on American battleship construction and on the fortification of Guam and the Philippines.

The Borah letter was reprinted in the Japanese press and stirred anti-American responses. Both the French and British ambassadors to Tokyo believed that the letter had "done a great deal of harm." At the League of Nations the letter had a more favorable reception; the Assembly voted in March of 1932 that it was incumbent upon members not to recognize any situation or treaty achieved by violation of the Kellogg-Briand Pact. After the League received the Lytton Commission report, Japan's course was condemned as a violation of the League Covenant by a vote of the Assembly. But rather than chastening the erring member state, the League action was followed a month later, in March of 1933, by Japan's withdrawal from this international organization.

Henry Stimson's approach to Japan in 1931–1932 failed. If threat and a clear readiness to go to war could have deterred Japan's expansionists and strengthened the moderates, the American position was too weak. Neither the President nor Congress were ready for such a sacrificial effort in behalf of issues which seemed peripheral to the nation's major interests. When the Borah letter drew belligerent support from some Americans, Hoover was moved in the other direction. The best that Stimson was able to do in defense of his position was to stave off until May of 1932 a statement, which the President issued through Undersecretary of State William R. Castle, renouncing any intention of an economic boycott against Japan. Stimson did succeed in putting up some "bluff of force" by keeping the Fleet based at Hawaii for some months in 1932 after it had completed its Pacific maneuvers. This action led some Japanese chauvinists to harangue against the American threat, and Stimson felt that it was probably useful as a restraint.

The Borah letter had been intended to warn Japan, encourage Britain and the League to take a stronger stand, and to educate Americans. In 1947 Stimson looked back and wrote, "The lines of division laid down so clearly in February, 1932, led straight to Pearl Harbor." Although the historical path was far from "straight" and would be better represented in terms of zigs and zags, advances and retreats, Stimson's statement was a basically sound generalization. But how did a lone Secretary of State, working with an unsympathetic President and a public and Congress absorbed in other issues, make such a great impact on American Far Eastern policy? In part the answer is to be found in Stimson's success in transmitting his viewpoint to the Franklin D. Roosevelt administration. In part the answer lies in Stimson's leadership and encouragement of an educated and influential elite who believed that their country was called to set foot on a new path in the direction to which Stimson pointed.

Stimson's supporters were largely made up of individuals who were convinced that the establishment of the League of Nations in 1919 had created a new international order. Moral judgments could and should be made about the behavior of the member states of this new order and these judgments should form a basis of national action. As the leading peace-loving nation in the world, it was America's duty to judge and act and, in the case of the Sino-Japanese dispute, to support the Chinese underdog. The United States was "naturally destined for a leader in the promotion of peace throughout the world," said Stimson in October of 1932. No nation in the world, he felt, had been so well provided by "Providence" with a secure position from which to promote good relations among nations. This was a twentieth century version of the "chosen people" concept which many great nations had held in the past in forms noble and ignoble.

In an American society which was still reacting to the barrenness of the results of participation in World War I and in which the quest for peace was still considered the highest ideal, Stimson's program with its emphasis on legality and morality had strong appeal. Few saw that it carried the implication of another war in behalf of peace. Few saw that the Sino-Japanese relationship was too complex for a simple moral judgment by western nations with a stake in the Asian status quo, acquired by methods in the nineteenth century similar to those of Japan in the twentieth century. Stimson's major opposition came instead from apathy and the simplified traditional view that any American intervention in international affairs was not in the national interest.

His supporters were strong in academic circles where a petition was circulated by the presidents of Harvard, the University of Michigan, and the University of Minnesota. Long lists of signatures were collected on campuses in favor of American co-operation with the League if economic sanctions were applied against Japan. The petition's goal was also supported by some prominent congressmen and newspapers. The American Committee on the Far Eastern Crisis was established with Communist support to rally religious and labor groups for the same ends. Nicholas Murray Butler, president of Columbia University, headed a third group, the Committee on Economic Sanctions with an impressive list of sponsors which issued a call for a conference of Kellogg-Briand Pact signatories to adopt a supplementary protocol to the Pact on economic sanctions. Chinese propagandists joined in the effort to stir American opinion with an appeal from "Chinese Women to the Women of America" for a feminine boycott on Japanese goods.

Despite these efforts it was only a small vocal minority of Americans who in 1932 concerned themselves with Japan's actions in Manchuria. Of these it was probably a minority who would have supported condemnation if they had foreseen that Stimson's path led to war. Even one of the initiators of the non-recognition doctrine, Walter Lippmann, wrote in February of 1932 that "The idea of war should be renounced clearly and decisively" in respect to Asia. Both presidential candidates in the summer and fall of 1932 concentrated on domestic issues which seemed likely to dominate the voters' thinking.

The defeat of Herbert Hoover and the election of Franklin D. Roosevelt was generally viewed as favorable to the improvement of Japanese-American relations. Roosevelt was not expected to permit the Far East to divert him from recovery measures. His new Secretary of State, Cordell Hull, was known principally for his interest in low tariffs, a policy which boded

no ill for Japan. The "brain-trusters" in the President's en-
tourage were almost entirely men who held traditional views
about the primacy of domestic over foreign affairs. In Japan
the press and informed public took an optimistic view of the
changes in Washington. "No more Stimson" was the remark
gleefully made to Ambassador Joseph Grew in Tokyo by an
embassy chauffeur and an embassy maid.

There were two qualities of the new President, little noted,
which were to prove very influential in the course of future
relations with Asia. The first was the strong, sentimental tie
which Roosevelt had to China; the second was his love of the
Navy and admiration for seapower. Both qualities were rooted
deeply. His reactions to any discussion which touched these
two areas had emotional overtones. As close associates learned,
his rationality was easily swayed when either China or the
Navy awakened in him a chain of associations from which he
derived warm satisfactions.

Roosevelt's attitude toward China was literally acquired at
his mother's knees. Her father, Warren Delano, was a New
England sea captain who had made a substantial fortune in the
Canton trade. Sara Delano was taken to China as a small child
by her father, an adventure which seems to have provided her
with many tales with which to later entertain her only child.
The fascination and lure of the Orient, so common to many
Americans of earlier generations, was accentuated in young
Franklin. Stories of his grandfather's career were recalled on
many occasions for the benefit of the President's associates.
That his family had gained so much from the China trade
seemed to leave Roosevelt with some sense of personal responsibility for China's future.

Henry Stimson discovered the Roosevelt soft spot when the
two men met to discuss foreign policy issues during the inter-
regnum of 1932–1933. Their first encounter took place in
Washington with President Hoover a few weeks after the elections and was not a favorable one from Stimson's point of view.

But on January 9, 1933, Stimson accepted Roosevelt's invitation and spent a day with the President-elect at the latter's Hyde Park estate. The retiring Secretary of State used much of the time speaking in support of his Far Eastern policy. He found that Roosevelt had what Stimson called "a personal hereditary interest" in China.

Stimson returned to New York assured that there would be no break in Asian policy. Several days later he secured Roosevelt's approval of a phone call to London to assure the British that the American position would not change on March 4. "That is one place where I think the two administrations will be entirely in accord," Stimson told the American embassy in London, referring to his non-recognition statement and the Borah letter. On January 17, Roosevelt made a guarded statement to the press, saying that he believed in policies which "upheld the sanctity of international treaties." This was generally viewed as an indirect endorsement of Stimson's doctrine and created some consternation among the New Deal supporters who were critical of Stimson's position. Two of Roosevelt's closest advisers, Raymond Moley and Rexford Tugwell, hastened to point out the dangers of commitment to what appeared to be a futile and legalistic policy. Roosevelt responded by telling them of his deep sympathy for the country with which his grandfather had traded. "How could you expect me not to go along with Stimson on Japan," he asked Moley.

Secretary of State Hull may have had views on the Sino-Japanese affair similar to those of the President, albeit without the family background. As Hull remembered it in 1948, he had entered the State Department with two convictions about the Far East. One was that it was in the American interest to block the extension of Japanese power, and the other was his conviction that Japan could not be trusted to uphold any treaties. Hull retained as his Far Eastern Division chief, Stanley K. Hornbeck, who had held that post since 1928 and who had been influential in interpreting Japanese policy for Stimson.

Although Hornbeck was initially reluctant in respect to the non-recognition program, he was one of those who believed that Japan could be forced to change course under the pressure of a boycott.

Some historians have concluded that the Stimson-Roosevelt conversations were of no significance for future American policy and did not influence the New Deal. Roosevelt, it is pointed out, failed to follow the logic of the Stimson position and made no effort to apply sanctions to Japan. Shortly after taking office the new President refused to fight in Congress for the type of arms embargo legislation which would have given him one means of exerting pressure on Japan. Nor was Roosevelt, any more than Hoover, willing to face the strong protests which the cotton industry and the silk industry would have made over any curtailment of trade with Japan.

The new administration did, however, continue to refuse recognition to Manchukuo although it was sympathetic to a *de facto* recognition policy in Latin America. American non-recognition did not substantially interfere with Japan's development of its satellite state, but it was an issue between the two nations which the Japanese were not allowed to forget. When in the winter of 1933–1934 rumors spread of a possible change of American policy, Stanley Hornbeck made a speech, widely reported in Japan, in which he was quoted as saying that his government would continue to refuse to recognize "governments made by swords." Ambassador Grew warned that such statements tended to undo efforts being made to ease trans-Pacific tensions. Franklin Roosevelt may not have needed Stimson to convince him that it was to America's interest to support China's cause, but to commit his administration in advance to a particular policy unpopular with many of his own supporters may well have been a tribute to Stimson's powers of persuasion.

Non-recognition of Manchukuo in time turned out to be a less important policy of the new administration than the impact

upon Japanese-American relations of Roosevelt's navalist outlook. Love of ships and an interest in seapower, like his attitude
toward China, can be traced to Roosevelt's formative years.
His family owned a sailing yacht and even as "a little mite,"
according to his mother, he declared himself "a seafaring man."
During Roosevelt's adolescence the writings of Alfred Thayer
Mahan stirred the minds of many outward-looking Americans.
For a Groton schoolboy with nautical interests, Mahan's ideas
had an added attraction. The fact that they were also ex-
pounded by an admired relative, Theodore Roosevelt, increased their appeal. As a Christmas present in 1897 Franklin
received a copy of Mahan's *The Influence of Sea Power Upon
History, 1660–1783* and, according to his mother, he pored
over this volume "until he had practically memorized the whole
book." A month later, on his sixteenth birthday, the future
president received a copy of Mahan's *The Interest of America
in Sea Power, Present and Future.* Other volumes of Mahan
followed and were added to a growing Roosevelt library of
naval histories and naval prints.

When Roosevelt was appointed Assistant Secretary of the
Navy in 1913, he "embraced the 'big Navy' cause" with a
wholeheartedness which startled Secretary Josephus Daniels,
according to Roosevelt's 1931 campaign biographer, Ernest
Lindley. As Assistant Secretary, Roosevelt also opened a correspondence with the retired Admiral Mahan and found that
he shared with him a strong concern over Japan as a major
threat in the Pacific. There is also some evidence that Franklin
saw himself playing the same dynamic role that Theodore had
in pushing the Navy into a state of readiness. "You remember
what happened the last time a Roosevelt occupied a similar
position," Franklin told a reporter shortly after he took office
in 1913.

After World War I, however, Franklin Roosevelt showed a
sense of balance in his thinking not found in other big Navy
boosters. When it was most impolitic for a Democrat to do so,

he supported Secretary Hughes and his achievement in the Washington Naval Limitations Treaty. He criticized Coolidge in 1927 for talking of an expanded cruiser building program and retained a belief, even after he became president, that the Washington Conference had made an important contribution to peace in the Pacific.

For his Secretary of Navy Roosevelt selected Claude B. Swanson, a man known for his faithful support of increased naval appropriations as chairman of the Senate Committee on Naval Affairs. At his first press conference in March 7, 1933, the new Secretary stated that his policy was to build as quickly as possible to the London Treaty limits set in 1930. On June 16, 1933, Roosevelt issued an executive order allotting $238 million of the National Recovery Administration's funds to a naval building program. Construction plans included four new cruisers, two aircraft carriers, sixteen destroyers, four submarines, and a number of auxiliary vessels.

Although the new ships would not bring American tonnage beyond the 1930 limits, Tokyo and some European capitals viewed the American program as again starting the world on a naval race. Naval construction had declined as national budgets were trimmed under the stress of the world depression. Japan's appropriations for new ships declined from $40.8 million in 1930–1931 to $33.5 million in 1931–1932 and were cut further to $26.9 million in 1932–1933. The American building program was the largest single construction undertaken by any nation since the end of World War I. There was some basis for critics, both foreign and domestic, charging that the Roosevelt administration was taking the initiative in reopening competition.

The Japanese press viewed the American expansion as being directed across the Pacific. The *Osaka Asahi,* one of the least chauvinistic papers, charged that the program "betrays the spirit of the London Treaty." Japanese naval expansionists, jealous of the large Army appropriations as a result of the Manchurian victories, used the American move as propaganda for their own budgets. The new American ships, they claimed, would upset the uneasy balance of power in the Pacific and pose a threat to the security of the Japanese homeland. This argument, spread through the Japanese press, helped the naval propagandists to win an additional appropriation of over a hundred million dollars from the Diet. In December of 1933 Japan announced plans to build 22 new ships to meet treaty strength.

London also viewed the American building program with concern. Britain feared a reopened naval building race which they would be regretfully forced to enter if Japan followed the American example. In September of 1933 the British Foreign Office approached Washington to ask if the United States would suspend laying down its new cruisers if the British could persuade the Japanese to do the same. Hull replied by stressing the economic function of the American program and denying that it had any relation to Japan or to Japanese building. There was "nothing to take us to the Orient, much less to induce us to make preparations for a naval conflict on account of any Oriental considerations," he said. When Prime Minister Ramsay MacDonald and Foreign Secretary John Simon raised the same proposal with Norman Davis, the State Department again refused to consider a moratorium in view of the need to "round out" the Fleet.

Was President Roosevelt thinking of a possible war with Japan when he acted to expand the American Navy in 1933? Harold Ickes whose New Deal agency handled the building funds boasted in 1943 that "we did start girding our loins for war early in 1933." Ickes doubted, however, that the President was looking forward to actual war and suggests that the building was begun because Roosevelt was "congenitally as well as by choice, Navy-minded." Another cabinet member, James Farley, writing in 1948, states that the President took up the issue of a possible war with Japan on March 7th, three days after taking office. Although the cabinet agreed that no action should be taken which might result in hostilities, Roosevelt reportedly lectured the cabinet on how the war could be fought. He recognized the problem of distance in a trans-Pacific conflict, but considered it possible to starve out Japan by a blockade in three to five years. He anticipated the temporary loss of the Philippines and the launching of bombing attacks on the Japanese islands from the Aleutians.

In the midst of the great banking crisis of March 1933 the President was probably not giving serious consideration to war. More likely he was indulging himself by playing naval strategist and demonstrating what he considered to be his competence in this area. But his building program does seem to have been directed at Japan. When a friend wrote to him in the summer of 1933 to express his concern about the impact of American naval expansion on Japan, Roosevelt stated his own concern about Japanese strength. He wrote to the Reverend Malcolm Peabody that he had discovered to his "dismay" that the Navy "was and probably is actually inferior to the Japanese Navy." He also defended his action by stating that "the whole scheme of things in Tokyo does not make for an assurance of non-aggression in the future."

In January 1934 the Roosevelt administration announced its intention of bringing naval strength up to the limits set by the London Treaty. Congress quickly passed an authorization for the construction of over a hundred ships to be built over a period of years at an estimated annual cost of $76 million. No battleships were planned, but the 1935 construction was to begin with an aircraft carrier, two light cruisers, 14 destroyers, and six submarines.

When the President signed the naval bill he assured Americans that it was not a law for the construction of any additional ships, but merely congressional approval for a tentative future program. His administration, said Roosevelt, still favored the limitation of naval armaments. Although it clearly involved considerable ambivalence on his part, Roosevelt, was genuinely interested in naval limitation as well as in expanding the fleet. Norman Davis, the American disarmament specialist, visited Roosevelt in late April of 1933 and advised that the United States and Britain go it alone in their building programs, since Japan could not be trusted. But the President insisted on another naval conference at the expiration of the London Treaty. He told Davis that he hoped to see a new ten-year treaty, keeping the present tonnage ratios between Britain, the United States and Japan, but making a 20 percent reduction in total tonnage. If Japan refused to accept this, Roosevelt spoke of extending the present treaty for another five years. When the preliminary conversations for a new treaty began, Roosevelt took a strong personal interest in their conduct, often bypassing his Secretary of State in setting the course of the negotiations.

In its Far Eastern policy, the Roosevelt administration dropped the note-writing program of Stimson, characterized by some contemporaries as "international nagging," but gave no other evidence of a change of position in regard to Japanese activities in China. Not only did naval construction strengthen the American position in the Pacific, but additional diplomatic strength was gained from the recognition of the Soviet Union in November of 1933. There were other important considerations which favored reopening of diplomatic relations with the Russians, but it was also clear to Tokyo that it cleared away a major obstacle to common action between Washington and Moscow to block Japanese influence in northern China. The Japanese military were particularly concerned over possible Soviet-American co-operation in view of the rumors of a new Russo-Japanese war. A month before recognition of Russia was announced, Ambassador Grew was approached by the Japanese with the suggestion that a good-will mission be sent to the United States. The Ambassador felt that there was no need for such a venture at that time and the State Department backed him up in rejecting Tokyo's suggestion. The United

States quickly discouraged another Japanese initiative the same month, when the Foreign Office sent up some trial balloons in behalf of a Japanese-American arbitration treaty. It was not a "propitious time" for such a treaty, Grew believed.

The Roosevelt administration was also opposed to any British rapprochement with Japan. A coolness had developed between London and Tokyo after the British supported the Lytton Commission report and refused to recognize Manchukuo. But the rise of Adolf Hitler and talk of German rearmament led some members of the MacDonald government to consider a new course. A new Anglo-Japanese alliance or even a non-aggression pact with Japan would strengthen Britain's hand in Europe by permitting naval and military concentration against future German strength. Neville Chamberlain, Chancellor of the Exchequer, argued in the fall of 1934 that the United States could not be counted upon to support Britain in Asia and would only go to war against Japan if Hawaii was attacked.

How seriously London considered a rapprochement with Japan must await further publication of British records before final determination. A rumor of negotiations was sent from Tokyo by Grew in May of 1934. Stanley Hornbeck thought the rumor a serious one and urged that it be countered by pushing ahead with the naval building program and by giving publicity to the progress made in warship construction. When Roosevelt heard the rumor, he was angry. He wanted Norman Davis to tell the British Foreign Minister that "If Great Britain is even suspected of preferring to play with Japan to playing with us," the United States would go over London's head and appeal directly to Canada and other Dominions for support. This was a bold threat which would have very likely backfired and, fortunately for the Roosevelt administration, was never attempted. It illustrated, however, the President's determination to maintain a diplomatic front of opposition to Japan's China policy.

In the atmosphere of "no war, but yet no peace" in the Pacific which characterized the first Roosevelt administration,

chauvinists and rumor-spreaders again became active in adding to the tensions. Spy stories became common in both countries as in the early twenties. Japan expressed what later appeared to be a clairvoyance in its fears of American bombing
planes, but which at the time could be dismissed as almost
sheer fantasy. When in 1932 the National City Bank of New
York asked its Japanese branch offices to collect photographs
of the business sections of the cities in which they were located,
a bombing scare ran through the press. Instead of being used
as an indication of economic growth, Japanese newspapers
charged that the photographs were wanted by the United
States government to aid in planning bombing raids. Innocent
American travellers taking pictures in Japan frequently found
themselves detained by police as spies, while their films were
confiscated.

Fears were stirred throughout Japan by press reports which
gave exaggerated significance to the flight of six U.S. Navy
flying boats from San Francisco to Honolulu early in 1934.
The same treatment was given later in the year to a mission of
ten Army bombers to Alaska. More concrete reasons for fear
were provided by the public testimony of the pioneer air force
enthusiast, Brigadier General William Mitchell, who in October
of 1934 stated that, "Japan is our most dangerous enemy, and
our planes should be designed to attack her." Mitchell called
for the construction of dirigibles and planes with a range of
more than 6,000 miles in order to bomb Japan. Cordell Hull
also reminded the Japanese Ambassador of the increasing vul-
nerability of his home cities when he lectured the diplomat on
the need of a changed foreign policy in May of 1934. Hull
pointed out that an American flier had flown from the United
States to Japan and around the world in eight days. Using
Britain as an island which once had security, Hull told the
Japanese that a fleet of 2,000 bombing planes from any western
European capital could now wipe out London. It is understandable that Grew could report from Tokyo that same year

that the Japanese people were "extraordinarily apprehensive of attack from the air" and thus quite concerned about the reported growth of Soviet air power and the building of American airplane carriers.

The American sensational press did its part to keep fear of Japan alive among its readers. A common rumor told of imminent Japanese conquest of the Philippines, helped by Japanese agents in the islands. Secret fortification of the mandated Pacific islands was another frequent report which was given credence in some American government circles, due to Japanese reluctance to authorize visits of American naval vessels to this area of the Pacific. Questions were frequently raised about "mysterious" Japanese in Mexico or about the loyalty of Hawaiian and Californian Japanese. When the future Secretary of the Navy, Frank Knox, returned from a visit to Hawaii in March of 1933, he wrote to the Deputy Chief of Staff of the U.S. Army in alarm. American security was being threatened by the growth in numbers and political power of "Japanese, Chinese and Philippino citizens [sic] who dictate to the political government." He suggested that the first move to take was to "intern every Japanese resident before the beginning of hostilities threatens."

Senator Arthur Robinson of Indiana warned Americans, in a popular magazine in March of 1934, that Japan was looking greedily at Alaska and that the Japanese Navy was more familiar with Alaskan waters than the Americans. Support was given this story by Representative William Sirovich of New York who told his fellow congressmen that while in Moscow he was shown Japanese documents, captured by Soviet spies, showing plans for the seizure of the Aleutian Islands.

In this atmosphere there was little hope for continued Japanese-American agreement on naval strength. Preliminary talks for the London naval conference began in October of 1934 and continued through to the end of the year without progress. Japanese delegates held that the 1922 ratio of 60 percent of American tonnage in capital ships no longer provided adequate security, due to the increased range of ships and planes. The United States was unwilling to agree to substantial modifications in the tonnage ratio, since this would only increase the odds against conducting a successful naval war in Far Eastern waters.

On December 29, 1934, Japan gave the stipulated two years' notice to the Washington Treaty signatories of the termination of the agreement. The same day that Japan gave notice, the U.S. Navy announced that the 1935 naval maneuvers would be held west of Hawaii. The timing of the Navy's announcement was viewed in Japan as a direct effort at intimidation, although the Navy Department claimed that it was mere coincidence. President Roosevelt regretted the timing when Japan's reaction was called to his attention, but when the Undersecretary of State suggested that the naval maneuvers be moved to the Atlantic or at least closer to the Pacific coast, the President refused to modify the Navy's planning. Before the maneuvers took place a petition signed by a number of prominent Americans as well as by more than 200 American missionaries to Japan appealed to the President to suspend this operation in the interest of easing the Pacific tensions which they seemed to be stimulating. National organizations such as the Federal Council of Churches joined in the appeal. The war games took place, however, directed at blocking an attempt to invade the American mainland, but using about 400 planes based principally in Hawaii, an aspect fully noted in Japan.

As Roosevelt completed his first four years of office, diplomatic relations with Japan were in a state of stasis as Stimson had left them, while the naval relationship was becoming a competitive one as it had been before 1922. Roosevelt's biographer, Ernest Lindley, summed up the situation in 1936 in his *Half Way With Roosevelt*. He praised the President for putting a stop to "inflammatory note-writing" to Japan and approved the naval building program as a deterrent, "a pointed hint to

Japan to go slow." But Roosevelt's Far Eastern policy was viewed as dangerous since it fell between two poles. One involved a staged withdrawal from Asia, done with as much dignity as possible, leaving the Japanese to set their course with China unhampered by American protests. The other meant a decision to face war and to seek definite commitments from Britain in order to utilize British bases and sea power to nullify the disadvantages of distance. The Roosevelt administration in 1936 seemed unwilling to opt clearly for either course.

Chapter XI

THE YELLOW TRADE PERIL

E CONOMICS AFFECTS the behavior of men and nations in circuitous ways. The pursuit of gain does not always produce logical acts directed toward realistic ends. Dreams may outweigh realities; a market in hand may be worth less than two seen dimly in the future. Decisions made in respect to national economic interests may involve very little objective weighing of the pros and cons.

The Americans who were willing to fight Japan on the issue of the Open Door in China knew that war and the destruction of the Japanese economy meant for some years the elimination of their country's best customer in Asia and the third largest purchaser of American exports. The Japanese who decided on war with the United States knew that this meant an end to trade with the largest buyer of Japanese goods as well as closing off the source of many important imports. Yet the leaders of both countries made their decisions at a time when foreign trade was regarded as vital to economic recovery and good customers were in themselves a major national interest.

For both Washington and Tokyo it was China that was the center of interests more important than their existing economic relations with each other or the preservation of peace in the

Pacific. "Security" and "responsibilities" were the words with which these interests were more often described than in terms of yen or dollars. Chinese communism did pose an ideological threat to Japan, while a powerful Soviet Union expanding in Asia might in time take revenge for the military defeat of 1905. Spokesmen for Japan's national mission also claimed for their country as the leading power in Asia the responsibility of guiding a chaotic China to stability and prosperity, free from western imperialist influences. But Japan's material investment in this area and China's importance as a source of raw materials also added up to a substantial economic interest.

For the United States it is easy to make a plausible case for more important non-material and material interests in Japan itself than in China. By the 1930's Japan had fully demonstrated its susceptibility to western technology and other aspects of American culture. Jazz, baseball, Hollywood movies, and American novels had all penetrated the language barrier and become a part of life in the major cities. Far more than the Chinese, the Japanese seemed open to the assimilation of American behavior patterns, although not always the most desirable ones. Optimists who still viewed the national mission as the Americanization of Asia could easily center their hopes on Japan.

For the more hard-boiled appraisers of American material interests, Japan provided an expanding market during decades when the Chinese consumption of American exports was insignificant. Both as an area for profitable investment and for trade, it was difficult to subordinate Japan, whose standard of living edged upward, to a China seemingly doomed to an eternity of poverty intensified by civil wars. In the depression years of the thirties, American sales to Japan ran four to seven times as large as the sales to China. Japan was also a more attractive center for American business to invest speculative capital. By 1936 American holdings in Japanese bonds and stocks reached over $164 million. The Philippines came second, despite its tiny population, compared to China which ranked third with a total investment amounting to about $100 million. With a population about four-fifths agricultural compared to Japan's approximate one-fourth, China imported less than three-fourths as much as Japan despite a population over seven times as large.

Despite these disparities in existing economic realities as well as in future prospects, the American view of China was almost completely impervious to the rival attractions of Japan. A thorough exploration of the sources of this persistent national bias would involve a broad and deep study of collective national attitudes and soon draw the investigator into areas where neither data nor generalizations exist to provide a basis for inquiry. At best a few hypotheses can be offered which seem to have some historical support from scattered data.

George Kennan once suggested that Americans have a tendency to create "hazy and exalted dreams of intimacy with other peoples," and this appears, prior to the disillusionments of 1949–1950, to have been most true of the Chinese. Despite the nineteenth-century west coast hysteria, in the twentieth century racial fears of the "yellow peril" variety were short-lived in their focus on Chinese. Japan easily became the substitute for nativist hostility. One obvious reason seems to have been the early termination of perceptible Chinese immigration, whereas anxiety was expressed over what seemed a dangerous influx of Japanese right down to the passage of the exclusion act in 1924.

Chinese immigrants and their children also seem to have concentrated in occupations or in the kinds of businesses—restaurants, laundries, import shops—which seem to have presented far less of a threat to white Americans. The Japanese-American farmer and businessman often operated in areas where he competed with previous generations of immigrants from Europe. He was attacked, usually with little or no justification, as an unscrupulous and vicious competitor demonstrating traits also attributed to the nation of his origin. This animosity, while regional in origin, was disseminated widely by the mass media. A book like Pearl Buck's *The Good Earth,* published in 1931, and the subsequent movie based on the book, disseminated a warmly sympathetic view of the Chinese peasant. No domestically produced counter-images were strong enough to nullify its impact. To present Japanese peasants to the American public with the same favorable view and with such widespread success would have been difficult if not impossible. In novels as well as in Hollywood films the Japanese was more likely to be portrayed as an internal or external threat.

The American impressions of the Chinese and Japanese response to Christian missionary efforts also helped to create a bias in favor of the former. Evangelical activity did create a minority of believers in Japan which included some distinguished individuals, but the island empire never appeared to be as fertile a field as China. The nominal conversion of Chiang Kai-shek to Christianity and the role of the Christianized Soong family in Kuomintang politics and finances were without a parallel in Japan. Probably by coincidence, the returned missionaries from Japan and their children seem not to have played such an influential part in American life as did such disparate individuals as Henry Luce, Walter Judd, and Pearl Buck.

In the economic realm, a more easily measurable set of factors worked against Japan. While the dream of China's profitable markets persisted in the minds of export interests, Japan was increasingly viewed not merely as a market, but as a tough competitor, threatening American overseas markets and pushing American-made goods off the shelves in the United States.

As in the case of military and naval development, the growth of Japan's export economy was aided by Americans. After the Meiji Restoration in 1868, a variety of economic prohibitions were removed and exports encouraged. As in China it was the British who led in handling this business, but it was the Americans who became consumers of Japan's exports to a total value far exceeding the British. Japanese green tea was preferred by Americans to the black tea of China, and almost all tea exports were consumed in the United States along with increasing quantities of raw silk and small items like fans, bric-a-brac, and lacquer ware. By 1880 the United States was buying over 40 percent of Japan's exports, compared to 10 percent by Britain. Japan's imports, however, at this date were still predominantly British, totalling over 50 percent, compared to the American share of approximately 7 percent.

From the earliest years Americans were optimistic about Japan's commercial and industrial prospects. Already in 1864 the *Annual Cyclopedia* informed Americans that foreign commerce had "struck deep roots and is acquiring influence" in Japan. President Grant in his annual message to Congress in 1869 mentioned Japan as one of the markets which should receive "our special attention." The American Minister to Tokyo, R. B. Van Valkenburgh, sought to guide Japan's economic course when in 1867 he advised the Foreign Minister to turn to the manufacture of silk goods for the American market rather than export raw silk alone.

When General Charles LeGendre was advising on Japan's foreign policy, he also gave thought to expanding the market for Japan's exports. Furniture made in European styles by cheap Japanese labor could, he believed, undersell all competitors on the American market. At his request samples of Japanese chairs were sent to the Philadelphia Exhibition in 1876 to attract buyers. Tea sets also interested the busy general who found that a 27-piece set, made and painted by hand cost only $2.75 in Japan, but could be sold in San Francisco for $15.00 to $20.00. He urged the Japanese to use machinery to give regularity of shape and size to these sets and to use lithographic processes for the design, cutting costs in half. He advised the Home Department Minister that a $40 million market for pottery existed in the United States, which could be dominated by Japan. He also sketched out ambitious plans for the conquest of the markets of Mexico and South America.

As the Japanese cotton textile industry began to increase the number of spindles in operation, a growing market opened for American cotton. The cotton sales were eventually to be a major factor in balancing American raw silk imports, but by 1890 imports from Japan were still totalling several times the value of Japan's purchases from the United States. Total trade figures, however, surpassed by this date the Chinese-American exchange.

The first fears that Japan was going to give the experienced Yankee some serious competition in the business world were expressed in the 1890's. The *San Francisco Chronicle* which took the lead in the attack on the Japanese immigrant also was the first to raise the economic issue. In an editorial in February of 1890, the *Chronicle* questioned the wisdom of allowing Japanese youth to be educated in the United States. Returning home, these individuals carried technical and business skills which the *Chronicle* feared would eventually produce a flood of cheap goods on the American market. Three years later a minority report of the House Committee on Ways and Means called for tariff raises to protect the silk industry from Japanese products produced by labor paid one-tenth of the wages of their American counterparts. But Van Valkenburgh's advice of some 20 years earlier that Japan produce its own silk textiles rather than export raw silk never produced a serious competitor.

In 1894 a Senate committee heard another of a long series of pleas from American producers for protection, this from the refiners of camphor who attacked the cheaply produced Japanese product.

As fears increased, fantasy began to produce wild rumors of new Japanese trade invasions. In 1896 business circles from New York to San Francisco discussed reports of the imminent onslaught of thousands of Japanese bicycles which were to sell for $12.00 each and drive the American-made product off the market. A similar story spread about the flood of Japanese buttons which were going to destroy all competitors by their low prices. Investigation of these stories showed that Japan had no bicycle plant capable of turning out more than 150 wheels yearly and these were of a quality far inferior to the American product. Austrian and German-made buttons were successfully competing on Japan's domestic market, and no shipments were being made to the United States.

In the atmosphere which pervaded some circles in the 1890's, it seems to have been sufficient for a few Japanese imports to arrive in any competitive field to stir fear. The ingenious Oriental, it appeared, had now learned how to get the best of his western mentor. An illustrative comment made in 1896 complained that:

> In early days of missionary work, the missionary wives used to hem moral handkerchiefs for the little heathen. Today the heathen Japanese have turned the tables on the Christian nations and cornered the world's markets for silk handkerchiefs, exporting within the last few years one hundred thousand of these useful articles.

The National Association of Manufacturers were concerned enough by 1896 to send a specialist to Japan to survey the areas of future competition. A report entitled *Commerce and Industries of Japan* was published by the envoy, Robert Porter, which warned that nothing short of absolute protection could exclude some Japanese products. These Orientals, Porter said, were completely dedicated to industrialization and determined to make their way in the international trade world. Their low wage scales in particular made them unbeatable. But a congressional committee established in 1896 to study the "alleged invasion of the markets of the United States" could still find no made-in-Japan manufactures of any quantity in American stores. Most of the imports consisted of handmade goods of a type which were unlikely to attract American producers.

If some American businessmen feared Japanese competition, others were anxious to profit from increasing the flow across the Pacific. These individuals occupied the role of middlemen, stimulating Japan's production of the most salable items, giving help in securing capital and machinery from the United States and in setting up wholesale networks to distribute the products. In time Japanese businessmen also learned many of the tricks of this trade and displaced many of these individuals, but the most capable were still able to profit from their role as agents of the feared competitor.

By the turn of the century, as the Japanese immigration question aroused hostility, fears of Japanese imports were used by the exclusionists to promote their own ends. The underpaid Japanese factory worker was equated with the immigrant who showed that hard work and a low standard of living made him a serious competitor to the white fruit and vegetable farmer even though the Japanese was forced often to develop the most arid and least fertile of the Pacific coast lands. Other interests also used the fear of trade competition to promote their ends. Protectionists of all varieties used Japan as they did Europe to promote a higher tariff policy with the American people and Congress. Even the free silver advocates found the Japanese issue a useful one. They held that Japan's price advantages came from paying labor in silver and selling on a gold market. An American bi-metalism was urged as an answer to the trade menace.

Hostility to Japan's economic growth was not characteristic of all business circles. Many importers welcomed Japanese goods and materials while exporters were happy over the expanding market. When a trade delegation from Tokyo visited the United States in 1904, it was enthusiastically received by export interests in New York and in other east coast cities. When the American Asiatic Association was founded, it viewed the "Muscovite" as the true peril of Asia and all the world, while Japan was the good customer.

After Japan's defeat of Russia in 1905 when the island empire's military and naval strength became a new matter of concern for American interests in the Pacific, the trade peril became more closely entwined with political fears and animosities. Economic growth was recognized as an important aspect of growth in power. The development of a Japanese merchant marine to compete for the carrying trade of the Pacific was seen as an aspect of naval power. A Senate Committee in 1900 reported that Japan's ambition for the creation of a big navy would not concern Americans half as much if it had not been paralleled by the declaration of some Japanese businessmen in behalf of "a big fleet of merchant ships competing for the transportation business of the world." An American writer warned in 1905 in the *North American Review,* "John Bull, be it remembered, drove the American merchantman from the Atlantic; and Japan may capture the carrying business of the Pacific." A survey of the growth of Japan's merchant marine in 1909 saw it as much of a power factor in the commercial world as the army and navy had demonstrated themselves to be in the military world.

As Japanese businessmen became sophisticated in competitive methods and learned how little ethics applied to the western capitalist world, frequent complaints were raised against the techniques used to sell. Products were sold using well-known American trade names or deceptively similar names. Badly copied American labels were put on products produced for the Japanese or Asian market in order to profit from the goodwill these American-made goods had among customers. Colgate's toothpowder was found by one correspondent in Manchuria in 1905 with a crude replica of the American label to which was added the claim that this powder relieved "teethache." Disregard for copyrights and patents began to create a stereotype of Japanese businessmen as unscrupulous traders, ready to steal the reputations and designs of the West. This was coupled with a stereotype of the Japanese workman, described by a Brooklyn newspaper in 1905 as "ingenious, artistic, inventive, industrious and intelligent, wearing almost no clothes and living on less than would support a mechanic's dog in this country."

Between 1910 and 1920 American exports to Japan jumped from approximately $21 million to over $450 million, while imports rose from $66 million to $527 million. A survey of the trade relationship prepared by an American businessman for the State Department in 1921 pointed out that Japan had "drifted into an unexpected dependence upon the United States." The latter country provided much of the raw material, machinery, and technical knowledge on which Japan's export economy was based. "We are their bankers, who finance their trade and with whom their surplus government and bankers balances are principally carried," the survey concluded. Henry Morgenthau, Sr., returning from a good-will trip to Japan a few years later, reaffirmed this trade relationship by pointing out that Japan was now buying more than 80 percent of its autos and lumber from the United States, over 70 percent of the building materials, and 50 percent of the needs for oil and machinery. In turn Americans bought over 90 percent of Japan's raw silk exports, over 50 percent of the brushes, and almost 40 percent of the pottery and toy exports.

In comparison Chinese-American trade still remained small. Sales to China's 400 millions were approximately half the value of those to Japan. Efforts at industrialization by the Chinese nationalists were feeble and hampered by the political strife. Yet the allure of the potential Chinese market remained strong. At the National Foreign Trade Convention held in San Francisco in 1920, a Japanese representative pointed out that his country's purchases of American goods amounted to $4.50 per capita compared to 10¢ per capita for China. But optimistic exporters were fond of thinking of what China's consumption would be if raised to the per capita level of Japan. Tobacco exporters pointed out that cigarette sales to China had grown from an average of only one smoke per Chinese per year in 1900 to 19 per year in 1920. If this trend could be encouraged to the point where adult Chinese averaged a cigarette a day, the market would obviously be gigantic. The keynote speaker at the Oriental trade session in 1920 used the time-honored phrases in speaking of the "undeveloped trade" of China as "beyond all bounds," and called upon exporters to be "reawakened to the vastness of its opportunities." The Irving National Bank issued a guide, *Trading with the Far East: How to Sell in the Orient,* in 1920 with a description of the China market as "potentially the greatest in the world" with an "almost limitless field for the sale of foreign goods" in the next 50 years.

The world depression gave the arguments of economic nationalists a new urgency when the prosperous decade of the twenties came to an end. As unemployment figures rose and factories closed, every foreign-made item on the shelves was construed as taking work away from American workers and business away from American businessmen. "Buy American" became a popular slogan, held to be the duty of every loyal citizen and directed at imports from any foreign supplier.

Even if the political tensions which followed Japan's Manchurian venture had not affected the American scene, Japan would have still come in for a major share of these attacks. Much, if not all, of the economically-produced animosity was unjustified. A United States Tariff Commission report in 1934 found only 8 percent of the total imports from Japan to be substantially competitive. The great bulk of American purchases were items which would not be produced in this country or raw materials which were used for domestic production. The competitive imports, however, were items which came quickly to public attention as they were displayed in 5-and-10-cent stores or in other shops dealing wtih the cheapest commodities. Matches, cotton rugs, cheap cotton cloth, pottery, glassware, brushes, pencils, toys, electric bulbs, and small rubber items like boots and balls were typical imports in this category. Many reached the markets through the initiative of Americans. When prices fell under the weight of the depression, buyers for chain stores carried samples to Japan which they invited producers to copy and to submit bids upon. Sometimes capital and machinery for production came from the United States. The first imported toothbrushes, for example, were produced in Osaka by an American-owned factory which shipped its entire product back across the Pacific in order to profit from the cheap labor of Japan.

In another respect the attack on Japanese imports was an outdated one. In 1932 the balance of trade which had long been in Japan's favor shifted to the United States and remained so for the rest of the decade. American sales to Japan increased steadily in a period of fading foreign trade. By 1937 they passed in value the pre-depression peak of 1928. American imports on the other hand declined from over $400 million in 1929 to half that figure in 1937. With the reopening of war in China, increased sales of oil, scrap metal, and other materials used by the Japanese war machine added to the favorable American trade balance.

Such statistics did not soften the attacks of the producers and interests who were hurt or believed they were hurt by Japan. This was particularly true of the cotton textile industry which watched importation of Japanese cottons move up from one million yards in 1933 to over 75 million in 1936. This was still a small fraction of the total market, where domestic production was of over seven billion yards in 1936. But in certain categories of cheap cottons, Japan supplied about half of the amount consumed in the United States.

The effort to counter this yellow trade peril took many forms. In newspapers and magazines, as well as on the floor of Congress, frequent alarms and calls to action were presented to the public. "Give a Japanese product an inch and it takes a mile," proclaimed a typical attack in the *Saturday*

Evening Post in 1934. Congress and the President received appeals to preserve the American economy. "If nothing is done to stop the flood of these imports it will mean that hundreds of American workmen will be thrown out of employment," a vice president of the American Lead Pencil Company wrote to Roosevelt in the fall of 1933. The loss of Latin American markets as well was predicted, as Japanese businessmen were accused of using strategically placed colonies of nationals to take over this trade.

Late in 1934 a concerted drive was launched by the National Association of Manufactures, the Cotton Textile Institute, and the Toy Manufacturers of America to bring together representatives of all suffering industries to pressure Congress and the President for action. Fifty members of New England Chambers of Commerce joined in the call. Some saw import quotas as the solution, but the manufacturers of matches, cotton rugs, pottery, and glassware wanted virtual exclusion. Representatives of these latter industries formed a "Made in America Club" in the spring of 1935. With the help of the Hearst newspapers, they publicized their demands for closing the door on Japanese goods. Some groups, such as the National Potters Association went further and actively supported the boycott movements which originated out of political motives.

Not all business groups dealing with Japan joined in the trade war. When a United States Steel Products Company representative complained about Japanese competition at the 1934 National Foreign Trade Convention, he was answered by a spokesman of the New York Cotton Exchange. The latter pointed out that Japan had increased its purchases by 60 percent in the past five years of otherwise declining sales, "the one vividly bright spot in the cotton trade picture." A representative of the Department of Commerce also reminded the convention that Japan was then buying more than was sold to the United States, and that this trade balance was not countered by unfavorable invisible expenditures such as American tourists in

Japan or payments to Japanese shippers. A former member of the Tariff Commission pleaded for a balanced view, since the complaints were largely over petty items. "I think we should try to bring emphatically to the minds of the American people that Japan is a good buyer," he said.

That goal was not achieved; China remained a more popular and attractive prospect. The opening address of the National Trade Convention in 1932, like that of 1920, dwelt on China's possibilities when "untold millions will be delivered into the laps of those whose foresight will have established the avenues that lead to her shores." In 1935 the National Foreign Trade Council joined the Asiatic Association in sending an 18-man economic mission to China for two months. When invited to Japan, they stayed only two weeks and returned with a report which advocated an extension of American political and economic commitments to China. During the thirties China also began to serve as a useful dumping ground for surplus American commodities. By extending credits, beginning with a $50 million Reconstruction Finance Corporation loan in 1933, the United States disposed of some 6½ million bales of surplus cotton and over 35 million bushels of surplus wheat by 1939.

President Roosevelt took a broader view of the situation than that of the special interests and refused at first to be pushed into extreme acts of economic warfare against Japan. He recognized the validity of the words of Ambassador Saito that "international trade cannot operate only one way." If a nation will sell, said the Ambassador, "it must also buy." American action was also hampered by the terms of the 1911 Japanese-American Treaty of Commerce which accorded Japan most-favored-nation treatment. With the co-operation of the State Department, representatives of some affected industries negotiated "gentlemen's agreements" with their Japanese rivals whereby voluntary quotas were set on exports to the United States. The threat of more drastic action was used to press the Japanese into these self-imposed restrictions.

Although some quotas were successfully established, the match and chinaware industry complained that they were still too high. American importers complained that quotas were set too low and crippled their operations. And as one southern congressional representative said in 1936, "We've got to sell our cotton somewhere and I will not be one to endeavor to drive away the best foreign customer the Texas cotton farmer has left."

When an effort to set a quota on imports of bleached and colored cotton cloths failed, President Roosevelt finally took direct action. In May of 1936 he invoked the flexible provisions of the tariff law and ordered an average increase of 42 percent in the duty on these categories of imports. By this date Japan's cotton goods had begun to suffer from restrictive measures taken by more than half of their other markets. Japanese xenophobia was further stimulated as tariff barriers against Japanese goods, like earlier barriers against Japanese immigrants, and presented a convincing picture of western encirclement. The most secure markets were those which Japan could control politically; an argument for further political expansion.

Momentum and the outbreak of war in China carried Japanese-American trade to a new peak in 1937, when American sales to Japan topped those of 1928 and American purchases almost reached the level of 1931. But the turn came in 1938 when Washington began to take a series of restrictive measures which culminated in the virtual embargo of Japan in the summer of 1941.

The extension of Japanese control over North China beginning in the summer of 1937 created another economic grievance. American exports to the Japanese-held areas were not seriously affected in 1938 and 1939, with some areas even showing an increase in imports from the United States. But resident American businessmen found themselves facing increasing Japanese competition while the Japanese government eliminated the special privileges which western businessmen had once enjoyed. American Chambers of Commerce in the major Chinese ports joined in urging the United States government to make a vigorous defense of treaty privileges in the Japanese-held areas and to protest the favoritism shown Japanese businessmen. Resident businessmen formed the American Information Committee which distributed propaganda in the United States, such as a booklet entitled *Japan's War on Foreign Business in China* as well as sending anti-Japanese press releases to American news services.

Did the clamor against Japanese goods in the United States and the complaints of business interests in China influence the Roosevelt administration in moving against Japan? A direct relationship would be difficult to prove, but that there was at least indirect influence seems likely. Public opinion was not immune to the reiterated attacks on the Japanese economic menace, while the occasional pleas of the cotton exporters received little attention. Hostility produced by Japan's exports blended easily with hostility aroused by Japan's foreign policy.

The economic measures taken against Japan from 1938 onward hurt some American interests, but the rise of exports to Britain and France as these nations began to rearm was ample compensation. Protests could be answered with the argument that the salvation of China offered a great reward for temporary losses in trade with Japan. A war against America's best customer in Asia was also a war for potentially the greatest future customer.

Chapter XII

THE CHINA COMMITMENT

A T PRESENT there is clearly no support in American public opinion for territorial possessions in the Far East," concluded Tyler Dennett, in 1936. "We are in a mood to get out, not to get in," he believed. Lack of interest in Asian issues was also demonstrated by the presidential campaign in 1936. Neither of the major party platforms mentioned Far Eastern policy. Foreign affairs were treated briefly in clichés; the Democrats pledged the maintenance of "a true neutrality," while the Republicans used the traditional phrase in promising to avoid "entangling alliances."

In the campaign oratory of the summer and fall of 1936, domestic issues were discussed to the almost total exclusion of all else. President Roosevelt and his opponent, Governor Alfred M. Landon, fought over the ground of unemployment and the state of the national economy. In one major speech devoted to foreign policy, made at Chautauqua, New York, in August, Roosevelt ignored the Far East to speak of his Good Neighbor policy in the Americas and of his determination to keep this nation isolated from European wars. Both candidates recognized that any hint of a stand in Asia or Europe which might lead to American involvement would lose votes.

In an oblique fashion the Roosevelt administration did prepare to take a position in the Far East by its decisions on naval construction. When the Japanese delegate withdrew from the London Conference in January of 1936, hopes for extending the naval limitations were dimmed. Future construction would depend on each nation's assessment of its security needs and the willingness of legislatures to make appropriations.

Some thought had been given as early as the fall of 1934 to the possibility that Japan would refuse to negotiate a new naval limitations treaty. Roosevelt at that date was adamant in opposing any agreement which would increase treaty tonnage, even if an increase was the only means of extending the life of the treaty. Roosevelt was unwilling, however, to meet Japan's demands for parity by promising not to maintain in peace time a stronger fleet in the Pacific. Admiral William H. Standley, Chief of Naval Operations, told the President that such a promise carried no serious consequences for the defense of the United States; Japanese strength would still be inadequate for operations outside of Asian waters. Peacetime parity in the Pacific, Roosevelt knew, meant, nevertheless, limited ability to exert diplomatic pressure backed by naval strength, and the maintenance of such a capacity he considered important.

Norman Davis read an opening message to the London Conference early in 1935 in which the President spoke of the 1922 Washington Treaty as "a milestone in civilization" and warned of the dangerous consequences of a return to competitive building. Davis proposed initially that all three navies reduce their tonnage by 20 percent, while keeping the old ratio system. But the Japanese had come to London to end an arrangement which carried implications of national inferiority. The 5-5-3 ratio of 1922 now seemed to mean "Rolls Royce—Rolls Royce—Ford," said Ambassador Saito. Since their economy was not favorable to the construction of a "Rolls Royce" navy, the Japanese were interested in scaling down British and Amer-

ican tonnage to a level closer to their own. Another aspect of
the Japanese program was the elimination of aircraft carriers
and battleships from all three forces, making each almost in-
vulnerable in home waters.

Acceptance of either or both of Japan's proposals would
still have left an Anglo-American naval force far greater than
that of Japan. But in actuality such a naval force was unlikely
to exist in the Pacific. Even if London and Washington could
agree to function as allies vis-à-vis Japan, the growing concern
of Britain for the strength of the Italians and Germans would
tie considerable naval tonnage to European waters. Anglo-
American forces might be then incapable of conducting an
offensive in the Far East or of backing up diplomatic moves.
Attempts to check future Japanese moves in China would be
ineffective. Although neither London nor Washington had any
intention in 1936 of conducting such a restraining operation in
China, neither was willing to accept a treaty which would
prevent such action if at some future date their national interests seemed to call for it.

There seemed to be no bridge between Japan's view of its
security needs and the British and American view of their
potential future role in Asia. After the Japanese delegates
withdrew, Britain and the United States concluded a new
treaty which stressed qualitative rather than quantitative limitations on new naval construction. The London Treaty of 1936
did little to hamper either signatory, since it contained ample
escape provisions to permit both to build to meet new Japanese
construction. The Roosevelt administration was now free to
consider a building program which met national needs.

Two schools of thought were apparent in Washington as to
the course of future naval construction. The first was exemplified by Stanley Hornbeck, chief of the Far Eastern Affairs
Division. Already in the fall of 1934 Hornbeck had argued that
the United States might be better served by a breakdown in
the treaty negotiations than would Japan. A new treaty, he

feared, might hamper naval reinforcement of diplomatic policy. In January of 1936, after Japan had withdrawn from the Conference, Hornbeck welcomed the return to unrestricted naval competition. The United States could now begin to build a big Pacific fleet whereas Japan, he believed, could not afford to enter a naval race and would be forced to take the initiative in asking for a new treaty. American delegates would be in a far better bargaining position at this point to secure continued treaty superiority to Japan. Hornbeck argued for his policy on the assumption which he had made earlier in advising Stimson on economic boycotts; Japan's economy had a precarious existence and was incapable of withstanding severe strains.

The Hornbeck point of view had many active supporters in addition to the expansionists within the Navy itself. Cordell Hull reached the conviction by 1935 that the United States should hasten the construction of a large Navy and that peace could not be secured through disarmament. In Congress naval expansion had the enthusiastic support of influential members like Key Pittman, chairman of the Senate Foreign Relations Committee. After the Japanese withdrew from the London Conference, Pittman made such a vigorous attack on their foreign policy that Hull was led to send Tokyo an official disavowal of having been consulted by the belligerent senator.

Norman Davis was for a time the spokesman of another school of thought. He accepted as valid the statements of the Japanese in withdrawing from London that they had no intention of initiating a new naval race. Despite rising Japanese nationalism, the 866 thousand ton Japanese fleet of July, 1936, had only grown since 1930 in ships built and building by 2.6 percent. This compared with a 2.3 percent growth for the American fleet of 1,368 thousand tons in mid-1936. Davis felt that continued restraint on American and British building would encourage similar action in Tokyo.

President Roosevelt, while continuing to express his hopes for a return to naval limitations, supported a construction program which inclined toward the Hornbeck school. The naval appropriation bill introduced by the administration in the spring of 1936 asked for over $500 million, the largest peacetime appropriation to date. Replacements were provided for over-age submarines and destroyers and authority was requested for the construction of two battleships, if the President determined that either Japan or Britain was engaging in similar construction.

A lively discussion took place in both houses of Congress in 1935 over the wisdom of continuing naval expansion. In 1936 Roosevelt's request for funds went through with little debate or questioning of fundamental naval policy. Senator Gerald Nye, supported by a few associates, raised the issue of the impact of new ships on relations with Japan, but his voice was that of a tiny minority. The President had set a useful precedent in 1933 by making naval construction a domestic recovery measure, and the interests of congressmen from seaboard and industrial constituencies in naval construction were primarily economic rather than concerned with foreign policy. Representatives from agricultural states were more likely to question naval expenditures, but in 1936 the need for a united front in a presidential election year was probably adequate to stifle Democratic criticism. A public opinion poll in December of 1935 also supported congressional action with figures showing that more than 70 percent of the individuals sampled favored a larger navy. This did not mean, however, that these individuals favored a stronger foreign policy in the Pacific; over 70 percent also viewed a stronger navy as more likely to keep the United States out of future wars.

By the end of 1936 the Secretary of the Navy was able to speak of "an unparalleled renaissance" of naval building with three aircraft carriers, 11 cruisers, 63 destroyers, and 18 submarines under construction. The Japanese nationalists viewed this expansion as a future threat in Far Eastern waters, and it served to spur their own building program. Admiral Osami

Nagano, Minister of the Navy, warned the Diet of a dangerous future after Congress passed the 1936 appropriation bill. Unless Japan expanded its construction program, Nagano estimated that fighting strength would shrink from approximately 80 percent of that of the United States to below 60 percent by 1941. He proposed an annual addition of 50,000 tons to keep a ratio of strength against the estimated 70,000 tons which the United States was going to build annually.

With the termination of the naval limitations treaty on the last day of 1936, Japan's building plans were no longer made public. Rumor quickly reported that super-battleships were to be constructed which far exceeded the old treaty ships of 35,000 tons and 14-inch guns. In January of 1937 President Roosevelt announced that he was approving the construction of two battleships to balance new construction in Britain, where two battleship keels were laid down the same month. In April of 1937 Congress voted a half billion dollars to continue the naval expansion according to the schedule set in 1934. The Navy shortly after requested additional funds to modernize aircraft carriers. In Japan keels were laid in 1937 for two battleships which were to be the largest and most heavily armed in the world. The naval race which had been checked in 1922 was on once more.

In the summer of 1937 political developments in the Far East gave new significance to the naval competition. Japan's economic situation failed to improve as exports struggled against an iron ring of tariffs. Militant nationalism continued to weaken the old political structure. Relations with China were marked with incidents which periodically aroused the chauvinists. In early July a minor brush took place between Japanese troops on maneuvers and Chinese forces stationed near the Marco Polo bridge in the vicinity of Peking. The Japanese had much larger forces in the Chinese capital to protect their embassy and nationals than did any of the western powers. Now additional troops were brought in as the Chinese refused to yield.

Chinese nationalism had also reached a point where compromise was no longer politically tenable. Full-scale but undeclared war spread through northern China.

American residents and American interests in China were roughly treated by the warring Japanese armies and a flow of protests began from Washington to Tokyo. On December 12, 1937, Japanese naval fliers bombed and sank the U.S.S. *Panay* on the Yangtze River above Nanking and also bombed three Standard Oil tankers nearby. The American naval vessel was clearly marked and the action of the Japanese in machine-gunning the survivors suggested a deliberate attack. Three American lives were lost. Headlines brought the news of Japan's action to American homes, while movie theaters heightened American feeling by showing a film record of the attack captured by an alert newsreel cameraman on board the *Panay*.

In Tokyo Ambassador Grew, who had found hope in the lack of enthusiasm for war among the Japanese people and government, now prepared for a break in diplomatic relations. The Japanese government quickly apologized, however, and paid an indemnity of over $2 million dollars. The genuineness of Japanese concern was also demonstrated by the action of thousands of citizens in sending contributions to the American embassy to aid the survivors of the attack and the families of the dead.

Hardly had the *Panay* incident left the headlines when Japanese invasion and occupation of Nanking brought new protests over damage to American property and mistreatment of American residents. The Japanese war machine was clearly not going to be hampered in its action by concern for the rights of Americans and Europeans in China, nor be chastened by the protests of foreign governments relayed through Tokyo. In Washington it was clear that in northern China, if not in all of China, Japanese power was jeopardizing the status of the United States, Britain, and other European powers. American dreams for the political future of China and American ambitions for the expansion of economic interests in Asia were being destroyed.

Calls for a re-evaluation of Far Eastern policy became common in 1937 and 1938. Some Americans claimed that Washington had no rational and consistent policy based on a clear assessment of national interests in Asia. Continued non-recognition of Manchuria and protest notes to Japan, possibly backed by an expanding American Navy, did not add up to a Far Eastern policy. "A combination of drift and bluff means disaster," historian Allan Nevins warned. In the Navy and in the State Department the need was felt for a statement of American goals and a selection of means in dealing with the turbulent Orient. The Navy believed that the enlarging Pacific Fleet was still too small to fight a successful war with Japan over China. "If we are going to back down, do it now when not challenged rather than later," Hull was advised by Admiral Standley.

The Secretary of State saw that his country was at what he called later "the Oriental cross roads of decision." One alternative was "to withdraw gradually, perhaps with dignity, from the Far East." But Hull felt that this meant the nullification of all American treaty rights, the abandonment of American citizens in China, the closing of the Open Door, and the relinquishing to Japan of an area in which lived nearly one-half the population of the world.

Other Americans did not see the consequences of withdrawal in such a dire light. "Little or no harm will come to us if we await the outcome for the initiative lies with China," Ambassador Nelson T. Johnson wrote from Peking in 1936. He told Hull that he was opposed to the use of force to save China from probable Japanese conquest. "It all seems so stupid to me," Secretary of Interior Harold Ickes wrote in his diary after a cabinet meeting in September of 1937 in which armed protection for American businessmen in China was discussed. Investment in foreign enterprises ought to be at the risk of the investor, Ickes believed. Pleading for "A Clarifying Foreign

Policy," historian Samuel F. Bemis claimed that the Open Door policy was itself "a protean error." Bemis believed that American trade would have been greater with a China partitioned or under British or Japanese protection, and that it was time to abandon the Open Door policy.

A policy of withdrawal and accommodation had both political and ethical strength in 1937 and 1938, since it represented the point of view of the great majority of Americans. Americans wanted a lien on the Chinese market, the chief of the State Department's Western European Division wrote to Norman Davis in the spring of 1937, if persuasion was the only price. "But if the price seems to involve a fight, the American people are patently unwilling to assume the risk for a possible profit," he concluded. Public opinion polls taken at this time gave ample support for this conclusion. In September of 1937, 55 percent of the people polled refused to express sympathies for either side in the Sino-Japanese conflict. Although in a month this neutrality had declined to 40 percent, over 60 percent stated that their sympathy for China was still not strong enough to keep them from buying Japanese goods. After the *Panay* affair, 70 percent of those polled believed that Americans in China should be warned to leave and the armed forces withdrawn from Chinese soil. A State Department study of public sentiment in late 1937 and early 1938 concluded that there was "a growing sympathy for China, but the controlling feeling of the country was the desire to keep out of war." Even those elements of society like veterans' organizations which were free from any pacifist taint and tended to express nationalist belligerency were opposed to Asian involvement. The annual American Legion convention declared for a policy of "absolute neutrality" in 1937 and 1938, while the Veterans of Foreign Wars in November of 1937 launched a campaign to secure 25 million signatures to a "Keep America out of War" petition.

Congress reflected the attitude of the general public. The

Panay sinking which some feared would produce the same belligerency and results as the *Maine* in 1898 was discussed with restraint in both houses. The chief concern of congressmen was the maintenance of neutrality. Some pointed to the earlier loss of American lives as a result of blunders of Chinese fliers and argued for complete withdrawal of American residents.

One display of the concern of Congress for the avoidance of war was the strong fight made for the Ludlow resolution. Introduced by Congressman Louis Ludlow of Indiana in 1935, the resolution called for a constitutional amendment which required the approval of the voters in a national referendum for a declaration of war in cases other than an actual invasion of American territory. For three years the Ludlow proposal had remained stalled in a House committee, but the *Panay* sinking quickly won for it 218 signatures, a majority of the House necessary for a vote on the discharge of the resolution. Even if discharged, the resolution still required a two-thirds vote of both houses of Congress plus ratification by 36 states. The enthusiasm for the move was so great, however, that the Roosevelt administration decided to try to block initial consideration. Alfred Landon and Henry L. Stimson were enlisted to appeal to Republicans, while Postmaster General James Farley warned Democrats that they would cut themselves off from patronage by supporting Ludlow. The administration won, but only by a narrow margin of 209 to 188, with 111 Democrats deserting the White House to vote for discharge. Even President Roosevelt's great popularity was challenged by the drive to keep domestic considerations before foreign.

Popular sentiment for withdrawal and non-involvement in Asia was largely based on traditional isolationism and the simple argument that the way to avoid war was to stay at home. Withdrawal was also supported by more sophisticated arguments made by those claiming to be realists. By the mid-thirties the Soviet Union had demonstrated marked recovery from the economic and political chaos left by the Revolution of 1917 and was again a factor to be reckoned with in Europe and Asia. There was evidence of a renewal of old Tsarist interests in northern China, with new allies in the form of the Chinese Communists. The strength of this movement was easily noted by observers who did not limit themselves to Chiang Kai-shek in their analysis of Chinese politics. Any protection of American interests which looked beyond day-to-day policies involved a return to the balancing technique which Theodore Roosevelt had attempted when he supported Japanese power as an essential counterweight to Tsarist influence.

The State Department was warned of this consideration in a brilliant memorandum prepared in 1935 by John V. A. Mac-Murray, former Chief of the Far Eastern Division, who acted on an official request. One of the conclusions was that:

> The defeat of Japan would not mean her elimination from the problem of the Far East. . . . It would merely create a new set of stresses and substitute for Japan, the U.S.S.R. as the successor of Imperial Russia as a contestant (and at least an equally unscrupulous and dangerous one) for the mastery of the East. Nobody except perhaps Russia would gain from our victory in such a war.

MacMurray discussed the contents of his report briefly with Stanley Hornbeck when it was delivered, but it was pushed aside and not circulated in the Department until January of 1938, when it was dusted off at the request of Ambassador Grew. How seriously its argument was considered at this date is not ascertainable from the documents.

Recognition of the importance of Russia and rising Chinese Communism was not confined to official circles. A widely praised study, published in New York and London in 1937 by a British scholar, issued the same warning as did Mac-Murray. The destruction of Japanese power, said G. F. Hudson in *The Far East in World Politics*, meant "the return of Russia and a new upsetting of the trembling balance of China's domestic politics with world wide repercussions." Whereas Japan's imperialist activity was circumscribed geographically, Hudson advised that "the triumph of Communism in China would stimulate anew the revolutionary forces in every country." The British Navy, Hudson believed, would not be used against Japan to facilitate the rise of Communist power in China.

Another argument for withdrawal which claimed consideration was that which evaluated the importance of Chinese nationalism. In the decade before 1931, this movement had given ample demonstration of its determination to end the privileged position of the West in political and economic life. "China for the Chinese" was a slogan not to be forgotten because of the rise of Japan's claims of "Asia for Asians." American policy had recognized this factor in the 1920's and it was not forgotten completely in the next decade.

Secretary of State Hughes had "the sanest conception of America's real interests in Asia," Samuel Bemis wrote in 1936, supporting Hughes' action in preparing for "a face-saving retreat." It was a "delusive hope," John MacMurray concluded, to hope that the elimination of Japan would make for closer understanding with China. "If we were to 'save' China from Japan and become the 'Number One' nation in the eyes of her people, we should thereby become not the most favored, but the most distrusted of nations," said MacMurray in 1935 with a clear view of developments a quarter of a century in advance.

Even if American interests in Asia might be worth fighting for, the strategic problems dissuaded others from considering war. The Philippines were scheduled to receive their independence, and many felt that they should make their own adjustments to their Asian neighbors. The elimination of Manila as an American naval base would leave Guam and Samoa as the major outposts of American power west of Hawaii and neither had prospects of being secure bastions. Even with the retention of bases in the Philippines, the weight of opinion among American strategists in the thirties was that these islands could not be held against a major Japanese attack. A successful war with Japan over China required a larger navy and more bases than dreamt of by even the most ardent naval expansionist. More than a few hundred American lives would be expended to protect American interests and this was an equation few dared to attempt to support in the mid-thirties.

An alternative which appealed to those who did not want to face up to a retreat or major sacrifice of lives and money was to protect American interests by measures "short of war." Japan, it was believed, could be pressured into giving due regard to American rights and even into withdrawing from China itself by a variety of pressures, chiefly economic. Peace and stability in Asia did not require war but the use of new techniques. This was a viewpoint which had great appeal for peace-minded Americans who did look beyond their borders and hoped that a contribution could be made to world affairs without adding to the existing amount of violence.

One category of opinion relied on "moral pressures." Worldwide condemnation of Japan's policies in China would, it was hoped, move the saner elements to check the excesses of their government and modify policies. The League of Nations was viewed as one important forum for chastening Japan; Hull's frequent lectures on the "sanctity of treaties" given to the Japanese Ambassador or sent to Tokyo in diplomatic pouches were viewed as another means. Japan should be made to see that its future lay in following the "orderly processes" of international relations and in preserving the Open Door in China.

A vigorous group of Americans viewed moral lectures as meaningless unless accompanied by economic pressures. The outbreak of war in 1937 led, as in 1932, to appeals for a private boycott of Japanese goods. A few days after the sinking of the

Panay two major 5-and-10-cent chains announced that they had stopped buying goods from Japan. The American Federation of Labor and the Committee for Industrial Organization both voted in their October 1937 conventions to boycott imports from Japan. Some 600 delegates of the American Student Union at Vassar College in January of 1938 took part in a mass burning of silk stockings and silk ties, chanting, "Make lisle the style, wear lisle for awhile." Peace groups, civic organizations, and manufacturers joined in the call to stop purchase of the products of the "Oriental aggressor."

When the boycotters expressed more than mere animosity they claimed that their actions would produce benefits in the Far East. Curtailment of overseas sales would make it difficult for Japan to secure the foreign exchange necessary for the purchase of materials with which to carry on the war in China. An effective boycott, it was estimated, would cut the market for 40 percent of Japan's exports and require a parallel cut in imports, hampering the war effort. The damage done to export industries and the resulting unemployment should bring home to the Japanese people the hostility which their government was creating all over the world.

It was even claimed by some that enough economic pressure would lead to a virtual collapse of the Japanese economy. This argument was supported by Freda Utley's *Japan's Feet of Clay*, which appeared in the spring of 1937. Admiral Yarnell, after reading this volume, advised Admiral William Leahy, Chief of Naval Operations, that it contained much material of value in planning moves against Japan. The message of the book was that Japan was putting up a big bluff to the world as to its economic strength. Without silk sales to the United States, cotton sales to the British empire, and credits from the western nations, the economy would collapse within a few weeks. Since Japan could not attack either the United States or Britain, the author assured her readers that "there is no reason at all why economic sanctions need lead to war."

Some believers in the utility of economic pressure saw private action as inadequate and called for an official embargo to do the damage necessary for the proper results. Henry L. Stimson was one of the best-known proponents of this view outside of government circles. In a letter to the *New York Times* in October of 1937, he appealed for government action to ban trade with Japan; a personal appeal to the same end was made directly to the President. Stimson did not believe in using American soldiers in the final resort, he said, since they would "do much more harm than good."

Another means of pressuring Japan which had some popular support was direct aid to China's effort to drive the island invaders off the mainland. This approach, it was claimed, was less likely to create hostile reactions in Japan and had the advantage of doing no harm to the American economy. Although the Neutrality Acts forbade the sale of arms and munitions or the lending of money to belligerent nations, this legislative ban was inapplicable, since neither China nor Japan were officially at war.

An alternative or supplementary method of putting pressure upon Japan was the continued and rapid expansion of the United States Navy. The threat of force spoke far more effectively, some argued, than economic pressures or lectures on international morality. Naval expansion did not mean, as Congress was frequently assured, that the United States was preparing for a war in the western Pacific. A large force in the Pacific was the best means of avoiding war by bringing the Japanese to their senses, and meant that American protests would be heard and acted upon.

The number of Americans who favored using the last resort of nations, war, as a means of defending their interests in Asia was very small in 1937 and 1938. Senator Key Pittman issued a personal declaration of war against Japan and Germany in December of 1938, but the erratic Democrat from Nevada represented no body of opinion in the Senate. In the Navy there were a few admirals who saw war as inevitable and wanted to fight Japan as soon as possible, but they seem to have been a minority. Secretary of the Navy Swanson, according to Ickes, called for war at the time of the *Panay* sinking, and some claims were made by the Navy that this was the best time for a quick victory with Japan preoccupied with China. Other than Secretary of the Treasury Henry Morgenthau, Jr., no other member of the cabinet is reported to have supported war in 1937.

All of the measures suggested as a basis of American policy had support among some members of the Roosevelt administration. Ambassador Joseph Grew for a long time represented the approach which probably came closest to that of the American public. Although policy was made in Washington and not in Tokyo, Grew had the friendship and respect of Roosevelt as well as the weight of his long years of diplomatic service in expressing his views in the State Department.

Grew's reluctance to see the United States involved in what he conceived to be a dangerous effort to pressure Japan was in large part a result of his evaluation of the situation as seen from long residence in Tokyo. The war in China was not a popular war, the Ambassador frequently reported, but it was an effort to defend what Japanese considered to be their vital interests and rights on the mainland. Patience, sympathetic understanding, and occasional reminders of the ill effects of the military path to power in Asia would eventually strengthen the moderate elements, Grew hoped, and enable them to restrain or even oust the militarists from control.

The Ambassador was not opposed to the maintenance of a strong American position, but he was concerned that strength not be used in such a way as to stir needlessly Japanese chauvinism and cut the lines of communication. As early as 1934 he had advocated building up the American naval forces in the Pacific as a means of earning respect in Tokyo. He objected, however, when that force was brandished in such a way as to evoke a similarly belligerent response from bellicose Japanese. Even verbal threats such as he construed to be contained in Roosevelt's October, 1937 "Quarantine" speech cut the ground from under diplomatic efforts. Roosevelt's action left him depressed and he wrote in his diary that he felt "my carefully built castle tumbling about my ears."

Grew's opposition to and warning against economic pressures probably served to postpone a decision on their use in Washington. Unlike some American analyses of the Japanese economy, Grew saw that it had great psychological strength in the patriotism of a people who were willing to make almost endless sacrifices in the interests of national security. It would not be a simple matter to cripple the war machine by cutting off its supply lines; further efforts to isolate economically a people who still resented discrimination against them as immigrants might only spur new efforts to expand by force. Grew came to Washington in the early summer of 1939 and warned Roosevelt that sanctions once begun would have to be carried through to the end and that could mean war. Sanctions lifted without achieving their end would "bring in their wake a loss of prestige and influence to the nation declaring them." Cutting Japan's supply of oil, he told the President, would probably lead the militarists into an attack on the Dutch East Indies in order to secure control of these petroleum resources.

On his return to Tokyo in the fall of 1939 Grew carried with him a message to the Japanese people which he delivered publicly to the America-Japan Society under the title, "Straight from the Horse's Mouth." It was an effort, supported by the President, to make clear the extent to which the American people had been alienated and aroused by the use of force in China. The Japanese Foreign Office requested that the text be released to the press and the Ambassador felt that he had made progress in educating the people and encouraging a reappraisal of foreign policy.

The events of the next year led the Ambassador to lose

hope. The fall of France and the jeopardy in which Britain was placed by German successes seem to have convinced Grew that the status quo in the Pacific deserved preservation until the European war was over. Not just private American interests were at stake in Asia, but "vital" national interests, he wrote. In September of 1940 Grew sent a long memorandum to Washington which the Far Eastern Division called his "Green Light" message. Some form of economic sanctions now seemed worth the risk. Whether or not they resulted in war would depend, he believed, upon the "do or die" temper of the Army and Navy who might act suddenly without the prior knowledge of the political leadership. Grew's change of position probably strengthened the arguments of the sanctionists in the State Department.

Stanley K. Hornbeck was one of the most influential believers in economic pressure as an instrument of American policy in Asia. Relieved of his position as Chief of the Far Eastern Division, Hornbeck was appointed Adviser on Political Relations to the Secretary of State in August of 1937. This promotion did not seem to change his perspective and three years later an associate, J. Pierrepont Moffat, described him as regarding "Japan as the sun around which her satellites, Germany and Italy, were revolving." An experienced and at times a cautious diplomat, Hornbeck in 1935 believed that war with Japan was in no sense inevitable. An Anglo-Japanese war, a Russo-Japanese war, or a civil upheaval might weaken Japan enough to make possible adjustment of relations with the United States. The best policy, he believed, was to develop a strong military machine, but avoid giving China any hope for armed assistance in settling relations with Japan.

When war broke out in July of 1937, Hornbeck at first warned against "saying those things which may tend to inflame the parties directly in conflict." He assumed that neither the United States nor Britain would intervene with force and told the Chinese Ambassador on August 2 that his country must stop expecting foreign powers to fight her battles or even take sides in the controversy with Japan. But the same month Hornbeck reported favorably on a Chinese request for an Export-Import Bank loan, although the Office of Arms and Munitions Control felt that such an action would violate the spirit of neutrality legislation.

A year later, in the fall of 1938, Hornbeck had become a proponent of economic warfare. In a series of memoranda for Secretary Hull he advocated action and argued that moral suasion had failed, leaving no alternative. In December of 1938 he proposed the denunciation of the 1911 commercial treaty with Japan in order to clear away legal difficulties. The American public now favored bold action, he said, which would deter Japan from going to extremes. The formulation and adoption of "a diplomatic 'war plan'," henceforth engaged Hornbeck's energies.

Secretary of State Hull stood somewhere between Grew's original position and the economic sanctionists. Possessed of the spirit of a Tennessee mountain feudist, Hull's animosity toward Japan seemed limitless. Ickes accused him in the spring of 1938 of deferring unduly to Hitler and Mussolini, but said that he "all but rattles the saber when it comes to Japan." But despite the vehemence of his verbal attacks on the "international bandits" of Asia, Hull was slow to join the camp of those calling for economic action. He even sympathized with Grew's objections to the "Quarantine" speech and wrote that it set back the State Department's efforts at educating the public in favor of international action by six months.

If it was not just temperament which restricted Hull to a faith in moral suasion, economic considerations were probably also important. Even if sanctions were applied in co-operation with Britain, Hull pointed out that the major burden on consumers and producers would be borne by the American economy. The blow which sanctions would deal to the southern cotton industry was probably a major consideration since the Secretary kept in close touch with his former colleagues in Congress from the southern and border states. His first major action was not taken until July of 1938 when an appeal for a "moral embargo" was made to American manufacturers and exporters of planes and aeronautical equipment. In view of the strong press coverage of Japanese bombings of Chinese cities, the exporters were asked not to sell to nations which engaged in air attacks on civilian populations.

President Roosevelt was an eclectic, and in his approach to foreign as in domestic policy he frequently took positions with little consistency or logical continuity. American economic recovery had a serious setback in 1937, and the political problems which continued to engage his administration in 1938 usually had top priority. Roosevelt was also fully aware of the strength of public feeling against military involvements and his public statements frequently did not correspond with his actions. He appears to some scholars to have moved far ahead of public opinion in foreign affairs, to others he seems to have lagged behind and overrated the unwillingness of Americans to take a stand. Navalism and a benevolent attitude toward China continued to form the basic framework of his thinking when he approached Far Eastern issues.

The outbreak of the Sino-Japanese war in 1937 seems to have put an end to the President's interest in naval limitation. On July 20, 1937, his specialist in this area, Norman Davis, gave Roosevelt notice that he was now ready "to advocate a temporary increase in expenditures in naval armaments." Davis suggested the construction of two or three additional battleships, while still rejecting the theory that the best way to preserve peace was to prepare for war. A bigger navy, Davis said, would mean more influence for disarmament. These views may have only reinforced Roosevelt's own convictions about the future of the United States Navy. On November 26, 1937, three weeks before the *Panay* sinking, the President advised Admiral Leahy to ask for four new battleships rather than the scheduled two in the next naval appropriations request.

The House of Representatives passed in January of 1938 the annual naval appropriations which provided, in accordance with the 1934 schedule, for the construction of two battleships, two light cruisers, eight destroyers, and six submarines. A week later Roosevelt delivered a special message on rearmament and appealed for an increase of 20 percent over the construction just authorized. Two more battleships and two more cruisers were included in the request. Admiral Leahy had advised that the United States was so superior in aircraft carriers to Japan and Britain that there was no need for additional tonnage.

Like the "Quarantine" speech three months earlier, the President's message aroused strong protests from those who viewed the new ships as preparation for further action in the Pacific. By coincidence, or more likely by plan, Roosevelt's rearmament appeal followed by one day the publication of a strong State Department protest to Japan, actually sent 11 days earlier, over disrespect for the American flag and rights in China.

In congressional committee hearings Admiral Leahy assured the critics of additional appropriations that it would require three times the projected increases to prepare for aggressive action in the Far East. The Navy was being built, Leahy said, strictly for defense against an attack on American shores. Advocates of the bill also pointed out that labor eventually received 85¢ out of every construction dollar spent and that the new ships required materials from every state of the union. Skepticism was not eliminated by these claims, and the number of negative votes in the House rose from 15 on the first appropriation bill to 100 on the second. The expansionists were still strong enough to make the President's recommendations for 3,000 naval planes the minimum rather than the maximum goal. Congress has been "exceedingly generous to the sea defenses in both money and authorization," Admiral Leahy wrote Admiral Harry Yarnell, Commander-in-Chief of the Asiatic Fleet. Leahy believed that the Navy would soon be strong enough "to take care of any foreseeable difficulties."

A year later after Germany had occupied Czechoslovakia, preparedness was far more acceptable to Congress and the naval appropriation in the spring of 1939 jumped from $644 million the previous year to over $900 million. There were still strong fears expressed when there was any suggestion that the Fleet might be used for anything but the defense of American soil. An effort to include a small appropriation for the dredging of the harbor at Guam for a submarine base was knocked out of the 1939 appropriation by a House vote of 205 to 168.

While the growth of the Navy gave support to the President's thinking about the use of this instrument of power against Japan, his political actions were cautious when compared to the steps urged upon him by some of his advisers. The "Quarantine" speech of October 5, 1937, had led his supporters and critics alike to expect some bold action. The bulk of the speech was devoted to a condemnation of war, probably directed as much at Germany and Italy as at Japan. What aroused the press was his use of the word "quarantine" in discussing the need to keep war from spreading to America. When a reporter the next day suggested that the President was thinking of economic sanctions, he responded, "Look, sanctions is a terrible word to use. They are out the window." Further questioning revealed that conferences were also "out the window." But the President claimed to have some method in mind.

One student of Roosevelt's foreign policy, William L. Langer, claims that Roosevelt was thinking of "an extreme form of sanctions." In a cabinet meeting the following December, after the *Panay* sinking when economic action was being considered, Roosevelt said, "We don't call them economic sanctions, we call them quarantines." But the "get tough" elements failed to win any immediate support from the White House for their programs.

A good example of the unwillingness of Roosevelt to take any economic initiative was his approach to the Brussels Conference held in November 1937. The United States and Britain co-operated in calling this meeting of all powers interested in the Far East after a similar proposal had been made in the League of Nations. Norman Davis, the chief American delegate, conferred with Roosevelt a week after the delivery of the Quarantine speech. Davis told the President of the two schools of thought which existed in the State Department:

> One was that if Japan conquers China she would not only later on take everything that the British and Dutch have in the Far East, but also the Philippines, and that war with Japan would become inevitable. The other school believes that while Japan can divide China, she can never conquer her, and that she will so exhaust herself in the effort that she would not become a menace to the United States. Furthermore, even if she does succeed, it would not make any great difference to the United States because she would have to trade with us, and that she could never successfully attack us in this hemisphere and that we have no interests in the Far East that would justify war.

Hearing of these two extremes, the President told Davis that he agreed with the first school of thought.

When it came to acting at Brussels on this assessment of the situation, the President advised that the major effort should be devoted to bringing about a truce between China and Japan and working out a permanent agreement. Hull asked, what if this effort failed? Should Davis come home or seek concerted effort in pressuring Japan? Hull and Davis both reminded Roosevelt that neither Britain nor Holland would be willing to join in any coercion of Japan unless the United States was willing to pledge to protect their possessions with the U.S. Navy. Roosevelt answered by saying that if Japan refused to be reasonable he was sure that public opinion in the world and in the United States would most probably demand that something be done.

Just before leaving for Brussels, Davis showed Roosevelt some proposals, one of which used the word "sanctions"; this drew an immediate presidential objection. Roosevelt did mention the possibility of supplying arms to China, although this would conflict with the Neutrality Acts. He also raised the possibility of having all neutrals break off relations and ostracize Japan. But the chief message to Davis seems to have been that in any co-operative effort, "we must avoid getting out in front alone."

The Japanese refused to come to Brussels and Davis was left in a dilemma. He was enjoined to see that something constructive was done, but at the same time to avoid leadership. Anthony Eden, the British Foreign Minister, would support anything the United States would do, Davis reported to Roosevelt, but the British had no enthusiasm for an embargo. The European situation also prevented the British Navy from moving to the Pacific in force to join in an anti-Japanese naval demonstration. Davis suggested that the President request a suspension of the Neutrality Act as something to alarm Japan and hearten the Chinese, but the White House ducked away from tackling such a difficult political task.

Only the Soviet delegate, Maxim Litvinov, talked strongly for collective action so the Conference closed after issuing a weak, face-saving statement. The principles of the Washington Nine Power Treaty of 1922 were reaffirmed and an appeal made to China and Japan to cease fighting. Sumner Welles reports that Davis returned to Washington disgruntled and found that any thought of a trade embargo, unilateral or collective, had been put aside.

After the *Panay* sinking, Roosevelt again talked of economic action against Japan. Welles recalls that for several months the idea of extending American territorial waters some 90 miles out to sea, off the coast of Washington and Oregon, interested the President. By this means Roosevelt felt he could exclude Japanese fishermen from the salmon catch and curtail Japan's foreign exchange. No action was taken; some realist may have described for the President the legal complications involved in making such a claim to the High Seas and the relatively insignificant role this fishing area played in the Japanese economy.

One of the most vigorous and belligerent of the presidential advisers was Secretary of Treasury Henry Morgenthau, Jr., who urged war at the time of the *Panay* incident. What was in effect an economic warfare division was established in the Treasury Department and from it the Secretary derived many ideas to press upon Roosevelt. On September 7, 1937, Morgenthau suggested to the State Department that the United States, Britain, and France refuse to accept Japanese yen or gold in exchange for dollars, sterling, and francs, with no explanations offered. The international financial chaos which such a move would create was recognized by the State Department and Morgenthau was rebuffed.

Before the Japanese paid the *Panay* indemnity, Roosevelt asked Morgenthau to see how, with or without legal authority, he could seize Japanese assets in the United States. Morgenthau found that these assets ran between $100 and $200 million and that a legal basis for seizure could be found by declaring an emergency and using legislation passed in 1933. Agreement was reached on the indemnity, but the President still considered seizing Japanese property to compensate for the loss of American property in China due to military "looting." Hull now cautioned Roosevelt that he could do this only to nations designated as "enemies" after the United States became a belligerent.

The Treasury Department next turned to an effort to aid

China's war with American credits and with expectation of White House support. The Treasury had authority under the Silver Purchase Act of 1933 to buy foreign silver in order to keep up the price earned by American mines. China, in August of 1937, requested a loan of $50 million from the Export-Import Bank. Although the State Department favored this action, the Bank decided to postpone action, possibly because of fear of congressional ire over loans to a belligerent power. Morgenthau decided to meet the situation by buying Chinese silver. Hull disapproved, but Roosevelt was willing in this case to risk congressional attack and the purchases were made.

After this decision was made in December of 1937, credits were extended to China in a variety of ways. Some were carried out in the guise of normal commercial transactions such as the arrangement completed in December of 1938 to give China a $25 million credit for shipments of tung oil to be delivered over a period of years. Maxwell Hamilton, Chief of the Far Eastern Affairs Division, argued against the project. China would probably be unable to deliver due to Japanese control of export centers; the project violated the intent of Congress in regard to American neutrality; it involved a dangerous commitment to China without vitally affecting the outcome of the hostilities, and it would be sure to worsen relations with Japan. Hamilton's arguments were also supported by Hull who opposed the project as an invitation to Japanese retaliation, pointing out that Tokyo would see through the alleged commercial character of American action. But again Morgenthau, with Hornbeck supporting him, won over the President and the credit was made.

Roosevelt's willingness to bypass neutrality legislation in aiding China was not immediately paralleled by a readiness to take direct action against Japan. Throughout 1938 the subject of economic sanctions was studied and discussed in the State Department, but no action was taken beyond Hull's request in July for a "moral embargo" on planes and aviation supplies. It was a year later, on July 26, 1939, that Hull finally informed Tokyo that the United States intended to abrogate the 1911 Commercial Treaty, six months from that date, the warning period required by the treaty itself. The sanctionists had won their argument, and the Japanese could now expect a variety of economic blows.

The occasion for American action, according to the Secretary of State, was a British move which suggested a willingness to come to terms with Japan over China. When the Japanese took control of the city of Tientsin, they surrounded a British concession with an investment reputedly in excess of $46 million. Conflict soon developed over British insistence on maintaining the rights granted them by the Chinese. After some harsh exchanges the Chamberlain government signed an accord, released on July 24, 1939, which "fully recognized" that the Japanese had special requirements for the security of their armed forces while war was on with China. Britain contracted not to countenance any acts prejudicial to these requirements. The text of the accord was ambiguous and Japan claimed that it applied to all of China.

Fears had been frequently expressed in the State Department that Britain might accept major compromises in a settlement with Japan in order to have a freer hand in Europe. Roosevelt now moved to stiffen the British position and with the knowledge that a resolution had been introduced in the Senate by a Republican leader, Arthur Vandenberg, calling for the abrogation of the 1911 Treaty. A public opinion poll taken the same month also suggested that a bare majority of Americans now favored stopping the shipment of war materials to Japan in an effort to protect national interests in China. A quarter of those polled still favored doing nothing, 18 percent were willing to rely on protests and only 6 percent were ready to go as far as war.

Aid to China continued to expand in 1939. In March Hornbeck had advised Hull that it was "easier to give assistance to

China than to place obstacles directly in the way of Japan."
In the fall of the year, after the outbreak of war in Europe,
Roosevelt instructed Morgenthau to "do everything we can
that we can get away with" in the form of help to China.

As 1940 opened the Commercial Treaty expired and the
Roosevelt administration was at last in a position to begin
full scale economic war against Japan. Public opinion had
been moved to the point where "measures short of war" against
Japan seemed to have majority support. Serious questions no
longer were raised within the Administration as to whether
national interests in Asia were worth the growing risk of war.
The opening of a potential front in the Atlantic, as British
and French forces stood behind the Maginot Line at war with
Germany, does not appear to have led to any tempering of attitudes toward the Pacific. The movement of Administration
thought had been from nominal neutrality to actual involvement. A course of action was launched with a potential on
which both Grew and Hornbeck agreed; if it did *not* succeed
the most likely result was war.

Chapter XIII

THE WANTED, UNWANTED WAR

W HILE SOME AMERICANS watched the flow of events in Asia, many more were preoccupied with Europe. Two traditionally great military powers, Britain and France, experienced their "Annus Terribilis" in 1940. After the speedy conquest of Poland in 1939, Hitler's armies faced the Allies, entrenched in their supposedly unassailable Maginot Line from which they did little more than stare across at the German enemy. This alleged "phony war" or *sitzkrieg* ended suddenly in early April of 1940 when German forces invaded Denmark and Norway. A month later, on May 10, Hitler's armies poured across the borders of Holland and Belgium to attack France on a weakly defended frontier. By late June the French had asked for peace, while the British retreated hastily across the Channel, leaving most of their arms behind them. An invasion was generally expected as the Home Guard drilled to repel the first wave of Nazis to come by sea or air.

Traditional American neutrality seemed to President Roosevelt to be inadequate to defend the security of the United States. He had proclaimed neutrality on September 5, 1939, but appealed for changes in the neutrality legislation which he claimed operated "unevenly and unfairly." At a specially called session of Congress, a revised Neutrality Act was pushed through both houses by early November after six weeks of debate. The new law repealed the embargo on sale of arms and munitions to nations at war which threatened to cancel almost $100 million in sales to Britain and France. The arms trade was put upon a cash-and-carry basis which permitted Britain and France to import their purchases only in their own ships. With British control of the surface of the seas, sales to Germany were impossible.

When the Nazi forces entered Holland and Belgium, Prime Minister Churchill appealed to Roosevelt to take part in the defense of Ireland, assume full responsibility for checking Japan, and to give military supplies rather than sell them. The President responded on May 22, 1940, by making available hastily declared "surplus" War Department arms and munitions, while his legal aides searched for some constitutional and legal basis for such an unprecedented action. On June 10, President Roosevelt went further in a speech at Charlottesville, Virginia, to make what Professor William Langer has called the "Great Commitment." Henceforth the material resources of the United States were pledged to "the opponents of force." Transfers of planes, destroyers, guns, and munitions followed, too late, however, to check the fall of France.

What was the meaning of German victory and the "Great Commitment" for American policy in the Far East? The balance of power in Europe, tipped to the advantage of Britain and British allies for more than a century, was destroyed. While the Soviet Union honored its Non-Aggression Pact with Berlin, German dominance of Europe was only matched historically by that of Napoleonic France. If peaceful coexistence was impossible with the German "New Order"—and this was the assumption of the President and many of his advisers—a great sacrifice of American manpower and resources was to be expected. For American war planners, Hitler had been designated "Enemy #1" with presidential approval even before the outbreak of war in Europe. Allocation of American resources favored maintaining only a "strategic defensive" in the Pacific; this was the military consensus. But in April of 1940 the main body of the American Fleet had been moved to the advanced post of Hawaii, where the President decided it should remain.

A substantial segment of American opinion favored taking strong economic measures against Japan. One poll taken in 1940 before the fall of France recorded 75 percent in favor of a ban on sales of arms and munitions to Japan. The great majority remained, nevertheless, unwilling to risk war with Japan in order to aid China. In July, 1940, only 12 percent agreed that the United States should take that risk to prevent the Japanese from conquering China.

The desire for a ban on arms' sales was in part the product of years of newspaper headlines, "JAPS BOMB . . ." with pictures of the resulting destruction. In the pre-television era news reels also helped stir American feeling against traffic in arms with Japan. A Japanese visitor stated his case against American movie houses in 1937.

> First comes Pearl Buck's "The Good Earth," which shows the Chinese at their best—polite, diligent and honest. Then comes the bombing of the Cathay Hotel [in Shanghai]. The bodies of the Chinese are seen strewn about the streets. The captions tell of the ravages of war and Japanese aggression.

Metro-Goldwyn-Mayer's *The Good Earth,* made on the basis of the best-selling novel in 1936, was a great boon to the Chinese cause. The first major film to bring a favorable image of Chinese peasants to the American screen, it was estimated to have been seen by some 23 million Americans. "March of Time" newsreels added to the anti-Japanese feeling. After viewing one of these reels in September of 1937, Admiral William Leahy noted that the shots were so arranged as to be "powerful publicity in favor of the Chinese."

The word "Jap" began to mean "cruelty" and "treacherous little yellow men" to many Americans. Hollywood recognized this attiude in 1938, when it dropped a series of detective films starring "Mr. Moto," played by Peter Lorre. Audiences no longer appreciated courage and astuteness displayed on the screen by a Japanese character. Hostility to Japan seemed more directed toward the people than the government, while the reverse seemed to be true when Americans were asked about their attitudes toward Germany. This difference, noted in a poll in February, 1939, persisted even after the United States went to war with both countries. In March of 1942 about 41 percent of Americans polled believed that "the Japanese people will always want to go to war to make themselves as powerful as possible." Only 21 percent believed that the Germans were naturally militaristic.

Although the White House was conscious of the weight of opinion against arms trade with Japan by the spring of 1940, Roosevelt supported the arguments of Ambassador Grew and the hesitancy of Secretary Hull in not expanding the "moral embargo." Economic considerations were still important enough to reinforce this position. Despite the spurt which sale of arms and munitions to Britain and France had given to the American economy, full prosperity was still "around the corner." In an election year with an unprecedented third-term bid for office, Roosevelt could not disregard the effect of a cut in exports on employment and business levels. Any ban on sales to Japan might also mean a cut in Japan's purchases of American cotton. Although sales of this commodity had declined since 1937, the disposal of more than a million and a half bales in 1940 was estimated to account for the employment of 350,000 Southerners with almost a million and a half dependents. Loss of tobacco sales to Scandinavia and to Belgium, Holland, and France after the German conquest gave cotton exports an even greater importance for some southern states.

The fall of France stirred some new talk of the value of a

settlement in the Pacific. Some suggestions came from isola-
tionists and critics of Roosevelt's foreign policy in aiding
Britain. Others came from well-informed supporters of that
policy who felt that it called for reconsideration of the American role in Asia. As France went down to defeat, Walter Lippmann in his widely-read newspaper column condemned the
thought of war with Japan as "suicidal madness" and argued
against the provocative attitudes expressed by some members
of Congress. "There is no conflict between Japan and the
United States which is not reconcilable by diplomacy," Lippmann advised. He urged immediate "friendly and conciliatory
and candid negotiations." Financial circles with interests in
Japan added another voice in support of a settlement. A
mission to Tokyo in the summer of 1940, sponsored by a New
York investment house and headed by Major General John F.
O'Ryan, returned home to urge concessions to Japan or at least
a passive attitude in regard to events in Asia until Hitler was
defeated.

Within the Roosevelt administration opinions differed in regard to future relations with Japan. Under Secretary of State
Sumner Welles frequently raised his voice against new proposals to pressure Japan further by stopping exports of oil and
scrap metal. Welles argued, as did Admiral Harold Stark and
General George Marshall on occasion, that an embargo on oil
would only encourage a southward Japanese move, in order
to compensate by acquiring the oil resources of the Dutch
East Indies. Maxwell Hamilton, Chief of the Division of Far
Eastern Affairs, supported Welles.

Ambassador Grew raised the possibility of a settlement in
China secured by offering some financial aid to Japan. Grew's
idea found some reinforcement in an approach made by a "Mr.
X," a prominent Japanese industrialist. The latter suggested to
the State Department that a victorious Germany would seek
to extend its power to Indo-China and the East Indies; to meet
this threat the United States and Japan should join together

for "mutual safety." There were ample opportunities for investment of American capital in Manchuria, the industrialist pointed out, where credits would be used to purchase heavy machinery and equipment from the United States needed for the long-range industrialization program.

While some skepticism was being expressed in Washington over the strength of "Mr. X" 's views in Japanese governmental circles, a shock was given American strategic thinking by the British. On June 27, 1940, the British embassy informed the Department of State that it could no longer risk a war in order to maintain the status quo in Asia. Completely absorbed by the German threat, the Winston Churchill government suggested two courses to Washington. Either the United States could attempt to maintain the status quo alone, by war if necessary, or try to "wean Japan from aggression" by concrete offers of negotiation. If a decision was made in favor of the latter course, Ambassador Lord Lothian said that his government was willing to "throw some material contribution into the pot."

British realism about their helplessness was seconded by the representations made to Washington by the Australian government at the same time. Ambassador Richard Casey told the State Department on June 26 that concessions to Japan would necessarily involve not "merely a shoestring, but something substantial, something according the Japanese what they want in China." The United States was frankly urged to take the initiative in a Far Eastern settlement which would free the fleet to move to the Atlantic. Whatever the concessions made, the Australians believed that they would "very likely be considerably less than Japan will be able to take by war."

The British Chiefs of Staff had informed His Majesty's government on June 25 that defense needs made it now impossible to send a fleet to the Pacific or to draw troops from the Near East for service in Asia. Yet Britain was committed to come to the defense of Australia and New Zealand in exchange for troop contributions to other fronts. British strategists felt that there was no alternative to sacrificing all outposts north of Malaya and to concentrating remaining strength on that area and Singapore in the hope of deterring any Japanese movement south of the Philippines and Indo-China.

As an initial step in readjusting relations with Japan, London accepted Tokyo's demands on July 12, 1940, to close the Burma Road to shipments of arms and munitions to China. Japanese forces by this date controlled all major Chinese ports and only three routes were left to supply the forces of the Kuomintang in the interior. One was the long, northern overland route from the Soviet Union which by the spring of 1940 was supplying the bulk of China's military imports. The other two routes went through British Burma from Rangoon to Kunming and through French Indo-China from Hanoi to Kunming. The defeated French had already agreed in late June to close the route through their Asian colony and had opened the way for Japanese penetration by agreeing to admit Japanese inspectors to enforce the ban. British action, taken for a trial three months, left Chiang Kai-shek with only the Soviet Union as a supply center over a route of limited capacity. Japan hoped that this shrinking of material aid would press China into negotiating a peace.

Meanwhile in Washington strong differences were expressed over the question of normalizing economic relations with Japan as a means to a political settlement. The expiration in January of the 1911 Commercial Treaty also made it possible to take further punitive economic action. In December of 1939 the State Department had asked American businesses to stop all deliveries on planes, manufacturing rights, or equipment for the production of aviation gasoline to "certain countries" bombing civilian populations. By this date the "moral embargo" had already stopped the sale of planes and aviation equipment to Japan.

The chief proponent of a "hard" policy in the State Department was Hull's Political Adviser Stanley Hornbeck. On May 24 he argued that the possibility for a dissolution of the Japanese war effort had increased; the Sino-Japanese conflict would "solve itself," he wrote, if the United States continued to assist China and withhold supplies to Japan. On June 12 he advised that the menacing events across the Atlantic did not "dissolve-out our interests and concern" with the Far East. He did concede that while German armies were consolidating their victory in France it was a time to "speak gently to Japan" to avoid giving chauvinists grounds for calling for new conquests. On June 26 he attacked the British and Australian proposals for the Far East as "appeasement policies" which had no more virtue in that area than when practiced in Europe in 1938. Ten dire results were listed in his memorandum for the Secretary of State, following any concessions to Japan as suggested by Britain. By July 19 he seems to have felt that the time to speak softly was past and he urged the cutting of aviation gas exports to Japan. On the 24th of the same month he advised strongly against withdrawing the Fleet from Hawaii where it could be used to back up the imposition of "substantial embargoes."

Hornbeck's faith in a "get-tough" program had strong support from Secretary of Treasury Morgenthau and two new cabinet appointees who took their seats in the White House in July of 1940, Henry L. Stimson as Secretary of War and Frank Knox as Secretary of the Navy. This addition of two prominent Republicans strengthened Roosevelt's hand in his third term electoral campaign and replaced two cabinet members who were out of sympathy with some of the measures the President was taking to aid Britain.

Henry Stimson, now in his seventies and with the experience and prestige of his earlier cabinet service under Taft and Hoover, was quick to add his weight to discussions of foreign policy. He had deep and firm convictions already expressed in frequent consultations with Hull and Hornbeck before he

joined the Roosevelt administration. Less than a year earlier
he had advised the State Department "to begin a frank attack
in Asia instead of Europe" since he had "always found the
American people much more willing to take an affirmative
policy in Asia than in Europe." Now as Secretary of War he
advised Lord Lothian in August of 1940 that "to get on with
Japan one had to treat her rough, unlike other countries." "She
doesn't understand any other treatment," he assured the British
Ambassador and complained about British "timidity" in Asia.
To a nation receiving the "rough" treatment from Germany's
Luftwaffe with their daily load of bombs, Stimson's remarks
may have seemed ill-timed, but the Secretary of War noted in
his journal that Lord Lothian "agreed with me."

In cabinet meetings and in talks with the President, Stimson
urged further embargoes on oil and iron and steel scrap shipments to Japan. To support his arguments on the effectiveness
of "rough" treatment he cited a number of what he believed
to be pertinent historical examples. The historian reviewing
them can only hope that this use of the past, as remembered
by policy makers, is not typical. In a long letter to Roosevelt
in October, 1940, Stimson recollected an incident which was
supposed to have taken place in Manila Bay in May of 1898
during the Spanish-American War. When a German naval
squadron threatened the American forces under Commodore
George Dewey, a British squadron moved alongside the Americans and between them and the German forces, forcing a
German retreat. This legend which originated in a newspaper
story in 1898 was subsequently thoroughly discredited by historical research, but it remained alive in Stimson's mind as an
example of what would happen if the American Fleet would
move from Hawaii to Singapore to prevent any union between
the Japanese and Axis naval forces from the Mediterranean.
Repayment for the kind act of 1898 would boost British morale, Stimson believed, and give the United States in Singapore
an excellent base for defensive or offensive action in dealing

with Japan. After the fall of Singapore in 1942 and the loss of Britain's newest battleship operating from that supposedly secure base, Stimson admitted that his potentially disastrous excursion into naval strategy had been based on an ignorance of Japanese air power.

Another seemingly pertinent historical analogy used by Stimson was Japan's good behavior, 1921–1931, which the Secretary said was the result of American strength gained in World War I. A third example of an effective "get-tough" policy was offered Stimson by the president of the American Committee for Non-Participation in Japanese Aggression. According to two memoranda which were subsequently sent to Roosevelt, the United States in 1919 "demanded" that Japan get out of Shantung and Siberia. Cotton sales and silk purchases were stopped by the War Trade Board, and Japan pulled back her troops "like whipped puppies." From this example the Secretary of War drew a "moral" for Roosevelt to the effect that Japan has:

. . . historically shown that when the United States indicates by clear language and bold actions that she intends to carry out a clear and affirmative policy in the Far East, Japan will yield to that policy even though it conflicts with her own Asiatic policy and conceived interest.

Although this version had more of a kernel of truth than the Manila Bay story in that the War Trade Board with the support of one of its aides, Major John Foster Dulles, did stop granting licenses for silk and cotton shipments for a few weeks in October and November, 1918, the claims for results were far-fetched. Japan made no such reversal of policy as claimed, and in his memoirs Stimson later admitted that the theory of his memoranda was not borne out by events.

Roosevelt's power to implement a "hard" policy was widened when on July 2, 1940 he signed "An Act to Expedite the

Strengthening of National Defense" which Congress had passed with little public attention. One provision of the new law gave the President authority to regulate all exports of commodities essential to the American military effort. By licensing measures exports could be limited or stopped entirely. Secretary Morgenthau pressed the President to use this device to stop all oil and scrap iron and steel shipments to Japan. In a cabinet meeting Sumner Welles, then Acting Secretary of State, fought the move. Roosevelt faced with the division refused to rule and asked the two men to work out a compromise which would then receive his approval. Morgenthau, Stimson noted in his diary, won "in substance." On July 26 aviation fuel and the highest quality of iron and steel scrap were brought under licensing control and shipments subsequently stopped.

Opponents of any compromises in the Far East strengthened their case, as the issues between Washington and Tokyo extended beyond the territorial confines of China and the settlement of the Sino-Japanese conflict. The fall of France and the Netherlands left their Asian colonies as inviting prizes for Japan. In early September, 1940, Japan took advantage of French weakness to secure an agreement under which troops were sent into parts of Indo-China. But by this date the State Department, with White House approval, had begun to give diplomatic support to the preservation of the colonial status of these areas. The Dutch East Indies with direct American interest in the oil and rubber resources was of some material importance, but the issue in Indo-China seems to have been a matter of principle alone. American concern for the French colony contrasted strongly with Britain's. On July 1, 1940, the British Ambassador told Sumner Welles that his government had no intention of fighting to preserve Indo-China for France and might be prepared to agree to its seizure by Japan. London believed at this point that France would soon have a government completely subservient to Germany and that colonial areas would have to fend for themselves.

The second issue which broadened the conflict with Japan was Tokyo's signature on September 27, 1940, of a Tripartite Pact with Germany and Italy. Each recognized the other's geographical spheres of leadership and agreed to assist the other with "all political, economic and military means" if any power was attacked by a nation not involved in the European War or the Sino-Japanese conflict. In effect this was a defensive alliance intended to deter American entry into either war. Since it still did not seem that the United States would take the first aggressive step to initiate open hostilities, either in the Atlantic or Pacific, the use of the term "attacked" gave each signatory some flexibility in its commitment.

The thesis that Nazi Germany, Fascist Italy, and Japan constituted an inseparable unit was well set forth by Stanley Hornbeck in June of 1940:

> . . . there is at present going on in the world one war, in two theaters; . . . there are two countries today opposing force to force, China which has been fighting for three years, and Great Britain which has been fighting for nine months.

Six months later in January of 1941, the President stated a similar thesis in a letter to Ambassador Grew. "The hostilities in Europe, in Africa and in Asia, are all parts of a single world conflict," the President wrote. He believed that "our strategy of self-defense must be a global strategy."

Postwar examination of German and Japanese records reveals that the political and ideological ties of the two regimes were far weaker than assumed in Washington. Conflicts of national interests between Tokyo and Berlin, dating back to World War I, were not obliterated by the prospect of facing common enemies. In addition the term "global strategy" needed further definition. Often it assumed that national interests were involved to the same degree *wherever* military expansion took place. This assumption which influenced American policy for the next two decades was a dangerous one since it ignored the logic imposed by the limits of national manpower and resources. If men and material were not to be dispersed thinly and ineffectively, priorities were necessary.

In the Army and Navy where assessments had to be made of national potential, the idea of a global war created considerable uneasiness. While the invasion of Britain seemed imminent in the summer of 1940, the War Plans Division had dropped all preparations for a war with Japan to concentrate on RAINBOW 4, the code name for plans for the defense of the Western Hemisphere. On September 25, 1940, when the survival of the British Isles looked more favorable, the War Plans Division still warned against a major military venture in the Far East for which "we are not now prepared and will not be prepared for several years to come." Two months later General George Marshall suggested that "we avoid dispersions that might lessen our power to operate effectively, decisively, if possible, in the principal theater—the Atlantic."

As early as the summer of 1939 work had begun on the possible invasion of Europe, RAINBOW 5, "to effect the decisive defeat of Germany or Italy or both." The events of the spring and summer of 1940 made it obvious that the defeat of these two nations would require a gigantic effort and the organization of an expeditionary force far larger than ever before contemplated. As late as September, 1941, when the German armies were involved in war with Russia, war planners assumed that if the 2 to 1 attack ratio were maintained it would take 700 American divisions or 22 million men under arms to invade Europe. Such a mobilization of American manpower was considered impossible and it was hoped that machines might compensate for failure to outnumber the enemy 2 to 1.

These realistic considerations seem to have been treated lightly by members of the Roosevelt cabinet and even by the President himself. While aid to Britain expanded, Roosevelt responded to a Japanese move into Indo-China by embargoing on September 26, 1940, all shipments of iron and steel scrap to Japan. Herbert Feis, State Department Economic Adviser, believed later that this was the "crossing of the bridge from words to deeds." The same month a new credit was extended to China; shortly after, Chiang Kai-shek was promised 50 modern pursuit planes. Help was also given American citizens wishing to join the Chinese Air Force.

By the end of 1940 licensing had stopped the flow of all war materials to Japan other than petroleum. In the next six months, Morgenthau, using devious measures, managed to progressively diminish the flow of oil. Appeals continued to be made to the President, from within the Administration and without, to squeeze Japan harder; this meant no oil and little else.

On July 26, 1941, Roosevelt acted abruptly to launch full-scale economic war against Japan. All Japanese assets in the United States were frozen. Britain, the Dominions, and British colonies followed suit. The Dutch East Indies put oil under export control and soon ended all shipments to Japan. With no source of substantial imports other than China, Japanese foreign trade came to a virtual standstill. Pressing the point home, oil continued to be sent to the Soviet Union via Vladivostok in American tankers which passed through Japanese waters.

The "get-tough" policy went into effect and Japan's economy received a serious, surprise blow. Tokyo viewed the joint action of the Americans, British, and Dutch as the final link in an encirclement effort which many believed was aimed at reducing Japan to the state of a minor power in Asia. In Washington it was now a matter of waiting and watching as Japan's reserves of essential materials dwindled away. Numerous intelligence estimates were made as to how long it would take before Japan surrendered or acquired new sources by moving southward.

The President's sudden consent to all-out action was stimulated in part by news of fresh Japanese troop movements into southern Indo-China. His original intent was that the freezing order would be followed by a release of some funds in order to resume a limited but easily controlled trade. When no strong domestic pressures developed for relaxing the freeze and while a vociferous minority was prepared to denounce any renewed trade as "appeasement," the order remained total. Only brilliant diplomacy or war seemed likely to change the American posture toward Japan.

The negotiations which culminated in the final break between the two nations began in February, 1941 and lasted until November 26. Admiral Kichisaburo Nomura was sent to the United States as ambassador in February because of his well-known American sympathies and an acquaintanceship with President Roosevelt which went back to his service in Washington during World War I. In the last weeks of negotiations Nomura was aided, at his request, by a skilled professional diplomat, Saburo Kurusu, who had an American wife and was well informed about American affairs. For the United States, Secretary Hull personally handled the bulk of the discussions, which were frequently carried on in the evening in the Secretary's apartment.

The exchanges were many and detailed. Genuinely intent upon avoiding a war with the United States, the Japanese took the major initiatives. After the freezing of assets in July, the tempo of the discussions was increased as Tokyo sought an American position which left Japan some alternative other than surrender or fighting. Hull, on the other hand, seemed confident of a position of superior strength as the talks dragged on while Japan's oil and steel reserves dwindled. The State Department was also in a position of tremendous advantage as the result of an American technical achievement. In the fall of 1940 a device was constructed which broke the Japanese diplomatic cipher, Purple, and by means of this electronic masterpiece, known as MAGIC, some 20 top officials were able to read daily the messages which passed between Tokyo and other diplomatic posts, including Washington, Berlin, and Rome. This flow of intercepts not only provided Hull with a report on his and other conversations as presented to the Japanese government, but enabled him to know the instructions given to the Japanese negotiators. It was a poker game in which both sides had a substantial number of chips, but in which one side was able to read most of the other's cards.

Between the first Japanese proposals in February and the final exchanges in November, there were no great changes in positions. Close study of the many notes and conversations shows some stiffening of the American attitude, while the Japanese, as time ran out, offered a little more in the way of concessions. The Tripartite Pact and the Japanese troops in Indo-China entered into the discussions, but the hard core of the differences between the two countries was still in China.

After four years of fighting on the mainland with no victory in sight, Japan was anxious to end the war with China. To get Japan out of China and Manchuria was the major American goal. Negotiations revolved around the circumstances and terms on which both parties were willing to accept a settlement with the Chinese government. Japan felt that the United States must end its aid to the Kuomintang in order to make a peace in which Japanese interests were protected. While making no demands for annexations or indemnities, Japan insisted on two conditions; protection of their national economic interests in China and "cooperative defense against communistic activities." Stability in China required the stationing of Japanese troops for an indefinite period in northern China where Communist strength was greatest. Troops were also to be stationed in Inner Mongolia where a number of border skirmishes were fought with Russian troops in 1938 and 1939. The United States was also asked to regularize its relationship with Japan's satellite state, Manchukuo.

Hull was skeptical of the possibility of reaching a satisfactory set of terms with Japan from the very beginning. At times the negotiations seem to have been chiefly an opportunity for him to lecture the Japanese Ambassador on how nations should behave. Wary in regard to Japanese intentions, his suspicions knew few bounds. Although the Secretary was personally violently anti-Russian, he seems to have dismissed completely Japan's concern over Communism and Russian influence in China. Security for Japan's economic stake in China for Hull meant only "imperialism" which would jeopardize the Open Door policy. Repeatedly he insisted that any agreement must begin with Japan's commitment to four general principles:

1. Respect for the territorial integrity and the sovereignty of each and all nations.

2. Support of the principle of non-interference in the internal affairs of other countries.

3. Support of the principles of equality, including equality of commercial opportunity.

4. Non-disturbance of the status quo in the Pacific except as the status quo may be altered by peaceful means.

These were standards of conduct which could arouse the support of most Americans, but which had been violated by every major power. The result was a curious one. The Americans, known for their pragmatism and tradition of hard-bargaining in domestic affairs, met the Orientals on a plane of abstraction, hesitant to deal with any concrete situation which might call for realistic compromises.

At the Atlantic Conference, held off the coast of Newfoundland, August 9–12, 1941, Churchill asked for a joint American-British-Russian ultimatum to Japan, threatening war if Japanese forces entered Malaya or the Dutch East Indies. Roosevelt was unwilling to go that far in committing the United States to a war which many congressmen would vote against as a defense of the British and Dutch Empires. But he did agree, as he later reported to Secretary of the Navy Knox, to "do some plain talking to Japan—not an ultimatum but something that very closely approximates that and can easily lead to it later if the Japanese do not accept our demands."

When Roosevelt returned to Washington, he called in the Japanese Ambassador and read him a prepared statement. Any further military advances by Japan, he warned, would mean that the United States would be "compelled" to take "any and all steps which it may deem necessary. . . ." Ambassador Nomura responded with an invitation from Premier Fumimaro Konoye for a personal meeting in which the two heads of state could talk directly. Roosevelt seems to have been initially receptive and began to explore the possibilities of such a meeting in Alaska or the Hawaiian Islands.

Secretary Hull viewed this Japanese initiative coldly. Any conference, he argued, could not be held until the terms of the settlement had been worked out in advance through the normal diplomatic channels. Roosevelt, who on many other occasions was to go over the head of his Secretary of State, accepted Hull's objections and by mid-October the idea of the conference was killed. The Konoye Cabinet which had the support of the Army and Navy in its last-ditch effort at diplomacy fell when the meeting failed of arrangement. Konoye was replaced as premier by General Hideki Tojo who was subsequently to represent for many Americans all that was evil about Japan.

The second attempt at a fresh approach was initiated in Washington almost at the end of the negotiations in November. Secretary Morgenthau offered Roosevelt and Hull some far-reaching proposals prepared for him by his brilliant aide, Harry Dexter White, whose pro-Soviet activities later made him a center of political controversy. White and Morgenthau seem to have agreed that it was essential that the American Fleet be moved into the Atlantic to fight Hitler's submarines and that this goal called for a grandiose settlement with Japan. On the one hand radical concessions were asked of Japan; the withdrawal of all troops from China and the sale of three-fourths of the annual production of war materials to the United States for use against Germany. In return the United States would withdraw the Fleet from the Pacific, work for the removal of old grievances such as the repeal of the Oriental Exclusion Act and meet Japan's economic needs by a 20-year credit of $2 billion.

Maxwell Hamilton, Far Eastern Affairs division chief, who apparently chafed under Hull's inflexibility, found the White proposal "the most constructive one which I've yet seen," and reworked it with some minor revisions into a more presentable diplomatic proposal. The same day, November 17, that he worked on White's terms, Hamilton also turned out a suggestion that the United States secure Japanese merchant ships and possibly warships by providing Japan with funds to purchase any number of territories including Manchuria, northern Indo-China, and northern Sakhalin from Russia and New Guinea. Hamilton's proposal seems to have been dismissed, but the White-Morgenthau plan was reviewed by both Admiral Stark and General L. T. Gerow, acting for General Marshall, and found generally satisfactory, although a number of revisions were requested.

Possibly stimulated by this radical effort, Roosevelt jotted down a four-point *modus vivendi* by which the United States would release funds for oil and rice purchases during six months and "introduce" the Japanese to the Chinese for peace talks. Japan was to agree to send no more troops to Indo-China or to the Manchurian border and to disavow the Tripartite Pact. Both drafts were then reworked and toned down by other individuals in the State Department. The suggestion for a six months' trial was cut to three, the unfreezing of assets was hedged with qualifications and instead of "introducing" the two belligerents to begin peace talks, the United States only pledged to "not look with disfavor" on such discussions. The White-Morgenthau plan was even more drastically revised so that it remained but a shell of the original. The new *modus vivendi* was then submitted to the British, Chinese, and Dutch for their consideration. Chiang Kai-shek responded quickly with an angry denunciation of any relaxation of the freezing order. Chiang's brother-in-law, T. V. Soong, launched an immediate campaign among administration officials and in the Washington press against "appeasers" who were being blackmailed by Japan. London's response was no more favorable and Prime Minister Churchill wired the White House that it left "a very thin diet" for Chiang.

In the meantime Japan had on November 20 submitted a final *modus vivendi*. In return for a restoration of oil shipments and suspension of aid to China while peace talks were in progress, Japan promised no further armed advances southward and to withdraw troops in Indo-China to the north. Washington learned that Nomura was warned that "in name and spirit this counter-proposal of ours is, indeed, the last." Failure to reach a quick agreement, Tokyo said, would mean that the relations of the two nations would be "on the brink of chaos."

The British embassy on November 25 informed Hull that the Japanese final proposals were "clearly unacceptable." Roosevelt and Hull, on the other hand, decided to drop the *modus vivendi* as a reply which would have attempted to prolong negotiations. The attacks made on this proposal by Chiang Kai-shek and Churchill, plus the charges within the administration that it constituted "appeasement," probably led to this crucial decision. After all the thought and time spent on this last-minute effort at a truce, Japan was presented instead with a drastic ten-point proposal which Tokyo viewed as an ultimatum. The framework for this final offering was the White-Morgenthau plan with the major concessions removed, while

Japan was asked for the equivalent of surrender on six of the ten points. This document was given to the Japanese on November 26.

Hull knew that the exchanges had come to an end. On November 27 he called Stimson and told him that he had washed his hands of the whole affair and that it was now a matter to be handled by the Army and Navy. Admiral Stark the same day sent a warning to the Pacific outposts that "an aggressive move by Japan is expected within the next few days." An intercept decoded by MAGIC removed any doubt about Tokyo's reaction; on the twenty-eighth Nomura and Kurusu were advised that in two or three days negotiations would be "ruptured" in response to this "humiliating proposal" from Washington. Another intercepted message ordered the destruction of Japanese code machines on American and British soil.

Within the Roosevelt administration there was considerable speculation as to exactly when and where Japan would make its next move. Roosevelt had been reassured by his cabinet early in November that an American declaration of war would be supported by Congress and the people, even if Japan attacked British or Dutch colonial territory rather than American soil. But the President also knew that under these conditions the country would remain disunited and that the war would be unpopular with those who would see it as shedding American blood in defense of disintegrating European empires. This probably was one consideration which led him to his discussion of November 25 with Stimson, Knox, Marshall, and Stark. The President, as Stimson noted in his diary, raised the question of how to maneuver the Japanese into firing the first shot without too much danger to the United States. That first shot would by preference be directed against American soil or against American military forces.

The same consideration may explain the President's direct intervention in Far Eastern naval operations. On December 2,

Admiral Thomas C. Hart, Commander of the Asiatic Fleet, received a presidential order to charter three small vessels under the American flag as "a defensive information patrol." The President stipulated that these ships were to be stationed off the Indo-China coast in the path of any Japanese advance on Malaya or the Dutch East Indies. Since Admiral Hart was already conducting what the Navy Department considered adequate reconnaissance by planes and submarines, this unusual request for picket ships suggested to one of their commanders that they were being sent out to provide an inexpensive *casus belli*. Due to difficulties in purchasing and dispatching these ships, none had reached their assigned posts before the Pearl Harbor attack provided a far less disputable *casus belli*.

The decoded Japanese intercepts gave many indications that a naval move was imminent. On December 2 Roosevelt told an aide, Donald Nelson, that he would not be surprised if war came by Thursday, December 4. In London where there was a British-operated MAGIC decoder, Ambassador John G. Winant decided on December 6 that the end was near and that he wanted to be with Prime Minister Churchill when the war began. He was dining with Churchill the next day when the news of the Pearl Harbor attack reached them by radio.

Outside of the small group of top officials who read the Japanese intercepts, there was also a belief that war was about to begin. One Honolulu newspaper on November 30 carried the headline, "Japanese May Strike Over Weekend," missing its warning by one week. "Pacific Zero Hour Near" was another Honolulu deadline on December 4. A high degree of prescience and overconfidence was demonstrated by the writers of *Time* magazine who filed their copy by December 1. The lead story in the issue dated December 8 began:

> Everything was ready. From Rangoon to Honolulu, every man was at his battle station. And Franklin Roosevelt had to return to his. This was the last act of the drama.

. . . One nervous twitch of a Japanese trigger finger,
one jump in any direction, one overt act might be
enough. A vast array of armies, of navies, of air fleets
were stretched now in the position of track runners, in the
tension of the moment before the starter's gun.

Subscribers received this report on the situation on December
4 and 5.

"Japan will commit national suicide, if necessary, to pursue
her plan of establishing peace in the Far East," Ambassador
Hirosi Saito told American newspapermen as early as 1934. His
nation would fight, he said, even if it meant war with both
Britain and the United States. Japanese naval strategy throughout the 1930's in considering such a war was primarily defensive, concerning itself with holding the western Pacific
against what might be overwhelming Anglo-American naval
superiority.

In January of 1941 Admiral Isoroku Yamamoto conceived
the bold plan of beginning the war with a lightning strike
across the Pacific in the tradition of Port Arthur and 1904.
Yamamoto was pessimistic about Japan's chances of winning
such a war, but he believed that the quick destruction of the
American forces at Pearl Harbor would long delay American
movement across the Pacific and make possible a compromise
peace. His plan remained a tightly held secret, while he fought
bureaucratic conservatism in order to get planners and resources allocated to his strategy. Ambassador Grew reported
to Washington that Japan was contemplating a Pearl Harbor
strike the same month Yamamoto put forth his plan, but there
is little likelihood that Grew's source was a real leak. In Washington Grew's message was dismissed as a fantasy.

Aside from some extremely chauvinistic elements there was
little enthusiasm in Japan for a new war by a people who for
four years had been drained of lives and resources by the conflict in China. The war potential of the United States was esti-

mated as seven to eight times that of Japan. A long conflict promised the defeat of Japan's forces regardless of their bravery and devotion to Emperor and nation. But many of Japan's leaders saw the American position as leaving no honorable alternative to such a disaster. Foreign Minister Shigenori Togo stated in the fall of 1941 that if Japan accepted American demands "all that had been achieved since the Manuchuria incident would have evaporated. . . . Japan would be compelled ultimately to withdraw entirely from the continent."

After the American freezing of assets in July, oil purchases were cut off and Japan's reserves dwindled by some 12,000 tons daily. As one Japanese expressed it, his country felt like a fish in a pond from which the water was being gradually drained away. Whether to try to seize the oil resources of the Dutch Indies only, risking an American counterattack, or to try to also knock out the American Fleet, was debated by Japan's military leaders through the summer. On September 6 an Imperial Conference approved full-scale preparations for war with the United States if diplomatic negotiations failed. But it was not until mid-October that hesitance over Yamamoto's proposal was finally overcome and the Pearl Harbor attack plan given formal approval.

On November 7 the date of the offensive blow against the United States was tentatively set for a month later. Shortly after, units of the Pearl Harbor Striking Force sailed north to assemble in the Kuriles and to await the outcome of the negotiations with Washington. Other forces moved to their bases and trained for their assigned strikes. Some 29 separate targets, including six on the island of Oahu, were to be hit at approximately the same time. Guam, Wake, the Philippines, British Malaya, and Hong Kong were all to hear the exploding Japanese bombs like a string of firecrackers. On November 26 the negative outcome of the diplomatic exchanges seemed certain enough with the American rejection of a *modus vivendi*.

The Pearl Harbor Striking Force was ordered to begin its move across the Pacific, still under orders to await the final word from Tokyo before launching its planes.

After a review of the diplomatic negotiations on December 1, the Japanese cabinet voted for war. The next day Admiral Nagumo, far out in the Pacific, received the message, "Climb Mount Niitaka." final approval of the Pearl Harbor strike. His mission could still be called off within 24 hours of the attack if there was an unexpected break of importance in the diplomatic impasse. A fourteen-point note, reviewing and ending the negotiations, was sent to Washington on December 6. At military insistence the Japanese envoys were not to deliver it to Secretary Hull until 1:00 P.M., Washington time, on Sunday, December 7, only a half hour before the attack on Pearl Harbor was scheduled to begin.

The surprise of the Hawaiian base was complete and the bombing brilliantly executed. Americans had demonstrated the theoretical soundness of the Japanese tactic in war games in 1932 and 1936. As late as March of 1941 this type of attack was described with accuracy in a defense plan prepared by the commanders of the Army and Navy air forces at Pearl Harbor. Launching some 300 planes from six carriers over 200 miles to the north, the Japanese caught the battleship fleet at rest and most of Pearl Harbor enjoying an inactive Sunday. At the loss of less than 30 planes, five American battleships were sunk and two more badly damaged; almost two hundred Army and Navy planes were destroyed and many damaged. The only unfavorable break was the absence of two aircraft carriers at sea which thus escaped attack.

Due to the later sunrise in the western Pacific, planes were scheduled to bomb Philippine bases some five hours after the Hawaiian attack. By jamming radio communications between Honolulu and Manila it was hoped to prevent a warning. The jamming failed and a heavy fog prevented Japanese planes from reaching their targets until nine hours after the news of the outbreak of war reached General Douglas MacArthur in Manila where he commanded the Army forces. American planes had looked for the Japanese and then returned to their air fields, where the attack caught bomber and fighter squadrons in neat lines. With one strike Japan was able to virtually eliminate American air power in the Far East.

In the south the British fared little better at the great Singapore base. Japanese soldiers, brought from Formosa and fortified by a meal of dried eels, landed in the dark and without detection on the Malayan coast. From there they moved south to take Singapore from its unprotected land side. Japanese planes on December 10 sank Britain's latest battleship, *Prince of Wales*, which Churchill had boasted a month earlier could "catch and kill any Japanese ship."

A shocked Congress voted on December 8 for the declaration of war after hearing Roosevelt's "Day of Infamy" speech, condemning Japanese treachery. One lone dissent was entered by Congresswoman Jeannette Rankin who had also voted against a declaration of war in 1917. Although the nation was now virtually united and Roosevelt's critics silenced by patriotic ethics, the problem of allocating American resources presented the administration with a most difficult situation. Germany, Enemy No. 1, still remained at peace with the United States, while the setback in the Pacific created pressures for a predominantly westward movement of men, ships, and munitions. The President seems to have been unwilling to ask Congress for a declaration of war, and Hitler hesitated in supporting Japan. Although there had been open warfare between American destroyers and German submarines in the Atlantic, the Germans chose not to make that war legal. But unless war with Germany became official, the Lend-Lease supply line would be pinched by the demands of active warfare against Japan. On Pearl Harbor day the former ambassador to the Soviet Union, Joseph Davies, was lunching with Ambassador Maxim Litvinov who had just arrived from the Soviet Union via Hawaii. When news of the attack reached them, Davies was elated since it was now "all for one and one for all." But Litvinov did not receive the news as good tidings, expressing fear that it would mean cutting the delivery of vital war materials to Britain and Russia.

Adolf Hitler saved the situation on Thursday, December 11, by joining with Italy in a declaration of war on the United States. The military planners were then freed to go ahead with their original plans for first priorities to the European war, while the Pacific could be reduced to second priority. German action also confirmed the view which Secretary of Interior Harold Ickes had confided to his diary in October of 1941, seeing the Pacific as the backdoor to war in Europe. Ickes wrote:

> For a long time I have believed that our best entrance into the war would be by the way of Japan. . . . Japan has no friends in this country, but China has. And of course if we go to war against Japan, it will inevitably lead us into war against Germany.

Even for a nation with lavish resources and substantial manpower, a policy needs be criticized which resulted in simultaneous involvement in wars with major nations across two oceans and which failed to prevent one of these wars from beginning with the loss of military outposts and substantial naval strength. Investigations into the limited field of the Pearl Harbor disaster were made by Army, Navy, White House, and congressional committees. Although individuals were selected to receive the major blame, chiefly the two commanding officers at Hawaii, Admiral Husband E. Kimmel and Major General Walter C. Short, many investigators recognized that the charge, "dereliction of duty" could be extended to military and political leadership in Washington as well.

For a number of questions raised, there are still partial or inadequate answers within the restricted framework of the Pearl Harbor disaster. Why was a MAGIC device not sent to

Honolulu as well as Manila? If one of these devices could not be spared for this major outpost, why was there not speedier decoding of the materials in Washington and the quick dispatch of at least the gist of the intercepts to Hawaii? These technical questions have particular bearing on the last 24 hours before Japan's attack. Saturday evening President Roosevelt was given the first 13 parts of the intercepted final Japanese message. Reading it, the President told his White House aides that it meant war, but no fresh warning was sent to the Pacific. The next morning the 14th and final part stipulated that the message was to be delivered at 1:00 P.M., Washington time. Assuming that something would happen then, at least one official, Col. Rufus Bratton, pointed out that the only place in the Pacific where dawn would be breaking at that hour was Hawaii. When this special threat to Hawaii was called to Admiral Stark's attention, he considered a direct phone call to Honolulu but then failed to carry out his action. General Marshall also considered a special warning to General Short, but sent it by a cable which used commercial lines and reached its destination only when the bombs were falling. Once news of the attack reached Washington direct phone communication was quickly established with Hawaii.

The usual defenses offered for these failures is the great concern for avoiding any leak which would suggest to the Japanese the existence of a successful decoding device, an asset which seems to have added little to the quality of American policy. Various war warnings had already been sent to Pacific commanders, and some fear was expressed of too frequently crying "wolf." Assaying the validity of these claims and the assumptions which lay behind them is made difficult by conflicting testimony, the disappearance of some documents and the security restrictions which prevent the use of others, leaving the story of Pearl Harbor still open to contradictory conjectures.

The historian can with more assurance raise broader criticisms of the policies which contributed to a war which in

China, at least, brought results as undesirable as some who had opposed the conflict predicted. Here the widely prevalent over-confidence in American power and underestimation of Japan's power and importance in the Far Eastern power structure explains a great many analyses which time has proven mistaken. Power breeds products other than corruption and, perhaps, the most important of these for America at peak power was an optimism which prevailed against all contradictory facts.

President Roosevelt exemplified the limits which this optimism and assurance imposed on the thinking of many Americans when they looked westward across the Pacific. Long before the Pearl Harbor attack he seems to have believed that it was the mission of the United States to stop Japanese expansion in Asia. In 1934 he told Henry Stimson that he had known about the Japanese threat since 1902 when a Japanese student at Harvard had confided in him his nation's hundred year plan of conquest drafted in 1889. Thirty years later the President remembered the details for Stimson and said that it included the annexation of Manchuria, a protectorate in northern China, the acquisition of British and American possessions in the Pacific, including Hawaii, and finally bases in Mexico and Peru to check the United States. By 1934 the President felt that many of the particulars of this plan had been verified by events.

If Roosevelt took this "plot thesis" interpretation of Japanese foreign policy seriously, it explains his efforts from his first months in office to build up the Navy. Along with his conviction that he grasped the secret goals of Japan was another, that he had the knowledge and competence to direct the naval operations necessary to counter Japan's policy. Like Winston Churchill who chose the code name of "Former Naval Person" in his correspondence with Roosevelt, looking back to his service during World War I as First Lord of the Admiralty, Roosevelt had a basis for his conviction in his service as Assistant Secretary of the Navy during the same period. He could also pride himself on having been an early student of the

writings of the great Admiral Mahan, the brilliant theorist who
had warned so strongly against a two-ocean war.

Assistant Secretary Roosevelt had sketched in 1913 a plan for
war with Japan by which a picket line of American ships across
the Pacific supply routes would starve that country into submission. Nothing that happened technologically, particularly
in the field of air power, seems to have shaken that conviction
about naval strategy in the next quarter century. In July of
1937 the President explained to Sumner Welles how such a
blockade could be used in peacetime against Japan. In December 1937, after the *Panay* incident, he told his cabinet that
with British co-operation such a blockade would be "a com-
paratively simple task," not requiring a great fleet, and would
bring Japan to her knees within a year.

While arguing for American naval needs in the Pacific, the
President must have been informed about the growth of Japanese strength. Since he does not seem to have given consideration to that growing strength in his own thinking about a future
war, he was either misinformed or selected that information
from his briefings which best fitted in with his own optimistic
assumptions. But one item noted by Henry Stimson even suggests that Roosevelt took no time to keep informed about the
Japanese Navy. Early in September of 1940 the Secretary of
War asked the President whether he had "any real knowledge"
as to what Japan had been doing in the way of secret fleet
building. Roosevelt told Stimson that he did not, but suggested
getting in touch with Secretary Knox and J. Edgar Hoover of
the F.B.I. to see if such information could be obtained. Stimson
left no record in his diary as to whether his quest was successful.

If the President only noted reports of Japan's naval weakness, he was probably able to find ample support for such an
illogical basis for optimism. Since Japan had built a cruiser in
the early thirties which had capsized, it was frequently claimed
by Americans that the Japanese vessels were top-heavy. A

common American cliché about Japanese having bad eyesight was used to deprecate their naval gunnery. Japan's abilities in the air were also generally underrated. Army intelligence estimates in late 1941 in regard to the Zero fell short as to its speed, range, and maneuverability. Even Japanese production of planes which was over 400 a month for combat types in December of 1941 was reported by American intelligence to be only 200.

There were more realistic assessments of Japan's fighting abilities in Washington files, but these may have been disregarded as inconsistent with general evaluations of Japan. Admiral Harry E. Yarnell, in command of the Asiatic Fleet, 1936–1939, had opportunity to watch the Japanese in action against the Chinese. Yarnell's Fleet Intelligence officer submitted a report in January of 1938 which should have demolished some illusions. Japanese naval officers and men were found to be "hardworking, studious, well-trained" and drilled in all weather and under the most adverse conditions. Naval vessels, guns, ammunition, and fire control were all rated "very good," not inferior to the U.S. Navy. While Japanese ships were not found to be as smart and clean as American, they were in good working condition with more hours devoted to combat drill than routine painting and polishing. Japan's naval aircraft were already considered "as good as planes in general service in the United States Navy" with bombing accuracy good, flight tactics very good, and aggressive action noted as "excellent."

Yarnell's evaluations were not kept from other commanders. In January 1938 he warned Admiral C. C. Block, the new Commander-in-Chief of the U.S. Fleet, then stationed in San Diego, against any attempt to move his forces to the Philippines after war began. The Japanese, he said, had a large force of submarines and aircraft which could operate from Formosa against any point in the Philippines. In December 1938, six months before he was relieved of his command in preparation for retirement, Yarnell wrote to Admiral Thomas C. Hart, then chairman of the General Board. The Japanese Navy, he said, was "a force which should not be despised," their cruisers and destroyers were "distinctly superior to ours in design," and operations were carried out "just as skillfully as we do." Through Admiral Leahy, Yarnell attempted to get his views on the Japanese Navy and the problems of future war read in the White House. On one occasion, Leahy reported back to Yarnell that Roosevelt had taken one of his memoranda along with him to be read while on a southern cruise.

Realistic evaluations like Yarnell's had some impact on naval circles, where there were no claims that a war with Japan would result in a quick and easy victory. As Secretary Stimson wrote the President in October of 1940, he found the heads of the Navy, "rather cautious—unusually cautious men." This caution came in conflict with Roosevelt's optimism when the President decided to keep the fleet at Pearl Harbor rather than on the Pacific coast. A temporary movement had been made to Hawaii in April 1940 to conduct war games, but when preparations were made for return in early May, orders came from Washington to postpone that return for two weeks. When that period expired, orders were received to remain indefinitely. When Admiral J. C. Richardson strenuously objected to Admiral Stark that the fleet was unprepared to maintain fighting efficiency at Pearl Harbor, he was informed that the orders came from the President himself.

In October of 1940 Richardson came to Washington to talk with the President who told him that the move 2,500 miles further west was made to deter possible Japanese moves southward. The fleet commander raised a number of objections to a political use of naval force which seemed to place it in jeopardy, but the President said he would "sit tight" on his decision. In March of 1941 Richardson was relieved of his command and replaced by Admiral Kimmel. Secretary of Navy Knox, Richardson reported, told him he was detached because he had hurt the President's feelings with his objections. In the congressional hearings Richardson charged that Stanley K. Hornbeck was exerting more influence over the disposition of the fleet than its commander.

The disposal of the fleet again came up for discussion in April and May of 1941. German submarines were operating in the Atlantic at such cost to the British supply lines that Stimson and Knox proposed to the President that the fleet be moved entirely to the Atlantic. The argument made by the two Secretaries was that Japan knew that the fleet in Hawaii was no real threat, since it could not be used offensively without ample warning. Roosevelt countered that the battleships were needed in Pearl Harbor for the defense of Hawaii itself. General Marshall was enlisted in support of Stimson and Knox and told Roosevelt that Hawaii was impregnable whether there were any ships there or not. The Army Air Force stationed in the islands was so strong, said Marshall, that Japan would not dare to attack such a long distance from home bases. Knox also claimed that Hawaii was unassailable even without the fleet, and this view, Stimson noted in his diary, "completely exploded the President's reason" for resisting the shift. Roosevelt then dropped back to the deterrent argument and said that the "mere presence" of the ships at Pearl Harbor protected the southwestern Pacific, including Singapore and the Dutch East Indies.

In the debate on this issue Roosevelt was not only torn between his "Europe-first" military and political commitments and his commitments to China, but he avoided talking with his war chiefs about the significance of increasing naval involvement in the Atlantic. Any force in the Atlantic, he told Stimson, "was merely going to be a patrol to watch for any aggressor and to report to America." Stimson reminded him that the real purpose was to report the presence of German naval forces to the British fleet. "I wanted him to be honest with himself," Stimson noted in his diary, stating his own willingness to recognize Atlantic patrols as hostile acts and to take the responsibility for them. The Secretary of War felt that Roosevelt was trying to hide his action by calling it "a purely defensive action which it really is not."

Secretary Hull opposed the naval movement to the Atlantic and the British supported his viewpoint in part. Some ships needed to be kept at Pearl Harbor, London said, to act as a makeweight against Japan moving freely on Singapore. The President compromised and sent approximately one-fourth of the Pacific Fleet to the Atlantic, including three battleships and one aircraft carrier. The remainder of the fleet was still based at Pearl Harbor on December 7, 1941.

"Uncle Sam and Britannia," Winston Churchill wrote in 1950, "were the godparents of the new Japan." By 1941 the godchild had grown up. No longer was it possible to win concessions with tactics which had been so effective 70 and 80 years earlier. And no longer could the defense of American and European interests in the Far East be achieved without regard to rising Asian nationalism and the rising human costs imposed by the spread of western military technology.

Six months after the war began, a Far Eastern publicist who supported the President's policy, Nathaniel Peffer, wrote that Pearl Harbor was "neither an accident nor a coincidence, but wholly in the logic of American history. Pearl Harbor was an effect, not a cause." That historical verdict seems likely to stand. Nor from an American viewpoint can there be much dispute about the cause as stated by Henry Stimson in 1948: ". . . it was American support of China—American refusal to repudiate the principles of Hay, Hughes, Stimson, and Hull— which proved the final cause of the breakdown of negotiations and the beginning of war." Aside from questioning the inclusion of Hughes in this list, the historian can only ask whether these principles, proclaimed to protect American interests, had not already been shown to be irrelevant in the face of rising Asian nationalism and the shifting balance of power in the Far East.

Chapter XIV

A NEW SUN RISES

THE KILLING of Americans and Japanese which began
with the attack on Pearl Harbor lasted for three and a half
years. Japan's decision to seek a military solution cost that
nation over a million lives in its armed forces. In addition over
a half million civilians died as American bombs levelled the
major Japanese cities and destroyed the industrial strength on
which the military effort was based. The end came on August
10, 1945, one day after the United States dropped the second
atomic bomb wiping out a major part of Nagasaki. General
Douglas MacArthur as Supreme Commander of the Allied
powers accepted the formal surrender and began the work of
occupying the Japanese islands and disarming a defeated
people.

The price in human lives was also great for those Americans
directly affected, although less than a tenth of that paid by
Japan. Battle casualties in the Army alone ran over 3,000 a
month through 1944 and rose to over 12,000 a month in the
final drives to oust the Japanese from the islands which blocked
the road to Tokyo. Total battle deaths for the Pacific, however,
were roughly 50,000, about a sixth of the total American losses
in World War II.

To this cost in lives must be added the political costs of a serious blow to constitutional liberties in the United States and the deleterious effect of the war against Japan on American war aims in Europe. This first cost involved over a hundred thousand individuals of Japanese ancestry living in California, Washington, and Oregon. In February of 1942 President Roosevelt conceded to West coast political clamor and the claim of military necessity and authorized the Army to conduct a mass evacuation of these individuals, aliens and citizens, children and adults alike, to concentration centers behind barbed wire in isolated areas of the inter-mountain West. Among these individuals were many whose sons were fighting in the American armed forces and a few who were veterans of World War I.

The old racial antagonisms were heightened by the Pearl Harbor attack and a variety of false rumors. One, given some support by the Roberts Commission report on the Pearl Harbor attack, claimed that there had been widespread acts of espionage by the Japanese residents of Hawaii. This further stimulated wild stories of treasonable activities among the Japanese-Americans of California, although no proved instance of sabotage or of espionage after Pearl Harbor among the West coast Japanese was ever uncovered. Economic interest groups anxious to rid themselves of their competitors of Oriental ancestry added to the hysteria which accompanied fears of a military invasion of the United States. Pressure from West coast congressmen and a false assessment of military necessity moved a pliable administration and War Department into ordering a mass evacuation.

Uncharged with any crime, some American citizens and their Japan-born parents remained behind barbed wire for the duration of the war. In 1944 the Supreme Court upheld the constitutionality of this mass abrogation of the rights of Americans to due process of law as guaranteed by the Fifth Amendment. Deprived of access to the War Department records which would have shown that Lieutenant General John L. DeWitt, commander of the Western Theater of Operations, did not consider a mass evacuation a military necessity, the Court justified its decision on grounds that "military urgency" and "proper security measures" demanded that all citizens of Japanese ancestry be "segregated." But with due perspective, this action appears to have been the greatest single violation of civil liberties in the history of the United States. The precedent established was incorporated in the Internal Security Act of 1950 which authorized the Attorney General to "detain" those persons in any future war "as to whom there is reasonable ground to believe they will probably engage in sabotage or espionage."

For the proclaimed aims of the United States in the war against the Nazi domination of Europe, the decisions to stand firm against Japan in Asia meant what may have been a crucial diversion of effort. Whatever the public statements about a global effort against one enemy, December 7, 1941 did not change the commitment and military plans of the Roosevelt administration which gave first priority to the defeat of Hitler. Winston Churchill had welcomed the entry of the United States into a common front against Germany by the way of the events of the Pacific. But when he visited Washington in late December of 1941 he was shocked to find "the extraordinary significance of China in American minds." Even at the top levels, he wrote, it was "strangely out of proportion." For Britain with the enemy but a few miles across the English Channel, it was difficult to grant equal status to the threat of Japan, thousands of miles from either Britain or the American mainland. Yet the fall of the Philippines and other defeats so moved the American public that opinion polls in 1942 and 1943 found twice as many individuals designating Japan as the major enemy as those who looked first to the defeat of Hitler. This national orientation with its political pressures combined with the strong demands of the Pacific commanders and the lack of a major front against Germany to counter the official priority system. In 1942 and 1943 about as many fighting men were sent to the Pacific as were sent across the Atlantic to face Germany.

A near-equal division of men and matériel between the two wars gave strength to the dominant British school of strategy which pressed for peripheral campaigns rather than opening a second front in France, as General George Marshall initially proposed. As a result, until June of 1944, American forces fought ground campaigns in North Africa and southern Italy while bombing German cities in an effort to weaken the German economy. Meanwhile the burden of coping with the bulk of German fighting forces was left to the Russians who slowly pushed the battle line off Russian soil and into eastern Europe.

When the war ended a year after American and British forces landed in France, it found the Russian forces in possession of most of eastern Europe and a major segment of Germany. Soviet leaders, having paid the highest price in blood for German defeat, were determined to maintain their hegemony far beyond their 1941 frontiers. For many Americans this meant a defeat for major objectives of the European war. A Poland, Czechoslovakia, Rumania, and Hungary freed from Nazi rule to become Communist nations was viewed as severe a blow to the freedom of small nations and to the balance of power in Europe as was German rule.

It is impossible, of course, to state with any certainty what would have been the course of the European war if the United States had entered the conflict directly in 1941 or 1942 with a compromise keeping peace in the Pacific. But since the shortage of matériel and manpower is frequently cited in the studies of the decisions to defer the cross-Channel invasion, an earlier and fuller engagement of German power seems very probable without the drain of the Pacific. A war which ended on the eastern frontiers of Germany, while exacting a greater price in American and British lives, would also have shifted the geographic balance in the postwar struggle for Europe.

Another price paid in connection with the Pacific War led to angry political recriminations in the United States. At the Yalta Conference in February of 1945 the American negotiators agreed that Russia's 1905 losses to Japan should be restored in return for Soviet participation in the war against Japan. The Soviet Union subsequently entered the Pacific War on August 8, 1945, just before its close, and was rewarded with the restoration of the southern half of the island of Sakhalin and adjacent small islands. The lease to China's Port Arthur and the cession of the Kurile Islands were also included in Russian gains. The subsequent presence of Soviet power in the Kuriles as well as in southern Sakhalin increased the threat to Japanese security from the north as well as jeopardized American hegemony in the northern Pacific. A further result of Soviet participation was the role assigned to Russian forces in taking the surrender of the Japanese army in northern Korea. Communist government was then installed in this area, leading to the division of Korea and to the costly Korean War which broke out in 1950.

Some broad outlines of the future peace with Japan had been laid down in wartime agreements of the Allies. At the Cairo Conference in November, 1943, Britain, China, and the United States stated that they were fighting to "restrain and punish the aggression of Japan" and agreed to demand "unconditional surrender." The defeated nation was to be stripped of the Pacific islands "seized or occupied" since 1914, of territories "stolen" from China, and of all other territories taken by "violence and greed." At Potsdam in July of 1945 it was agreed that Japan would be subject to military occupation until "a peacefully inclined and responsible government" had been created by the "freely expressed will of the Japanese people." The objectives of the Occupation were stated as including the elimination from power of the war leaders, the punishment of war criminals, the dismantling of the war industries, and the establishment of respect for fundamental human rights.

As the fighting came to an end in the Pacific another battle raged in Washington over how these aims were to be carried out. One group of specialists, identified by some as "the China crowd" and including many writers and scholars associated with the Institute of Pacific Relations and the journal *Amerasia,* argued for a rigorous and thorough reconstruction of Japan. They favored a complete purge of the ruling class and also of the *zaibatsu,* the great industrial and business families who were charged with being the allies of the militarists. In general this group favored a "hard peace," an end which had strong public support as a result of the bitter fighting and mounting casualties in the final months of the war.

The other group, called "the Japan crowd" by their opponents, was headed by former Ambassador Joseph Grew, director of the Office of Far Eastern Affairs in the last year of the war. Grew and his supporters believed that Japanese traditions and institutions retained values and forms which were worthy of preservation and which could be used in reconstructing a peaceful nation. The Emperor was seen as an asset in securing acceptance of the surrender and in easing the task of the new military rulers. The ousting of Hirohito, attacked by some of the "China crowd" as "War Criminal Number One," was viewed as opening the way for political chaos which would present endless problems for the Occupation authorities.

Neither school succeeded in making a deep imprint on Occupation policy. General MacArthur and his aides viewed with suspicion men who had special knowledge of Japan and the Far East. The General disregarded almost completely the Far Eastern Commission of the Allied powers and paid little attention to the advisers and directives sent from Washington. He set about to democratize Japan with the help of the men he relied upon, men who had been trained in war and experienced in military operations rather than in government. If the Occupation had any comprehensive theory as a guide, it was that "what was good for the United States must be good for Japan."

The Meiji Constitution by which Japan had begun parliamentary government was put aside, and the Occupation authorities wrote a new constitution which was adopted by the Japanese Diet. Guarantees were provided for a number of democratic rights, including a free press and free speech. To prevent re-militarization an article was included in the constitution by which Japan renounced forever the right to make war and banned the maintenance of land, sea, and air forces.

The Occupation then functioned by means of directives which were dutifully incorporated into law by the Japanese Diet and carried out by the Prime Minister. By such means the police force was decentralized in the hope of preventing future political control; the same was done for the school system which had been so effectively used as a means of indoctrination. Large landholdings were broken up, and some effort made to curtail industrial combines and to collect reparations from the Japanese economy. Political parties along American models were strongly encouraged.

By the spring of 1947 General MacArthur and his aides could look back upon an imposing list of laws and decrees. The General thought that he had completed his task and spoke of the spiritual revolution which had taken place in Japan as "probably the greatest the world had ever known." Democracy, he believed, was firmly implanted in Japan, and this nation would henceforth be "the Switzerland of the Pacific," MacArthur told newspapermen.

The Occupation continued, however, long after MacArthur believed that his work was completed due to the unwillingness of both Stalin and Chiang Kai-shek to sign the peace treaty proposed by the United States. The outbreak of the Korean War in the summer of 1950 turned the Pacific Commander to military tasks, and it was his successors who saw the Occupation terminated in 1952, after President Truman removed MacArthur from his post. The optimistic view of American achievements in rebuilding Japan which characterized communiqués issued from Tokyo has remained the official version of the seven years' accomplishments. When the Crown Prince and Crown Princess visited Washington in September of 1960, President Eisenhower spoke of Japan as a proud country which "with us believes in the democratic ideal of life." The President's gracious greeting ignored the fact that he had been prevented from paying an official visit to Tokyo by anti-American riots in May and June which contrasted with his friendly reception in Seoul, Manila, and Taipeh.

It is too early to appraise the permanent effects of indirect American rule, but it also is obvious that the character of the changes in Japan falls short of the official American and Japanese claims. If Anglo-Saxon political institutions are transferable to another culture they are slow to root and in growing take forms produced by mutations. More than a century's effort at transplanting the North American political forms to Caribbean and Central American states strongly suggests that it is very difficult if not impossible to disseminate the Bill of Rights and the two-party system among peoples of radically different cultures and living conditions.

Some of the Occupation's work has been undone since Japan recovered full sovereignty, while the Occupation itself retreated from some of its goals before withdrawing. The primary influence in the change of course was the growth of Russian-American and American-Chinese antagonism. The first effect was to make Japan's Communists and left wing parties, originally tolerated and even encouraged by the Occupation, a threat to the model Japan which Americans hoped to create. General MacArthur agreed to the curbing of some democratic freedoms which were used excessively by the Communists; the Japanese conservatives who dominated the post-Occupation governments went further. Civil servants and teachers, for example, had been guaranteed political freedom to prevent their becoming the helpless tools of the party in power. But when many of these individuals took part in Communist-led strikes and demonstrations, they found their freedom of political action withdrawn. Both the police system and the educational system have been recentralized since the restoration of sovereignty.

Some positive influences remain in effect. Many of the Occupation's critics grant that the American-sponsored land reform program went far in eliminating rural indebtedness and farm tenancy. Rural discontent was one of the major sources of the strength of the militarists. The change in the status of the Japanese woman also seems likely to remain one of the major accomplishments effected by the Occupation legislation and further facilitated in indirect ways by association with the thousands of lonely male Americans serving and working in Japan.

The presence of large numbers of Americans, both military and civilian, along with their dependents, may in time be seen to have exerted an even greater influence on Japan than the directives of the Supreme Commander. The mass culture of America—the juke box with its "pop tunes," television with its serials, the teenage set with its many fads—came to Japan. Those American cultural imports which existed in pre-war Japan were reinforced by the Occupation. Change also brought social disorganization; juvenile delinquency, theft, violence, sexual assault, which some of the older generation view as the evil products of Americanization and the destruction of traditional Japanese values. These complaints seem unlikely, however, to promote a successful purge of the imported elements which have fused in a variety of patterns with the indigenous culture.

One major goal of the Occupation, the creation of a neutral, unarmed nation without military leaders, has been almost completely discarded. The shift from a drastic demilitarization policy was begun by MacArthur. Faced with what seemed increasingly powerful Communist and Socialist demonstrations, the Occupation authorities began to fear an attempt at revolution. The Japanese government had only a minimal police force to protect itself and the Occupation leaders were hesitant about using American troops against Japanese civilians. General MacArthur agreed in 1950 to the establishment of a National Police Reserve of 75,000 men to cope with threatened subversion and public disorder. Trained and equipped initially by the American Army, this force soon rose to over 100,000 and drew its officers from the old Japanese Army. Renamed the National Security Force and expanding its arsenal of weapons to include tanks, this organization became the nucleus of a new army. Socialists challenged this development as a violation of the constitutional ban on armed forces, but the Japanese courts twice upheld the constitutionality of the new force.

American policy changed even further when it favored the growth of Japan's armed forces beyond the level needed for internal policing. The new goal was the creation of military forces which would once more make Japan a factor in the politics of the Far East. Following the ratification of the peace treaty a "Self-Defense Air Force" and naval force were created. The Air Force was equipped initially with American planes and trained by American pilots. The first class to graduate in the operation of jet aircraft included a lieutenant colonel who had taken part in the bombing of Pearl Harbor. By 1960 the new force had grown to include a thousand fliers and was headed by an airman who had played a key role in planning the successful air strikes of 1941.

The new navy began as it had almost a century before with American vessels. With congressional approval, the U.S. Navy in 1954 loaned Japan a number of small ships, including two destroyers. New vessels were soon built in Japan's own shipyards; by 1960 the flag of the Rising Sun flew again over 14 new destroyers and was painted on the fuselages of a small naval air force. In January of 1959 the new navy paid its first visit to Pearl Harbor, greeted this time with grass-skirted hula girls. Stirring of unpleasant memories was avoided as much as possible during the two-weeks' visit to the Hawaiian Islands; the Japanese reportedly firing their salutes outside the entrance to the harbor to avoid even ceremonial exchange of guns within the harbor. A tribute was paid to the hulk of the battleship *Arizona* which rests on the bottom, where it was sent in 1941 by Japanese bombs.

The nationalist forces of the older Japan have given their support to the development of military power on the foundations laid by the former enemy. The decision to give Japan a role in the Cold War and to use the islands as bases off the coast of Communist China cannot help but reinforce the belief of extreme nationalists that the nation's mistake was not the course adopted in 1931, but the failure to create enough strength to carry it out. The same developments add to the resentments created by the Japanese War Crimes Trials at which 25 major war leaders, led by General Tojo, were sentenced to death or life imprisonment by a tribunal created by the victorious allies. Tojo and six others were hanged. In August of 1960 a national monument was unveiled to these "Seven Martyrs" with an inscription charging that their execution had been by "ex post facto law after the nation was compelled to surrender when the United States used atomic weapons and the Soviet Union violated its non-aggression pact." The monument was built on a mountain side facing the United States and bears the pointed charge, "Let us cast our eyes far in the direction of the Pacific and probe who was responsible for the war."

Hostility toward the United States, which before the war was largely the expression of conservative and reactionary parties, became a major characteristic of the Socialist and Communist parties. Their hostility was chiefly directed at the security pact negotiated in 1951 which gave the United States the exclusive right to retain military bases on Japanese soil for mutual defense. A year after the Occupation was formally terminated, there were still over 150,000 American soldiers and their dependents on Japanese soil. The growing sense of national independence was constantly confronted with the foreign troops and strengthened the argument of the government's critics that it was the puppet of the Americans. The retention of Okinawa as a major base, granting Japan only "residual sovereignty," added to this political hostility. Although American ground forces were withdrawn in 1958 and the security pact renegotiated in 1960 on a more favorable basis for Japan, the provisions for continued American air and naval bases set off the massive anti-American demonstrations of May and June of 1960 which led to the cancellation of President Eisenhower's visit.

The growth of Communist China's prestige as a world power also strengthened those who claim that only the United States influence prevents a closer relationship between Tokyo and Peking. The existence of an even greater Chinese market than was available in the 1930's moved some conservative Japanese businessmen to join with their political opponents in favoring recognition of China. The prosperity which Japan gained in the 1950's and early 1960's was based on marketing outlets in the United States, Southeast Asia, and Africa. Any curtailment of these markets through an American recession or restrictive trade practices would make the pressure for the expansion of relations with China almost irresistible for even a conservative Japanese government.

The future of American relations with Japan within the Cold War framework is not likely to be a stable one. The strength of the Socialists and Communists has been greatest in the ranks of urban youth, organized workers, and the educated classes, sectors of the population growing faster than those elements such as farmers and older age groups who vote conservative. Unless Japan's prosperity can be maintained and extended in such a way as to weaken or reorient the parties on the left, the likelihood is great that they will in time have an influence on foreign policy which will disrupt the American security pact. A pro-Chinese or even a neutral Japan, insisting on the evacuation of bases in Japan and of Okinawa, would mean a major setback to American military strategy in the western Pacific.

The possibility of a new clash between the national interests of Japan and those of the United States does not seem to have been given serious consideration by American policy makers in the second decade following Japan's surrender. An attitude of forgive and forget, while assuming permanent partnership in the future, seems to mark American opinion as well. In April of 1962 the chairman of the United States Joint Chiefs of Staff awarded a Legion of Merit medal to General Minoru Genda for his outstanding services as Chief of Staff of the Japanese forces since 1959. Genda was the brilliant naval air officer who was consulted by Admiral Yamamoto in 1941 and who convinced the Admiral that an air attack on Pearl Harbor was feasible technically. Interviewed in 1961, Genda expressed his regret as a tactician that the attack had not been bigger and more destructive so as to eliminate the American carrier forces as well. The honors given to such an influential former enemy evoked no outcry from even the most extreme chauvinist elements in American society.

The available data on the rapid change in the attitude of the American public toward Japan in the post-Hiroshima decades suggests a continued close correlation with official American policy. In the last year of the war public opinion polls showed a rising hostility toward Japan, possibly produced by accounts of the savage last-ditch efforts to hold Pacific islands which also were dramatized by rising American casualties. But once the Japanese authorities surrendered and the peaceful occupation began this antagonism quickly subsided. Asked early in

1946 which nation would still most like to dominate the world, Americans picked their former allies, Russia and Britain. Japan ranked fourth after Germany and was suspected of retaining expansionist ambitions by only 9 percent of the respondents. In December of 1944 a majority of Americans felt that the Japanese would always be a warlike people; by 1946 this view was held by less than a third.

Even the old hostility of the West coast states seems to have been neutralized when comparisons are made with other regions of the United States. In a poll in early 1953, 64 percent of the respondents on the West coast expressed unequivocally friendly feelings toward Japan. This was 8 percent higher than the national average in the same poll. It was the South, perhaps influenced by the competition of Japanese textiles or by racist associations, which expressed the highest percentage of ill-will toward Japan.

Other aspects of the pre-Pearl Harbor stereotypes of Japan seem to have disappeared in the face of official sponsorship of the new Japan. The buck-toothed, grinning but threatening Japanese has been removed from the American political cartoonists' standardized portrayals. The renewed Japanese trade competition with American products failed to produce the type of "scare articles" which were a favorite stock piece of American magazines and Sunday newspaper supplements in the 1930's. Articles about Japan were more likely to be titled, "Land of Strangeness and Charm," "The Exquisite Enigma," "The Quiet Beauty of Old Japan" or even "Cool Cats and Samurai," to select a few titles from the 1960's. Even the amazingly rapid growth of Japan's economy was viewed more with wonder and admiration than fear of future competition. "Japan's Miracle," "Prosperity Unlimited" and "Free and Easy Trade" were typically friendly titles used in describing this economic transformation.

For a new generation of Americans who know World War II as a set of pages in history texts, the image of Japan is almost completely free of the older, hostile stereotypes. The word, "Japanese," evoked such adjectives as "exotic," "graceful," "picturesque," and "polite," from college students in the 1960's far more than it did, "sinister," "fanatic" "slant-eyed," and "treacherous."

Some of these changes in attitudes can be ascribed to what appear to have been obvious influences in the postwar decades. A series of exceptionally fine art films exported by Japan made circuits throughout the United States; Hollywood also found the new Japan with films which featured beautiful gardens, temples, and geisha girls; a renewed interest in Japanese art; the great interest in some circles in Zen Buddhism; an American tour by a *kabuki* troupe—all these may have strengthened impressions of Japan as the center of a great and attractive culture. Many Americans also came to know Japan personally during the Occupation, more than had ever visited Japan in previous periods as visitors. Their letters to friends and relatives, their personal accounts when they returned frequently added to the image of Japanese as a polite, co-operative, and likeable people. Of some 400 business and professional leaders who visited Japan in the postwar years, only 2 percent, according to a 1959 poll, returned with a bad impression of their hosts.

In the framework of American foreign policy the changed view of Japan has been as complete. An Assistant Secretary of State for Far Eastern Affairs, addressing the Japan-America Society in 1961 on "The American Image of Japan," said that the romantic post-Perry view had been dropped at the close of World War I. Americans now regarded Japan, he said, as a democracy, a major world industrial power, a center of culture, a leader in Asia, and a partner of the United States.

Japan has changed in many ways in the more than a century and a half of its relationship with the United States. The national character and the national outlook have not, however, changed as drastically and as frequently as have American impressions of that character and outlook. Nor can the changes in American views be closely related to increased information and knowledge of Japan. Ignorance and superficial acquaintance have produced some unrealistic judgments, but knowledge and close contact have not prevented equally unrealistic images from gaining currency. The experience with Japanese immigrants was no doubt a formative influence for Pacific coast Americans. But overriding all these considerations seems to have been the official relationship between Washington and Tokyo. When Japan's foreign policy is harmonious with American aspirations and interests in Asia, the Japanese people were seen as exotic but peaceful and hard-working individuals, loving beauty and nature. When interests have clashed seriously, all Japanese energies seem to have been directed at aggrandizement and the national pride in cultural achievements has been seen as Oriental arrogance. There is some evidence to suggest that a Japanese study of national stereotypes of the Americans might also find some rough correlation between the character of the relationship of the two powers on a governmental level and the Japanese image of the American national character. In both instances there are probably some residual attitudes which have gone deeper in the national consciousness and which change very slowly. The polling techniques in use, however, do not seem to probe successfully into this lower layer of bias and prejudgment.

The development of stereotypes, even though they seem flexible enough to change with the shifts in the character of trans-Pacific relations, still contributes to the production of unwanted results in foreign policy. To the extent that stereotypes are unrealistic and blot out contradictions and diversities, they are obstacles to objective analysis. In the post-Hiroshima decades they have supported the assumption of American policy that the new Japan is a natural and permanent ally. The obvious generalization that Japan has a set of national interests, produced by a geography, economy, history, and culture different from that of the United States, and that these differences will produce a clash of interests, seems to be frequently ignored. Clashing interests need not create new enmities but they do prevent a long-term alliance, more to the interests of one nation and possibly even against the interests of one partner. As an insular power Japan can no more turn her back upon the Asian mainland than can Britain disregard the countries lying across the English Channel. Jet planes and missiles have cut the distance between Washington and Tokyo, but they have not eliminated the proximity of Tokyo to Shanghai and Vladivostok. To hold to an image of Japan which bars the possibility of neutrality or alignment with the new nationalisms of Asia invites a blow to American confidence comparable to that suffered in 1949 when Chinese Communists completed their mainland defeat of the Kuomintang.

The flight of Chiang Kai-shek to Formosa was an even greater disaster for American policy than Pearl Harbor, a disaster which nullified the military victories of American power in the Pacific, 1942–1945. The American policy which led up to Pearl Harbor, it must be recalled, was not directed at achieving the transmission of American values to Japan nor at converting that nation from an opponent to an ally. The political end of the war was that proclaimed in 1941, the maintenance of a favorable balance of power in Asia in the interests of preserving the Open Door. The preservation of the treaty system, of the Kellogg-Briand Pact, and of the orderly processes of change, whatever their desirability as general goals of national policy, were also means for the maintenance of a status quo which seemed most favorable to the continuance of the Open Door. This term in itself had become almost a meaningless catch-all, at bottom, said Walter Lippmann in 1944, "a short name for the American way of life, projected abroad."

Few Americans ever pointed out that the doors were to be kept open for the advantage of foreign interests, not primarily Chinese interests. Implicit in the Open Door concept was the assumption that China, unlike other sovereign nations, had no right to bargain and to close or open its doors to whatever nations seemed to China's best advantage. The rise of Chinese nationalism in the 1920's clearly pointed to the time when China would close its doors to special privileges for Europeans and deny the United States its self-assumed role of protector. Only the growth of Japanese interests permitted this development to be ignored as a consideration of American policy.

The closing of the Open Door came, ironically, at a time when that great market of four hundred million impoverished customers had grown to over six hundred million who were at last promised that they would become, like Europeans, substantial consumers. Whatever the limitations of the "Great Leap Forward" led by Mao Tse-tung with its totalitarian-mindedness, China has begun its industrialization and its quest for a higher material standard of living. At the point when this turn came, the United States, embittered by the defeat of Chiang and Communist anti-Americanism, turned its back upon the trading possibilities which the new China might offer. Secretary of State Dean Acheson stated the new position in the spring of 1950 when he warned China's new rulers that their market for American goods was now viewed as so small that it could not be used to win political concessions. Exports to China, said Acheson, were "less than 5% of our total exports and our purchases from China were a mere 2% of all that we bought abroad." The United States was willing to leave it to the test of experience, according to the Secretary of State, to prove to the Chinese how little it depended on that trade.

In 1890 Henry Adams wrote to his friend, Henry Cabot Lodge, "On the whole I am satisfied that America has no future in the Pacific." Neither Lodge nor his successors who supported the larger American policy would consider Adams' statement as anything but unrealistic pessimism. But to Americans of the 1960's, looking back on the chastening experience with China, the Korean War with its limited victory, and the difficulties in maintaining friendly governments in Vietnam and Laos, there was more reason to examine Adams' views. Was America's great empire of influence, prestige, trade, and power to decline in Asia as drastically as have those earlier territorial empires of Britain, France, and the Netherlands? Was the United States, which always felt that it was holding out a helping hand to Asians, to fare no better than the European rivals whose ends seemed clearly to be crassly exploitive?

Fear that the answer to these questions might be in the affirmative raised cries of "What went wrong?" Had this country, as some charge, been betrayed by enemies in its midst? Had the key to China been turned over to Moscow or to Mao Tse-tung by American Communists and fellow-travellers? Were good intentions and good deeds to be swept off the balance by an evil spawned by Karl Marx and exported across Siberia to Peking? Such simple questions led, unfortunately, to oversimplified answers. Demonology rather than historical analysis was too readily used to give explanations which could be grasped without too much thought.

Any probing for an answer should initially see the American debacle as a segment of the broader story of the downfall of the European and of his efforts to rule and shape the future of Asia and Africa. It must note that the forces of nationalism which the European introduced and stimulated by his presence become in their development resistant to outside control. The intensity of the xenophobia which the nationalists, Communist and non-Communist, propagate is also related to historic grievances, real or imagined. In China and Japan the Taiping and Boxer rebellions and the "Expel the barbarians" movement attest to the nineteenth-century grievances. Even the most impeccable behavior by the European powers in the twentieth century may have been ineffective in diverting this nationalist hostility without curtailment of major interests.

Whatever the differences in aim and method, the United States was generally identified by Asians with the old order and European imperialism. As early as 1922 that percipient student of Far Eastern policy, Tyler Dennett, warned of this relationship in his classic work.

> Each nation, the United States not excepted, has made its contribution to the welter of evil which now comprises the Far Eastern question. We shall all do well to drop for all time the pose of self-righteousness and injured innocence and penitently face the facts.

These historic factors circumscribed the scope for successful advancement of American political and economic interests; the performance of recent American foreign policy and diplomats must be judged against estimates of the limited rather than unlimited possibilities of success.

Within these limits it is very probable that a wise policy could have avoided war with Japan without national humiliation and surrender of vital national interests. Wise policy ought also to have been able to have avoided the state of near war, the breakdown of political and economic relations with China after 1949. Avoidance of both of these two critical developments might have made possible the preservation of a minimum of economic interests in China and checked the anti-Americanism of Japan which poses difficulties for the future. The affairs of men are manageable to this extent by wise leadership and it is the failure to achieve these limited ends which provides a legitimate field for *post hoc* inquiry.

The inability of leaders to recognize and work within the limits of power to achieve the achievable seems to be a common psychological weakness of men who direct the behavior of nations. Although it is a well-known adage that a coat must be cut to fit the cloth, in the process of tailoring national policy the assumption tends to be that there is unlimited cloth. This is particularly true as a nation grows in strength and when the early, essential caution of a weak power begins to be lost.

The result of this lack of caution, of unlimited optimism is always overextension; the establishment of national interests and policies which are incompatible with existent national strength. Even when overextension is belatedly recognized, it is still difficult to effect a strategic retreat or change of course before being challenged and routed. Prestige and national pride frustrate the efforts of prudent heads to trim commitments and pare off untenable policies. The history of international relations is a grim gallery of this sort of failure to act before being routed in what may be a heroic but futile gesture. The defeat of France in Indo-China and of the French efforts to retain Algeria offer only a well-known recent example.

In the second century of its national history the United States seems to have become as susceptible as older nations to this flaw of character. The first hundred years saw new territory added to the holdings of 1789 at the rate of over 60 square miles daily. The total cost of these tremendous acquisitions was only a few thousand battle deaths and some $70 million in purchase payments. The men who planned the acquisition of the Philippines and who proclaimed the Open-Door policy could look back at the successful conquest of the continent against British, French, Spanish, and Mexican rivals without straining the national treasury or the national will to sacrifice blood and energy. But to conduct a war in China and to defend the Open-Door policy across the Pacific required an escalation of expenditure which could not be considered of the same order as fighting a war against a backward Mexico or enforcing the Monroe Doctrine against Maximilian's French troops in Mexico.

The defense of the Philippines and the maintenance of American economic interests in China against all rivals, including the Chinese, might have been possible with a surplus population used to create military outposts and with a ruling class willing to send their sons into colonial service for the greater part of their lives. Lacking these components of the Roman and British empires, the defense of the new trans-

Pacific interests still required a militarized nation, willing to maintain a large peacetime army and navy. Theodore Roosevelt, Elihu Root, and young Henry Stimson worked to this end. They met with the resistance of a public which preferred the pursuit of private gain and happiness to sacrificing for an empire in which they did not believe and for a world role which they only half wanted. These limits on the national will to sacrifice placed a check on national power as real as the lack of steel mills and a large population of conscript age places on small, less well-endowed nations.

Theodore Roosevelt by 1907 seems to have glimpsed the state of overextension in his well-known reference to the Philippines as the American heel of Achilles. None of Roosevelt's successors dared face the dilemma boldly, either by calling for the high taxes necessary to build and maintain a large army and navy or by renouncing the commitments which could not be adequately supported. The realistic retreats of the 1920's were never drastic enough and easily nullified by the Stimson Doctrine in 1931.

Neither Stimson nor Franklin Roosevelt dared say what they seem to have believed at some stages, that a policy of preserving the Open Door against Japan would quite likely call for a war for which major sacrifices ought to be made in advance. Such a statement in the 1930's would have had tremendous political repercussions and might have meant the loss of control over Congress in the next elections, if not of the White House itself. It was far easier to stick to the policy without spelling out its costs. If war came there was always hope for victory "on the cheap." Even Roosevelt's policy of building up the Navy had to be disassociated from a forward policy in the Pacific. The same reluctance to jeopardize political popularity by straining the nation persisted once the United States was in the war, with both the White House and Congress insisting on "guns *and* butter" while fighting a global war.

World War II should have been an object lesson in the impossibility of doing everything everywhere at the same time, but the lesson seems to have been quickly forgotten by the policy makers. The atomic bomb, "the ultimate weapon" as it was quickly named, in the sole possession of the United States again gave rise to an extension of the range of "national interests" abroad on a vast scale which exceeded the boldest of the nineteenth-century expansionist dreams. The "American Century" envisioned by Henry Luce in 1940 seemed about to open, any voices of caution were easily dismissed as vestigial "isolationism" or "neo-isolationism." National interests were by many identified as being also the interests of the rest of the world in such a way that American expansionism and idealistic internationalism were fused. The containment policy inaugurated in 1947, determined to counter Communist pressure wherever it was exerted and without explicit priorities, was in conception again a policy which assumed unlimited national power, endless cloth for infinite coats.

The beginning of a reassessment and a recognition of the limits of American power came in 1949. First came the announcement of the explosion of a Soviet Russian atomic weapon, ending the security and advantages which the United States had had as sole possessor of this devastating force. Later the same year came the flight of the Kuomintang to Formosa and the Communist victory on the mainland of China, as the American government with public support refused to send an expeditionary force to fight in the civil war. The next year saw the opening of the frustrating Korean War, the first "limited war" fought by the United States with a limited victory. Optimism still died slowly and the presidential campaign of 1952 was marked by claims for "containment plus" or "liberation" by which the Communist forces were not only to be checked in their expansion but rolled back to earlier boundaries. Recognition seems to be coming, however, of the real limits of national power in an age of missiles which range half way across the globe. It is this belatedness of recognition by three or four decades which was of first importance in the undoing of American policy in Asia.

Given the wreckage left by mistakes of the past, what is left for the American role in Asia? In 1950 Dean Acheson attempted a fresh statement of American aspirations:

> . . . we are interested in the people of Asia as people. . . . we do not want to use them for any purpose of our own. . . . we want to help them in any sensible way we can to achieve their own goals and ambitions in their own way.

Within this framework, and probably in this framework alone, the United States can still establish a constructive relationship with the new Asian governments and their restless peoples. Years of exaggerated claims and misuse of American values and culture traits does not nullify forever any universal importance they may have. A twentieth-century Matthew Perry, seeking to reopen the closed doors of China, could find within the multiplicity of American thought, technology, and folkways a substantial cargo from which Asian peoples might benefit. Although American production techniques are based on material plenty rather than scarcity, there may be many which, with adaptations, are still suited for the task of expediting Asia's drive for the elimination of scarcity. And when the level of the Asian masses begins to rise above that of mere survival, the American concepts of the individual, embedded in the Bill of Rights, may still make their way across the Pacific.

BIBLIOGRAPHIC ESSAY

THERE IS NO COMPREHENSIVE and scholarly study of Japanese-American relations which covers the period from the earliest contacts down through the postwar American occupation. Payson J. Treat's *Diplomatic Relations Between the United States and Japan* (3 vols., Stanford, 1932–1938) covers the period from 1853 to 1905 on the basis of manuscript materials in the Department of State. Although a pioneering study, these volumes suffer from a narrow concentration on diplomatic exchanges, describing many trees but never the forest. There are a number of brief, popular studies of Japanese-American relations which aim at a broader perspective. The best of these is by an able populizer, Foster Rhea Dulles, *Forty Years of American-Japanese Relations* (New York, 1937), although now out-dated in many respects, still worth reading. Edwin A. Falk's *From Perry to Pearl Harbor* (New York, 1943) is marked by wartime animosities. Kosaku Tamura's *Genesis of the Pacific War* (Tokyo, 1944) is a Japanese effort written in the same nationalistic framework and using chiefly American materials. L. H. Battestini's *Japan and America From Earliest Times to the Present* (New York, 1954) suffers from superficiality and faulty scholarship.

For the broader picture of American policy in Asia as well as chapters on Japan, the reader is well advised to return to Tyler Dennett's *Americans in Eastern Asia* (New York, 1922) and A. Whitney Griswold's *The Far Eastern Policy of the United States*

(New York, 1938). Many monographs have subsequently expanded or modified these classic works on specifics, but they both remain outstanding pieces of scholarship, rich in wise judgments.

For the other side of the Pacific, George Sansom's *Japan: A Short Cultural History* (New York, 1943) is an excellent introduction to its subject, while the same author's *The Western World and Japan* (New York, 1950) presents a broad picture of Japan's reactions to western culture down to the late nineteenth century. Chitoshi Yanaga's *Japan Since Perry* (New York, 1949), while relying on secondary sources for American relations, uses a great many Japanese monographs to provide a solid, factual history of Japan. Hugh Borton's *Japan's Modern Century* (New York, 1955) offers a more interpretive account of the same period as well as the best of recent American scholarship. Edwin A. Reischauer's *The United States and Japan* (2nd ed., New York, 1950) deals primarily with Japan despite its title and is a useful, brief volume with a good bibliography. Further reading on Japan now has a fine guide in John W. Hall's *Japanese History* (Washington, 1961), a pamphlet in the American Historical Association's series for teachers.

Chapter I: THE FIRST ARRIVALS

The most comprehensive study of pre-Perry relations between Japan and the United States is that of Shunzo Sakamaki, *Japan and the United States, 1790–1835* (Tokyo, 1939), with major emphasis on Japanese sources and an appendix listing all western ships entering Japanese waters in this period. An earlier and still valuable account using American naval records is included in Charles O. Paullin's *Diplomatic Negotiations of American Naval Officers, 1778–1883* (Baltimore, 1912), dealing only with official contacts.

There are a number of accounts of individual commercial voyages to Japan. H. W. S. Cleveland, *Voyages of a Merchant Navigator* (New York, 1886), tells the story of the visit of the *Massachusetts;* Amasa Delano, *Narrative of Voyages and Travels* (Boston, 1817) includes an account of the amazing William Stewart. In the *Historical Collections of the Essex Institute,* "The First Voyage to Japan," Vol. II (June, 1860), pp. 166–69 presents the journal of George Cleveland of the *Margaret* in 1800 and 1801, while "The First Voyage to Japan" in the same publication, Vol. II (Dec., 1860), pp. 287–92 is a record of the visit of the *Franklin* in 1800. Henry F. Graff summarizes the early American interest and knowledge of Japan in the introduction to his *Bluejackets with Perry in Japan* (New York, 1952).

Ranald Macdonald's story, based on his 1888 manuscript, was finally published by William S. Lewis and Naojiro Murakami, *Ranald Macdonald* (Spokane, 1923). Nakahama Manjiro's visit to America has been the subject of a number of volumes. Masuji Ibuse, *John Manjiro: The Castaway* (Tokyo, 1941) is a fictionalized account; Hisakazu Kaneko, *Manjiro: The Man Who Discovered America* (New York, 1956), and Emily Warriner, *Voyager to Destiny* (New York, 1956), utilize the scanty materials to reconstruct his life. A readable survey of Japan's early relations with foreigners down to the 1860's is provided by Harry E. Wildes' *Aliens in the East: A New History of Japan's Foreign Intercourse* (Philadelphia, 1937).

Admiral Yamamoto recalled his boyhood wish in a 1915 interview according to Willard Price, "America's Enemy No. 2, Admiral Yamamoto," *Harpers*, Vol. 184 (April, 1942), pp. 449–58. Congressman Elliott made his expansionist statement in a debate over the Louisiana Purchase, *Annals of Congress*, 8th Cong., 1st Sess., Vol. XIII, p. 451. The economics of the voyage of the *Empress of China* are described by Clarence L. Ver Steeg, "Financing and Outfitting the First United States Ship to China," *Pacific Historical Review*, Vol. XXII (Feb., 1953), pp. 1–12.

Chapter II: TRADE, RELIGION, AND THE NATIONAL MISSION

Good surveys of the European penetration of the Far East can be found in the opening chapters of G. F. Hudson's *The Far East in World Politics* (New York, 1937) and in E. R. Hughes, *The Invasion of China by the Western World* (New York, 1938). The American role is well summarized in Tyler Dennett's volume mentioned in the introduction, while China's response is described by Earl Swisher, ed., *China's Management of the American Barbarians, 1841–1861* (New Haven, 1953), the bulk of which consists of translations of Chinese documents of the period. Chief attention is given to the British role in John K. Fairbank's *Trade and Diplomacy on the China Coast: The Opening of the Treaty Ports, 1842–1854* (2 vols., Cambridge, 1953), a major work which includes some material on the United States as well.

The first proposal for a Japanese expedition is treated by Allan Cole, "Captain David Porter's Proposed Expedition to the Pacific and Japan, 1815," *Pacific Historical Review*, Vol. IX (March, 1940), pp. 61–65. Aaron Palmer publicized his own role in his *Documents and Facts Illustrating the Origin of the Mission to Japan* (Washington, 1857).

The various documents produced by congressional interest in Japan remain uncollected and must be sought in their original prints. Congressman Pratt's resolution in behalf of an expedition to Japan is to be found in House Document 138, 28th Cong., 2nd Sess., and Palmer's letter to President Buchanan in House Document 96, 29th Cong., 2nd Sess. Documents on the pre-Perry visits were published in House Executive Document 84, 31st Cong., 1st Sess., and Senate Executive Document 59, 32nd Cong., 1st Sess.

The official account of the Perry mission was edited by Francis L. Hawks, *Narrative of the Expedition of an American Squadron to the China Seas and Japan* (3 vols., Washington, 1856). Additional materials are printed in Executive Document 34, 33rd Cong., 2nd Sess. Some corrections of the official account are made by Hunter Miller in Volume VI of *Treaties and Other International Acts of the United States of America* (8 vols., Washington, 1931–1948). A well-written and entertaining account, based on recent scholarship, is Arthur Walworth's *Black Ships Off Japan: The Story of Commodore Perry's Expedition* (New York, 1946) with a useful bibliography. There are a number of additional first-hand records of the expedition; Allan B. Cole has edited *A Scientist with Perry in Japan: The Journal of Dr. James Morrow* (Chapel Hill, N.C., 1947) and *With Perry in Japan: The Diary of Edward Yorke Mc-*

Cauley (Princeton, 1942). Shio Sakanishi edited *A Private Journal of John Glendy Sproston, U.S.N.* (Tokyo, 1940), and two seamen's journals are published by Henry F. Graff in *Bluejackets With Perry in Japan* (New York, 1952). One of the most critical participants was S. Wells Williams, "A Journal of the Perry Expedition to Japan," *Asiatic Society of Japan Transactions,* Vol. 37 (1910), pp. 1–260, with some supplementary materials in Frederick Wells Williams, *The Life and Letters of Samuel Wells Williams* (New York, 1889).

A unique Japanese account of the Perry mission, "Diary of an Official of the Bakufu" is printed in *Asiatic Society of Japan Transactions,* Series II, Vol. VII (Dec., 1930), pp. 98–119. Perry's visit to Okinawa was recorded in the diary of a British missionary and published by William L. Schwartz, "Commodore Perry at Okinawa," *American Historical Review,* Vol. LI (June, 1946), pp. 262–78. A pioneering biography of Perry still worth reading is William E. Griffis, *Matthew Calbraith Perry* (Boston, 1877).

Chapter III: JAPAN'S WALL CRUMBLES

Contemporary evaluations of the Perry mission are to be found in the work of an early American scholar, Richard Hildreth, *Japan As It Was And Is* (Rev. ed., Boston, 1860). A British view is presented by Charles MacFarlane, *Japan: An Account. Geographical and Historical* (2nd ed., Hartford, 1856), and by Talbot Watts, *Japan and the Japanese* (2nd ed., New York, 1852), reprinting some European editorials on the authorization of the American expedition. An early interpretation by a Japanese scholar is to be found in Inazo Nitobe's *The Intercourse Between the United States and Japan* (Baltimore, 1891). Nitobe, (1862–1932), was one of the first Japanese scholars to do graduate work in the United States, and his later work with the League of Nations made him one of Japan's leading emissaries to the West. The work of the Ringgold-Rodgers expedition and their records are collected by Allan B.

Cole in *Yankee Surveyors in the Shogun's Seas* (Princeton, 1947). A valuable contribution to the understanding of the politics behind the Japanese reactions to Perry has been made by W. G. Beasley in his introduction to *Select Documents on Japanese Foreign Policy, 1853–1868* (London, 1955).

Chapter IV: WARSHIP DIPLOMACY AND "CURIOS"

General Grant's visit to Japan is reported by John Russell Young, *Around the World With General Grant* (2 vols., New York, 1879). According to Tyler Dennett, "American Good Offices in Asia," *American Journal of International Law*, Vol. XVI (1922), pp. 1–24, Grant recommended the formation of a Sino-Japanese alliance against the western imperialists.

British diplomatic activity in Japan down to 1858 is ably treated by W. G. Beasley, *Great Britain and the Opening of Japan* (London, 1951). The negotiation of the first British treaty is described in Laurence Oliphant's *Narrative of the Earl of Elgin's Mission to China and Japan* (2 vols., New York, 1860). Other basic sources for British diplomacy are Sir Rutherford Alcock's revealing *The Capital of the Tycoon: A Narrative of Three Years' Residence in Japan* (2 vols., New York, 1863), a fine memoir in the nineteenth-century imperial tradition and the second volume of Stanley Lane-Poole's *Life of Sir Harry Parkes* (2 vols., London, 1894). Alcock was the British Minister, 1858–1861 and 1864–1865, while Parkes served from 1865–1882. Sir Ernest Satow's *A Diplomat in Japan* (London, 1921), covers the period 1862–1869 and is the work of the first outstanding British student of Japan.

Townsend Harris left behind a journal covering the period, 1855–1858, edited by Mario E. Cosenza, *The Complete Journal of Townsend Harris* (Rev. ed., Rutland, 1959). Harris has also had two biographers. The first was William E. Griffis, *Townsend Harris: First American Envoy to Japan* (Boston, 1885) and the second Carl Crow, *He Opened the Door of Japan* (New York, 1939). An amusing Japanese view of Harris is presented by a drama written by Kido Okamoto, *The American Envoy* (Kobe,

1931). Harris' negotiation of treaties is covered in detail by Hunter Miller in his treaty series, *op. cit.*, Vol. VII.

Interesting glimpses of Harris and other westerners are to be found in Harold S. Williams' *Shades of the Past or Indiscreet Tales of Japan* (Tokyo, 1959); by an anonymous writer, "An American in Japan in 1858," *Harpers,* Vol. 18 (Jan., 1859), pp. 223–31; and by two seamen, Alexander W. Habersham, *My Last Cruise* (Philadelphia, 1857) and Lt. James D. Johnston, *China and Japan: A Narrative of the Cruise of the Steam Frigate Powhatan* (Philadelphia, 1861). Harris' letter to Alcock was printed in *Parliamentary Papers,* 1861, Lords, Vol. 18, pp. 43–44.

Of the formal histories of this period, the most rewarding are those of westerners who knew the Japan of the late nineteenth century through residence. James Murdoch's *History of Japan* (3 vols., London, 1903–1926) was the work of a Scot who came to Japan in 1889 as a teacher, with the third volume covering the Tokugawa epoch. M. Paske-Smith, *Western Barbarians in Japan and Formosa in Tokugawa Days, 1603–1868* (Kobe, 1930) is the product of a British consul, while William E. Griffis who wrote, *The Mikado's Empire* (2 vols., 1st ed., New York, 1876) was an American who came as a teacher in 1870. E. M. Satow translated *Kinse Shiriaku: A History of Japan* (Yokohama, 1876), which deals with the period 1853–1869.

The first official Japanese visit to the United States is entertainingly described by the America-Japan Society's *The First Japanese Embassy to the United States of America* (Tokyo, 1920), a volume which includes the journals of a Japanese member of the mission and one of the American naval officer escorts, along with contemporary newspaper comments. Additional views are presented in Chitoshi Yanaga's "The First Japanese Embassy to the United States," *Pacific Historical Review,* Vol. IX (June, 1940), pp. 113–38, in "The Private Journal of Henry A. Wise, U.S.N.," edited by Allan B. Cole, *Pacific Historical Review,* Vol. XI (Sept., 1942), pp. 319–29; and more recently with additional local color by E. Taylor Parks, "The First Japanese Diplomatic Mission to the United States, 1860," *Dept. of State Bulletin,* Vol. XLII (May 9, 1960), pp. 744–53. Some of the highlights of the second venture to the West, the 1862 mission to Britain, are told by Carmen

Blacker, "The First Japanese Mission to England," *History Today,* Vol. VII (Dec., 1957), pp. 840–47.

The story of other Japanese who came to America, usually as students, and returned to distinguished careers was written by Charles Lanman, *The Japanese in America* (New York, 1872) and reissued in Tokyo in 1926. Lanman, who was a Washington newspaperman and librarian, included in his volume some delightful essays on America written by these students. An edition edited by Y. Okamura under the title, *Leaders of the Meiji Restoration in America* (Tokyo, 1931), includes some biographical notes on the later careers of the individuals mentioned. James Murdoch edited *The Narrative of a Japanese by Joseph Heco* (2 vols., Tokyo, 1895) which tells the story of Hekozo Hamada who reached San Francisco in 1851 after a shipwreck, attended college and became a naturalized American in 1858, and in 1865 started the first American newspaper in Japan. Jerome D. Davis' *A Sketch of the Life of Rev. Joseph Hardy Neesima* (New York, 1894) deals with an immigrant who reached Boston in 1864, attended Andover Theological Seminary and returned to Japan to become a Christian leader. Bradford Smith's *Americans from Japan* (New York, 1948) is a popular treatment largely devoted to the later migration, but with some material on the pioneers.

The argument over the Shimonoseki expedition and the use of Japan's indemnity can be followed in a group of pamphlets; E. H. House, *The Shimonoseki Affair* (Tokyo, 1875), David Murray, *Japanese Indemnity* and Joseph Morrison, *Comprehensive Statement of the Circumstances Surrounding the Exaction of the Japanese Indemnity* (Washington, 1880) which supplement the materials in the Department of State archives.

The question of treaty revision is handled in detail by Payson Treat in the work mentioned earlier, with some scattered references to the American position to be found in the diary of Hamilton Fish in the Library of Congress. A strong plea was made for Japan by James K. Newton, *Obligation of the United States to Initiate a Revision of the Treaties Between the Western Powers and Japan* (Oberlin, Ohio, 1887).

Japan's cultural impact upon the United States is treated in part by Robert S. Schwantes in *Japanese and Americans: A Century of Cultural Relations* (New York, 1955), along with the biographical sketch of Ernest F. Fenollosa in his *Epochs of Chinese and Japanese Art* (Rev. ed., New York, 1921) and in Van Wyck Brooks, *Fenollosa and His Circle* (New York, 1962). Clay Lancaster, "Japanese Buildings in the United States before 1900," *The Art Bulletin*, Vol. XXXV (Sept., 1953), pp. 217–25 deals with the impact on architecture.

Some parts of this chapter draw on the papers of William E. Griffis in the Rutgers University library, particularly the materials collected for a book on Americans in early Japan which Griffis never wrote, although he completed and published several individual biographies.

Chapter V: ARMING WITH AMERICAN AID

The standard work of western scholarship on the Meiji Restoration is E. H. Norman's *Japan's Emergence as a Modern State* (New York, 1940), although some of its interpretations are being revised by recent scholarship. Along with George Sansom's *The Western World and Japan* (New York, 1950), it still provides a basic picture of this period.

There is no substantial work in western languages on the history of the Japanese Navy. Gustav Jensen's *Japan's Seemacht* (Berlin, 1938) is a German doctoral dissertation with some materials on the nineteenth century. Short surveys of the navy's origins are provided by the chapter written by Admiral Makoto Saito in *Japan and the Japanese*, edited by Alfred Stead (London, 1904); the chapter by Hironori Mizuno in *Western Influences in Modern Japan*, edited by Inazo Nitobe (Chicago, 1931); and the chapter in *Fifty Years of New Japan*, edited by Count Shigenobu Okuma (2 vols., London, 1909–1910) which was written by Count Gombey Yamamoto. Additional materials are found in John R. Black's *Young Japan: Yokohama and Yedo* (2 vols., London, 1881), the work of an English newspaperman who edited English language papers in Japan. The economic aspects of Japan's militarization are treated by U. Kobayashi, *Military Industries of Japan* (New York, 1922).

American contributions are dealt with specifically by Capt. J. M. Ellicott's "Japanese Students at the United States Naval Academy," *U.S. Naval Institute Proceedings*, Vol. 73 (March, 1947), pp. 303–15, and in the same journal, Lt. Commander Robert H. Barnes, "Japan's First Submarines," Vol. 69 (Feb., 1943), pp. 201–4. The Naval Academy's leading Japanese graduate is the subject of Katsunobu Masudo's *Recollections of Admiral Baron Sotokichi Uriu* (Tokyo, 1933). Edwin A. Falk's biographical work, *Togo and the Rise of Japanese Sea Power* (New York, 1936) deals with the origins of the new navy in the opening chapters. H. W. Loweree, "Long Islander Started the Japanese Navy," *Long Island Forum*, Vol. II (March, 1948), pp. 43–57, is a brief note on the work of Capt. Elbert Stannard.

A survey of American technical aid to Japan is included in Merle Curti and Kendall Birr, *Prelude to Point Four: American Technical Missions Overseas, 1838–1938* (Madison, Wisc., 1954). The same subject is dealt with by Robert S. Schwantes, "Perspectives on Point IV: The Case of Japan," *Far Eastern Survey*, Sept. 1953 and in the same author's broader work on cultural exchanges cited earlier.

William E. Griffis wrote a biography of his friend, *Verbeck of Japan: Citizen of No Country* (New York, 1900). Eli Sheppard and Henry W. Denison are without published biographies, but glimpses of Sheppard's role in Japan can be obtained from his papers in the Library of Congress which include some memoranda he drafted for the Japanese Foreign Office.

Some materials in this chapter have been taken from the *Annual Reports* of the Secretary of Navy for the period and from Senate Executive Document 33, 37th Cong., 3rd Sess., dealing with the sale of American ships in 1862.

Chapter VI: VENTURES IN IMPERIALISM

The factors leading to the development of the nationalist spirit are well analyzed by Delmer M. Brown's *Nationalism in Japan* (Berkeley, 1955) which utilizes a rich variety of sources. Also of value are Hilary Conroy's "Japanese Nationalism and Expansionism," *American Historical Review*, Vol. LX (July, 1955), pp. 818–29; "Government vs. Patriot: The Background of Japan's Asiatic Expansion," by the same author, *Pacific Historical Review*, Vol. XX (Feb., 1951), pp. 31–42, and his very thoughtful volume, *The Japanese Seizure of Korea, 1868–1910* (Philadelphia, 1960).

Charles LeGendre deserves a biography, but the published materials include only fragments which appeared in *The Far East*, Vol. III (Oct.–Nov., 1877), pp. 87–94, 96–101 and the brief sketch in the *Dictionary of American Biography*. The best source remains the LeGendre manuscripts in the Library of Congress. Edward H. House, *The Japanese Expedition to Formosa* (Tokyo, 1875) is an American eye-witness account which appeared in part in the *New York Herald*. Of interest are LeGendre's *How to Deal with China* (Amoy, 1871) and his *Progressive Japan: A Study of the Political and Social Needs of the Empire* (New York and Yokohama, 1878).

By the 1880's and 1890's the growth of American interest in the Pacific encouraged much fuller journalistic treatment of Japan, and the many articles in American periodicals reflect a common image of the Land of the Rising Sun.

Chapter VII: THE FIRST ABRASIONS

The rise of American nationalism has been described in a series of essays by Merle Curti, *The Roots of American Loyalty* (New York, 1946). Curti's work has been supplemented in its ideological aspects by Edward M. Burns, *The American Idea of Mission* (New Brunswick, 1957). One of the most interesting efforts to analyze the expansionist nationalism of the 1890's is Richard Hofstadter's essay, "Manifest Destiny and the Philippines," in *America in Crisis*, edited by Daniel Aaron (New York, 1952). Mahan's views and his contribution to the expansionist ideology are treated fully by William E. Livezy, *Mahan on Sea Power* (Norman, 1947). Some material was also taken from the Mahan papers at the Library of Congress. The political background of conflict is fully treated by Hilary Conroy, *The Japanese Frontier in Hawaii, 1868–1898*

(Berkeley, 1953). The first naval encounters in Hawaii are described by Ernest K. Wakukawa, *A History of the Japanese People in Hawaii* (Tokyo, 1938). The general story of American naval expansion in this period is admirably told by the latter chapters of Harold and Margaret Sprout's *The Rise of American Naval Power, 1776–1918* (Princeton, 1946) and by Donald W. Mitchell's *History of the Modern American Navy* (New York, 1946). The period is treated in more detail by Gordon C. O'Gara's *Theodore Roosevelt and the Rise of the Modern Navy* (Princeton, 1943). William R. Braisted's *United States Navy in the Pacific, 1897—1909* (Austin, Texas, 1958) is a significant contribution in pointing out the way and extent to which Far Eastern interests began to affect military planning. Some of the same ground is covered by an earlier volume, Outten J. Clinard's *Japan's Influence on American Naval Power, 1897–1917* (Berkeley, 1947), but without the benefit of the naval archives materials used by Braisted. Some additional details in this chapter have been gleaned from the Naval Intelligence files in the National Archives.

For the diplomacy of this period Payson Treat's third volume has now become outdated in most respects. Thomas A. Bailey's *Theodore Roosevelt and the Japanese-American Crises* (Stanford, 1934) has become a standard work along with the masterful contributions of the chapters dealing with Far Eastern issues in Howard K. Beale's *Theodore Roosevelt and the Rise of America to World Power* (Baltimore, 1956).

The literature on the Open Door policy is substantial and the interpretations widely divergent. Tyler Dennett's *John Hay: From Poetry to Politics* (New York, 1934) is a good introduction, along with the pertinent pages in A. Whitney Griswold's *The Far Eastern Policy of the United States* (New York, 1938). Paul A. Varg has written a life of W. W. Rockhill who was influential in the writing of the original note, *Open Door Diplomat* (Urbana, Ill., 1952). A different view of the origins of the policy is offered by George F. Kennan, *American Diplomacy, 1900–1950*. The economic factor is described by Charles S. Campbell Jr., *Special Business Interest and the Open Door Policy* (New Haven, 1951). An even stronger economic interpretation is given to the policy by William A. Williams in his iconoclastic volume, *The Tragedy of American Diplomacy*

(New York, 1959). The Navy's disregard for the notes is described by Seward W. Livermore, "American Naval-Base Policy in the Far East, 1850–1914," *Pacific Historical Review,* Vol. XII (June, 1944), pp. 113–35. Raymond A. Esthus, "The Changing Concept of the Open Door, 1899–1910," *Mississippi Valley Historical Review,* Vol. XLVI (1959), pp. 435–54, initiates the sort of evolutionary study which needs further extension.

The Japanese question in the United States itself has produced a voluminous literature of which the most recent is J. tenBroek, E. Barnhart, and F. Matson, *Prejudice, War and the Constitution* (Berkeley, 1954) with a fine historical treatment. A French view is to be found in Louis Aubert's *Americains et Japonais* (Paris, 1908), Prew Savoy, *La Question Japonaise aux Etats-Unis* (Paris, 1924), and Jean Pajus, *The Real Japanese California* (Berkeley, 1937). All three see the economic and ethnic threat as exaggerated. The same conclusion was reached by Sidney L. Gulick who presented a pro-Japanese account, *The American-Japanese Problem: A Study of the Racial Relations of the East and West* (New York, 1914), based on first-hand investigation. Still valuable as an introduction is Raymond Leslie Buell's "The Development of the Anti-Japanese Agitation in the United States," *Political Science Quarterly,* Vol. 37 (Dec., 1922), pp. 605–38.

There is need for a general study of the development of Japanese-American war scares. One contribution is that of Eugene K. Chamberlin, "The Japanese Scare at Magdalena Bay," *Pacific Historical Review,* Vol. XXIV (Nov., 1955), pp. 345–59. *Japan in American Public Opinion* by E. Tupper and G. McReynolds (New York, 1937) is a broad survey of limited value, since it makes little effort to evaluate its materials or to provide a valid sample. The dangers of accepting general impressions of public opinion are illustrated by Winston B. Thorson's "American Public Opinion and the Portsmouth Conference," *American Historical Review,* Vol. LIII (April, 1948), pp. 439–64 which disposes of the widely-held belief that American opinion became pro-Russian during the course of the negotiations. Sidney L. Gulick's *Anti-Japanese War-Scare Stories* (New York, 1917) is a rich collection of wild rumors.

President Taft's Far Eastern policies are treated by Henry Pringle in *The Life and Times of William Howard Taft* (2 vols.,

New York, 1939), Vol. II, and by Charles Vevier, *The United States and China, 1906–1913* (New Brunswick, 1955). Wilson's first encounter with the Japanese problem is described in detail by Arthur S. Link's *Wilson: The New Freedom* (Princeton, 1956). Roger Daniels' *The Politics of Prejudice* (Berkeley, 1962) is a brief but richly detailed analysis of the anti-Japanese agitation in California.

Chapter VIII: RELUCTANT ALLIES

After many years without fresh analyses, the foreign policy of the Wilson administration is now the subject of a number of solid monographs using the Wilson papers and archival materials. Further knowledge of this period can be expected with the projected publication of the Wilson letters and the completion of a major biography begun by Arthur S. Link. Tien-yi Li's *Woodrow Wilson's China Policy, 1913–1917* (New York, 1952) presents an interesting view of the pre-war years. Roy W. Curry's *Woodrow Wilson and Far Eastern Policy, 1913–1921* (New York, 1957) is a useful doctoral dissertation. Arthur Link's third volume, *Wilson: The Struggle for Neutrality, 1914–1915* (Princeton, 1960), has some materials on the Far East which supplement his chapter on "missionary diplomacy" in his *Woodrow Wilson and the Progressive Era, 1910–1917* (New York, 1954).

Josephus Daniels' two volumes, *The Wilson Era* (Chapel Hill, 1944–1946) are useful on naval policy. Paul S. Reinsch's *An American Diplomat in China* (Garden City, 1922) presents the strong views of a well-informed China-firster.

The question of the Twenty-one Demands was treated from a strongly pro-Chinese view by G. Zay Wood, *The Twenty-One Demands* (New York, 1921) and in the same author's *The Chinese-Japanese Treaties of May 25, 1915* (New York, 1921). The fullest treatment is the work of an Italian scholar, Mario Toscano, *Guerra diplomatica in Estremo Oriente* (2 vols., Rome, 1950). The best Japanese work in English of this period remains Tatsuji Takeuchi's *War and Diplomacy in the Japanese Empire* (Garden City, 1935). A more recent contribution is that of Marius B. Jansen, "Yawata, Hanyehping and the Twenty-one Demands," *Pacific Historical Review,* Vol. XXII (Feb., 1954), pp. 31–48.

The Lansing-Ishii negotiations were treated by Julius Pratt in his chapter on Robert Lansing in *The American Secretaries of State and Their Diplomacy,* edited by S. F. Bemis (10 vols., New York, 1927–1929), Vol. X. Lansing has found a strong defender in Burton F. Beers' *Vain Endeavor: Robert Lansing's Attempt to End the American-Japanese Rivalry* (Durham, N.C., 1962), a study which finds the Secretary of State more realistic about Far Eastern interests than the President. The best American study of the Lansing-Ishii negotiations is an unpublished doctoral dissertation by Francis C. Prescott on this subject (Yale, 1949). Viscount Ishii presented his views of the negotiations in *Diplomatic Commentaries* (Baltimore, 1936). The French diplomatic scholar, Pierre Renouvin, views the Japanese effort at a treaty as the first timid attempt to establish an Asian Monroe Doctrine in his *La Question d'Extrême-Orient, 1840–1940* (Paris, 1946), a valuable study of the power struggle in Asia. Japan's subsequent policy is treated by Frank C. Langdon, "Japan's Failure to Establish Friendly Relations with China in 1917–1918," *Pacific Historical Review,* Vol. XXVI (Aug., 1957), pp. 245–58.

Japanese-American issues at Paris are fully treated by Russell H. Fifield, *Woodrow Wilson and the Far East: The Diplomacy of the Shantung Question* (New York, 1952). Typical of the journalistic polemics which that question aroused is Thomas F. Millard's *The Shantung Case at the Conference* (Shanghai, 1921). A defense of the peace conference decision was made by Kenneth S. Latourette, "An Unpopular View of the Shantung Question," *Atlantic Monthly,* (Nov., 1919), pp. 708–13 and again by the same scholar in "Two Years After Paris," *Pacific Review,* Vol. II (Sept., 1921), pp. 287–98. The debate in Washington is touched on by Robert E. Hosack, "The Shantung Question and the Senate," *South Atlantic Quarterly,* Vol. XLIII (1944), pp. 181–93.

A great deal of scholarly energies have recently been turned on the subject of the Siberian intervention. Betty M. Unterberger, *America's Siberian Expedition, 1918–1920* (Durham. N.C., 1956) and John A. White's *The Siberian Intervention* (Princeton, 1950) both point to the anti-Japanese aspects of American participation. James W. Morley's *The Japanese Thrust into Siberia* (New York, 1957) rejects the older thesis that Japan was eager to seize this Russian territory. George F. Kennan's *The Decision to Intervene* (Princeton, 1958) puts the Siberian affair in the framework of Russian-American relations. Christopher Lasch, "American Intervention in Siberia: A Reinterpretation," *Political Science Quarterly,* Vol. LXXVII (June, 1962), pp. 205–23 argues for a return to the original claim for the expedition as being directed in some vague manner against the Germans.

The role of the missionary which seems of importance in this period is studied by Paul A. Varg, *Missionaries, Chinese, and Diplomats* for the period, 1890–1952 (Princeton, 1958). An earlier study still of great value is John W. Masland's "Missionary Influence upon American Far Eastern Policy," *Pacific Historical Review,* Vol. X (Sept., 1941), pp. 279–96. The missionaries also had their American opponents, one example is B. W. Williams, *The Joke of Christianizing China* (New York, 1927), which scoffs at claims of great successes.

Chapter IX: A NEW ASIAN POLICY

The part played by Secretary of State Hughes in shaping Japanese-American relations is discussed by two recent biographers, Merlo J. Pusey and Dexter Perkins. Pusey's two volume, *Charles Evans Hughes* (New York, 1951), written with the cooperation of Hughes and using his papers, is unfortunately quite uncritical and lacking in fresh interpretations of Hughes' diplomacy. Perkins' *Charles Evans Hughes and American Democratic Statesmanship* (Boston, 1956) is a more thoughtful evaluation although underrating Hughes' contribution.

The Washington Conference has produced considerable literature, but as yet nothing approaching a definitive study. The organized campaign which preceded the conference itself has been studied by C. Leonard Hoag, *Preface to Preparedness* (Washington, 1941), while two journalists provided contemporary accounts which catch the spirit of the times, Mark Sullivan's *The Great Adventure at Washington* (New York, 1922) and Raymond L. Buell, *The Washington Conference* (New York, 1922). Captain Dudley W. Knox wrote a strong criticism of the conference from the point of view of the U.S. Navy, *The Eclipse of American Sea Power* (New York, 1922). A Japanese view was offered by Yamato Ichihashi, *The Washington Conference and After* (Stanford, 1928), but without access to classified Japanese materials. The best recent account is to be found in Harold and Margaret Sprout's *Toward a New Order of Sea Power* (Princeton, 1946), using materials unavailable to previous writers. John C. Vinson has studied the Senate's ratification of the final treaty in *The Parchment Peace* (Athens, Ga., 1956). An interesting French view which sees the treaty as a major defeat for Japan is that of Pierre Renouvin in the relevant section of his *La Question d'Extrême-Orient, 1840–1940* (Paris, 1946). The official documents released at the time of the conference have now been greatly supplemented by the 1922 volume of *Foreign Relations*. One specialized study which merits attention is Russell H. Fifield's "Secretary Hughes and the Shantung Question," *Pacific Historical Review*, Vol. 23 (Nov., 1954), pp. 373–85. Another is J. Chal Vinson's "The Annulment of the Lansing-Ishii Agreement," *Pacific Historical Review*, Vol. XXVII (Feb., 1958), pp. 57–69. Herbert Yardley, *The American Black Chamber* (New York, 1931), reveals the story of American code-cracking at the Washington Conference.

The Geneva and London Conferences of 1927 and 1930 still await thorough study, but they are well summarized on the basis of the published materials in Benjamin H. Williams, *The United States and Disarmament* (New York, 1931). Further details on the basis of unpublished materials are added by Robert Ferrell's chapter on the London Conference in his *American Diplomacy in the Great Depression* (New Haven, 1957) and by Raymond O'Connor, *Perilous Equilibrium: The U.S. and the London Naval Conference of 1930* (Lawrence, Kan., 1962).

The American Navy's orientation to Japan is discussed by Gerald E. Wheeler, *Prelude to Pearl Harbor: The U.S. Navy and the Far*

East, 1921–1931 (Columbia, Mo., 1963), and by Louis Morton, "War Plan ORANGE: Evolution of a Strategy," *World Politics,* Vol. XI (Jan., 1959), pp. 221–50.

The passage of the Oriental Exclusion Act still awaits detailed study based on the archival materials and congressional debates, but two older studies are useful, W. Rodman Paul, *The Abrogation of the Gentlemen's Agreement* (Cambridge, 1936) and R. D. McKenzie, *Oriental Exclusion* (Chicago, 1928). The chapter on "Immigration" in A. Whitney Griswold's *The Far Eastern Policy of the United States* (New York, 1938) still remains a good summary of the diplomatic background.

American reactions to Chinese developments have been described for part of this period in Dorothy Borg's *American Policy and the Chinese Revolution, 1925–1928* (New York, 1947). A unique interpretation of this period in American Far Eastern policy is that of William A. Williams, "China and Japan: A Challenge and a Choice of the Nineteen Twenties," *Pacific Historical Review,* Vol. XXVI (Aug., 1957), pp. 259–79.

Some materials in this chapter have been drawn from the periodicals of the period, the most useful being *Current History,* which in this decade achieved a high level of journalistic reporting on international affairs.

Chapter X: NON-RECOGNITION AND NAVALISM

Henry L. Stimson has been the subject of fine quasi-official biography which, while uncritical of his political decisions, provides excellent insights on the nature of the man, *Turmoil and Tradition: A Study of the Life and Times of Henry L. Stimson* by Elting Morison (Boston, 1960). Supplementary are Stimson's own *The Far Eastern Crisis* (New York, 1936) and an autobiographical volume written with McGeorge Bundy, *On Active Service* (New York, 1948). Richard N. Current's *Secretary Stimson: A Study in Statecraft* (New Brunswick, 1954), is a valuable critical survey of the major decisions. Robert H. Ferrell's *American Diplomacy in the Great Depression* (New Haven, 1957) deals with Stimson's

Far Eastern policy in the broad setting of the period and has a bibliographical essay of great value to students. Relman Morin's *East Wind Rising* (New York, 1960) is a journalistic account of relations with Japan which benefits from the use of the diaries of Stimson and William R. Castle and contains some perceptive sketches of Stimson. Richard N. Current's "The Stimson Doctrine and the Hoover Doctrine," *American Historical Review*, Vol. LIX (April, 1954), pp. 513–42, attempts to distinguish between the views of the President and his Secretary of State.

The Japanese-Chinese conflict is described by G. R. Storry, "The Mukden Incident of Sept. 18–19, 1931," in *Far Eastern Affairs* edited by G. F. Hudson (London, 1957), using Japanese materials to trace the origins of the first exchange to the officers of the Kwantung Army. Japan's subsequent successes and failures in the occupation of Manchuria are analyzed by F. C. Jones, *Manchuria Since 1931* (New York, 1949). The case for Japan is made by K. K. Kawakami, *Japan Speaks on the Sino-Japanese Crisis* (New York, 1932) and in his sequel, *Manchukuo: Child of Conflict* (New York, 1933). Hirosi Saito, *Japan's Policies and Purposes* (Boston, 1935) is a collection of addresses given by the Japanese Ambassador to Washington in 1934–1935.

A detailed analysis of British public and press reaction to the Far Eastern crisis was made by R. Bassett, *Democracy and Foreign Policy: A Case History, The Sino-Japanese Dispute, 1931–1933* (London, 1952). The controversy at the League of Nations was studied in detail by W. W. Willoughby, *The Sino-Japanese Controversy and the League of Nations* (Baltimore, 1935). Sara R. Smith with little supporting evidence argues that strong American support for the League would have checked Japan, *The Manchurian Crisis, 1931–1932* (New York, 1948).

The American mood of the thirties is discussed by Selig Adler, *The Isolationist Impulse: Its Twentieth Century Reaction* (New York, 1957) and by Robert A. Divine, *The Illusion of Neutrality* (Chicago, 1962). The same outlook is defended by Charles and Mary Beard in the final chapters of *The American Spirit* (New York, 1942).

The transition of the Stimson Doctrine from the Hoover to Roosevelt administrations is treated by Robert Ferrell in the volume mentioned above and more recently by Bernard Sternsher, "The Stimson Doctrine: F.D.R. versus Moley and Tugwell," *Pacific Historical Review*, Vol. XXXI (Aug., 1962), pp. 281–90, an article which emphasizes the opposition of Roosevelt's two advisers.

The background of Roosevelt's navalism is scattered through the first two volumes of Frank Freidel's thorough biography, *The Apprenticeship* (Boston, 1952) and *The Ordeal* (Boston, 1954), and pointed up in two monographs by William L. Neumann, "Franklin Delano Roosevelt: A Disciple of Admiral Mahan," *U.S. Naval Institute Proceedings*, Vol. 78 (July, 1952), pp. 712–19; and "Franklin D. Roosevelt and Japan, 1913–1933," *Pacific Historical Review*, Vol. XXII (May, 1953), pp. 143–53. A clear contemporary view of Roosevelt was published by Ernest K. Lindley, *Half Way with Roosevelt* (New York, 1936). The reopening of the naval building race is described in the final chapters of George T. Davis, *A Navy Second to None* (New York, 1940) and brilliantly analyzed in a pamphlet written by Walter Millis, *The Future of Sea Power in the Pacific* (New York, 1935).

Diplomatic relations with Japan in this period can be viewed through the eyes of the American Ambassador, Joseph Grew, *Ten Years in Japan* (New York, 1944), as well as retrospectively through the self-righteous eyes of the Secretary of State, *The Memoirs of Cordell Hull* (2 vols., New York, 1948). Bits of interest are to be found in other New Deal memoirs; Raymond Moley's *After Seven Years* (New York, 1939), James A. Farley, *Jim Farley's Story* (New York, 1948) and Harold Ickes *Autobiography of a Curmudgeon* (New York, 1943).

Two special studies are pertinent, Robert P. Browder's, *The Origins of Soviet-American Diplomacy* (Princeton, 1953) with a chapter on the role of the Far East in respect to recognition of the Soviet Union and Gerald E. Wheeler's "Isolated Japan: Anglo-American Diplomatic Cooperation, 1927–1936," *Pacific Historical Review*, Vol. XXX (May, 1961), pp. 165–78, which concludes that by 1935 the United States was committed to parallel action with Britain.

Interesting contemporary analyses and descriptions of the events of this period are to be found in the annual volumes of *The United States in World Affairs*, sponsored by the Council on Foreign Relations, along with the annual British volumes of the *Survey of International Affairs* edited by Arnold Toynbee. *Foreign Relations of the United States* becomes more and more voluminous in these years and has to be read in conjunction with the two volumes, *Japan, 1931–1941*, published by the Department of State in 1943.

This chapter has also drawn on the unpublished materials in the Department of State archives, the papers of Frank Knox, Nelson T. Johnson, William D. Leahy, and Norman Davis in the Library of Congress, the Roosevelt papers at Hyde Park and the Stimson papers at Yale University. Julius Pratt's *Cordell Hull* (2 vols., New York, 1964) is a valuable, if seldom critical, supplement to Hull's memoirs.

Chapter XI: THE YELLOW TRADE PERIL

The economic history of Japan has been well surveyed by western scholars and most recently by William W. Lockwood's *The Economic Development of Japan, 1868–1938* (Princeton, 1954) and G. C. Allen and A. G. Donnithorne's *Western Enterprise in Far Eastern Economic Development: China and Japan* (New York, 1954). But the financial and trade relations with the United States deserve study by an economic historian competent in both languages.

Some treatment of the earliest trade is to be found in Inazo Nitobe's *The Intercourse between the United States and Japan* (Baltimore, 1891). Charles F. Remer, *Foreign Investments in China* (New York, 1933) and Ethel B. Dietrich, *Far Eastern Trade of the United States* (New York, 1940) are both useful. Fears of Japanese competition are noted in E. Tupper and G. McReynolds, *Japan in American Public Opinion* (New York, 1937). Some valuable data was collected by Philip G. Wright, *The American Tariff and Oriental Trade* (Chicago, 1931).

Two well-written but unpublished doctoral dissertations were used in this chapter; Richard A. Thompson's "The Yellow Peril, 1890–1924" (University of Wisconsin, 1957), and John W. Masland, Jr., "Group Interests in American Relations with Japan" (Princeton, 1938). Some of the results were published by Masland in "Commercial Influence upon American Far Eastern Policy, 1937–1941," *Pacific Historical Review*, Vol. XI (Sept., 1942), pp. 281–99 which sees no direct commercial influence in these years.

This chapter drew upon the *Congressional Record*, tariff hearings, and American periodical literature.

Chapter XII: THE CHINA COMMITMENT

American foreign policy during Roosevelt's second term is treated in detail and with substantial attention to the Far East by W. L. Langer and S. E. Gleason, *The Challenge to Isolation, 1937–1940* (New York, 1952), a work based on extensive archival research and free access to classified materials. Written to prevent the disillusionment and "confusion of mind" which took place over American entry into World War I, its judgments of the Roosevelt administration are seldom critical, and then implied criticism rather than direct. At the other extreme is Charles C. Tansill's *Back Door to War* (Chicago, 1952), utilizing the State Department archives but not the collections of papers at the Roosevelt Library. Tansill's book, which begins detailed treatment of foreign policy in 1931, is in the muck-raking tradition of the "disillusionist" books of the 1930's with a hypercritical tone that frequently produces *non sequiturs* from its very substantial documentation. Two other volumes dealing with Roosevelt's foreign policy which belong to what Professor W. A. Williams has called the "Era of Violent Partisanship" are Charles A. Beard's *American Foreign Policy in the Making, 1932–1940* (New Haven, 1946) and a reply by Basil Rauch, *Roosevelt from Munich to Pearl Harbor* (New York, 1950). Beard's volume contrasts Roosevelt's words with his actions, while Rauch's work largely defends Roosevelt's actions as being in the best national interest.

In addition to Hull's memoirs and Ambassador Grew's diary mentioned earlier, materials on Far Eastern policy are scattered through John M. Blum, *From the Morgenthau Diaries: Years of Crisis, 1928–1939* (New York, 1959) and Nancy H. Hooker, ed., *The Moffat Papers* (Cambridge, Mass., 1956), which contain interesting sidelights on the attitudes of Hull and Hornbeck by

J. Pierrepont Moffat, and in Harold Ickes' *Secret Diary: The Inside Struggle* (New York, 1954), covering 1936–1939. Sumner Welles' *Seven Decisions That Shaped History* (New York, 1951) contains a chapter on Far Eastern policy, 1937–1941.

By the time Roosevelt began his second term, a considerable literature had begun to accumulate on the coming naval war for the conquest of the Pacific. Hector Bywater's *The Great Pacific War* (New York, 1932) was the work of a British naval authority. Tom Ireland, *War Clouds in the Skies of the Far East* (New York, 1935), was critical of the American role. S. Denlinger and C. Gary, *War in the Pacific* (New York, 1936) was an imaginative American study, while Tota Ishimaru, *The Next World War* (London, 1937), predicted its outbreak by 1940. Gregory Bienstock's *The Struggle for the Pacific* (New York, 1937) was a geopolitical study of the major power conflict.

F. C. Jones, *Japan's New Order in East Asia* (New York, 1954), deals with Japanese policy for the period 1937–1945, as well as the American actions, and is the work of a British scholar. David J. Lu, *From the Marco Polo Bridge to Pearl Harbor* (Washington, 1962) is a study of Japan's road to war based on Japanese materials. The role of the militarists in their rise to power is studied by Y. C. Maxon, *Control of Japanese Foreign Policy: A Study of Civil-Military Rivalry, 1930–1945* (Berkeley, 1957), and by an able English scholar, Richard Storry, *The Double Patriots: A Study of Japanese Nationalism* (New York, 1958). Still of value for its emphasis on the background economic factors is Albert E. Hindmarsh, *The Basis of Japan's Foreign Policy* (Cambridge, Mass., 1936). In addition to the manuscript and archival materials drawn on for Chapter X, this chapter benefited from the papers of Admiral Harry E. Yarnell in the Library of Congress for the period 1936–1939, when he was Commander-in-Chief of the Asiatic Fleet.

Chapter XIII: THE WANTED, UNWANTED WAR

The two years before Pearl Harbor are covered in the second volume of W. L. Langer and S. E. Gleason, *The Undeclared War*,

1940–1941 (New York, 1953), with all the value and limitations of the previous volume. Herbert Feis, *The Road to Pearl Harbor* (Princeton, 1950) begins in 1937, but becomes more ample in handling 1940 and 1941. A work based on the State Department archives it also benefits by Mr. Feis's long years in the Department, but is similarly restrained in pointing out any errors in diplomacy or statesmanship other than those committed by Japanese. Charles Tansill's volume, mentioned earlier, also treats in detail these years, but presents the obverse side of Feis in centering its many criticisms on the Roosevelt administration alone.

Two more detached studies which focus on the weakness of the Tokyo-Berlin axis are Frank W. Ikle, *German-Japanese Relations, 1936–1940* (New York, 1956) and Paul W. Schroeder, *The Axis Alliance and Japanese-American Relations, 1941* (Ithaca, N.Y., 1958). The latter volume argues that Japan's ties with Berlin were so weak that they should not have prevented an American compromise with Japan over the Chinese issues.

Major emphasis is put upon Japanese diplomacy in the final two years by David J. Lu in the volume mentioned in the previous chapter and by F. C. Jones's section in *The Initial Triumph of the Axis* (New York, 1958), edited by Arnold and Veronica Toynbee.

A number of Japanese memoirs have contributed to the story of the final years of peace. Mamoru Shigemitsu, *Japan and Her Destiny* (New York, 1958) is the work of a diplomat and foreign minister; Shigenori Togo, *The Cause of Japan* (New York, 1956) was written by a man who served as foreign minister at the time of Pearl Harbor. Tohikazu Kase's *Journey to the 'Missouri'* (New Haven, 1950) is by an American-educated Japanese diplomat who also writes of the war years. Shigeru Yoshida, *The Yoshida Memoirs* (Boston, 1962) is the work of a postwar prime minister.

Frederick Moore, *With Japan's Leaders* (New York, 1942) presents the views of a man who served as counsellor to the Japanese Foreign Office for over 14 years. Robert Butow's *Tojo and the Coming of the War* (Princeton, 1961) is replete with details from Japanese sources on the role of the wartime prime minister.

Tetsuma Hashimoto's *Untold Story of Japanese-American Negotiations* (Tokyo, 1946) deals with the private efforts in behalf of peace in 1941. More details are added by Mitsu Kakehi's "Nine Years After," *Contemporary Japan*, Vol. XIX (July–Sept., 1950), pp. 389–402. Takeshi Haruki, "Matsuoka and the Japanese-American Negotiations, 1941," *Aoyama Keizai Ronshyu*, Vol. X (March, 1959), pp. 1–31 (in English), uses Japanese materials to describe the role of this foreign minister who is also studied by John Huizenga, "Yosuke Matsuoka and the Japanese-German Alliance," in *The Diplomats, 1919–1939* (Princeton, 1953), edited by Gordon A. Craig and Felix Gilbert. An official wartime view of the causes of the conflict, largely based on American materials, was produced by the Greater East Asia Inquiry Commission, *The American-British Challenge Directed Against Nippon* (Tokyo, 1943).

The literature on the Pearl Harbor disaster itself and the decisions of the last few weeks is becoming voluminous. One guide is that of Louis Morton, "Pearl Harbor in Perspective: A Bibliographical Survey," *U.S. Naval Institute Proceedings*, Vol. 81 (April, 1955), pp. 462–69. The same scholar's "Japan's Decision for War," in *Command Decisions* (New York, 1959) is a good short survey of Japan's moves which should be read with Mark S. Watson's *Chief of Staff: Pre-War Plans and Preparations* (Washington, 1951) for the American military planning.

The official Navy view of the attack and the moves preceding it are presented by Admiral S. E. Morison, *The Rising Sun in the Pacific, 1931–April 1942* (Boston, 1948), a volume in the U.S. Naval Operations History. Walter Lord's *Day of Infamy* (New York, 1957) is a dramatic account of the events of December 7, while Walter Millis, *This is Pearl!* (New York, 1947) extends his account over the final year.

Two specialized studies of the diplomacy of the last weeks are Richard N. Current's "How Stimson Meant to 'Maneuver' the Japanese," *Mississippi Valley Historical Review*, Vol. XL (June, 1953), pp. 67–74, and C. Y. Immanuel Hsu, "Kurusu's Mission to the United States and the Abortive Modus Vivendi," *Journal of Modern History*, Vol. XXIV (Sept., 1952), pp. 301–7.

A very interesting effort to analyze the failure of the intelligence system is that of Roberta Wohlstetter, *Pearl Harbor: Warning* and Decisions (Stanford, 1962). In the same framework is Benno Wasserman's "The Failure of Intelligence Prediction," Political Studies, Vol. VIII (June, 1960), pp. 156–69.

The effort to counter the black and white wartime picture of the causes of the war began with two pamphlets, John T. Flynn's The Truth about Pearl Harbor (New York, 1944) and William L. Neumann's The Genesis of Pearl Harbor (Philadelphia, 1945), with the latter making the first use of the two volumes, Japan, 1931–1941, published by the State Department in 1943. The Pearl Harbor congressional investigation at the end of the war threw the question of responsibilities into the area of domestic politics and produced George Morgenstern's polemical Pearl Harbor: The Story of the Secret War (New York, 1947) and a counter-attack on this volume by S. F. Bemis "The First Gun of a Revisionist Historiography for the Second World War," Journal of Modern History, Vol. XIX (March, 1948), pp. 55–59.

Charles A. Beard published his second volume, President Roosevelt and the Coming of the War, 1941 (New Haven, 1948), again contrasting the President's campaign pledges and political speeches with the diplomatic and military story opened up by the Pearl Harbor hearings. Admiral Morison fired a number of shots in return, "Did Roosevelt Start the War?", Atlantic Monthly, Vol. 82 (August, 1948), pp. 91–97. The debate was heightened by the publication in 1953 of a number of critical articles collected and edited by Harry Elmer Barnes, Perpetual War for Perpetual Peace (Caldwell, Idaho), one of which by Percy L. Greaves, Jr., discusses the various investigations and inquiries into the disaster by government boards. Rear Admiral Robert A. Theobald defended the role of Admiral Husband E. Kimmel in The Final Secret of Pearl Harbor (New York, 1954) and Kimmel offered his own defense the following year, Admiral Kimmel's Story (Chicago, 1955). A reply to the various charges was presented by Herbert Feis, "War Came at Pearl Harbor: Suspicions Considered," Yale Review, Vol. XLV (Spring, 1956), pp. 378–90.

Examination of some of the principal documents bearing on the controversy has been facilitated by two collections, The Puzzle of Pearl Harbor, edited by P. S. Burtness and W. U. Ober (Evanston, Ill., 1962) and What Happened at Pearl Harbor (New York, 1958), edited by H. L. Trefousse. Another collection, *Pearl Harbor: Roosevelt and the Coming of the War* (Boston, 1953), edited by G. M. Waller consists of articles by historians on this issue.

An interesting recent contribution to the total picture is Rear Admiral Kemp Tolley's "The Strange Assignment of U.S.S. *Lanikai*," *U.S. Naval Institute Proceedings*, Vol. 88 (Sept., 1962), pp. 71–83. Tolley was commander of one of the picket ships sent off the coast of Indo-China under presidential orders.

For scholars, the 40 volumes entitled *Pearl Harbor Attack* must remain a basic source, particularly as important Army and Navy files remain classified along with some White House files. These volumes contain the reports of previous investigations, along with a great many materials collected by the Joint Committee on the Investigation of the Pearl Harbor Attack of the 79th Congress. Since good historical writing is always revising views of the past, whether on the basis of new materials or new perspectives and insights, "revisionist" histories of the road to war in 1941 will continue to find their way into print.

Chapter XIV: A NEW SUN RISES

The military history of the Japanese-American conflict, 1941–1945, is outside the scope of this volume, but John Toland's *But Not In Shame* (New York, 1961) must be cited as an excellent journalistic account of the disasters and human suffering which followed Pearl Harbor as American strategy wrote off the Philippines and other areas of the Pacific as expendable under the burdens of a two-ocean war. The problems created by the Pacific in respect to commitments in the war against Germany are discussed by several volumes in the official series, *United States Army in World War II*, in R. M. Leighton and R. W. Coakley, *Global Logistics and Strategy, 1940–1943* (Washington, 1956); M. Matloff and E. M. Snell, *Strategic Planning for Coalition Warfare, 1941–1942* (Washington, 1953); and the companion volume, *Strategic Planning for Coalition Warfare, 1943–1944* by M. Matloff (Washington, 1960).

The end of the war and the decision to use the atomic bomb

are the subjects of a rapidly expanding literature, but two basic studies are Robert J. Butow's *Japan's Decision to Surrender* (Stanford, 1954) and Louis Morton's "The Decision to Use the Atomic Bomb," in *Command Decisions* (Washington, 1959) with ample footnotes to provide a full bibliography to the date of publication.

The other controversial and disgraceful decision, the internment of Japanese-Americans, has also produced a number of books. One of the earliest efforts to publicize the plight of these individuals was published in wartime, Carey McWilliams, *Prejudice: Japanese-Americans: Symbol of Racial Intolerance* (Boston, 1944). Two thorough postwar studies are Morton Grodzins, *Americans Betrayed: Politics and the Japanese Evacuation* (Chicago, 1949) and J. tenBroek and others, *Prejudice, War and the Constitution* (Berkeley, 1954).

A lively study of the Occupation is Harry E. Wildes, *Typhoon in Tokyo* (New York, 1954). A more thorough study, but less critical, is Kazuo Kawai's *Japan's American Interlude* (Chicago, 1960). Robert B. Textor's *Failure in Japan* (New York, 1951) centers on the work in education. One of the Occupation prime ministers in his memoirs is critical of some aspects, but considers the effort on the whole as a success, *The Yoshida Memoirs* (Boston, 1962). The process of peacemaking was studied by Bernard C. Cohen, *Political Process and Foreign Policy: The Japanese Peace Settlement* (Princeton, 1957), with an excellent survey of American public opinion for which this chapter is greatly indebted.

General MacArthur's personal role is treated in two pietistic biographies, both written by Occupation officials: Charles A. Willoughby, *MacArthur, 1941–1951* (New York, 1954), and Courtney Whitney, *MacArthur: His Rendezvous with History* (New York, 1955).

Of the many studies of postwar Japan's politics and foreign policy orientation especially valuable for this chapter were Sir Esler Dening's *Japan* (New York, 1961), a British study with two-thirds of the pages devoted to the period after 1945. Douglas Mendel, *The Japanese People and Foreign Policy* (Berkeley, 1961) contains the results of many polls of opinion since 1952. I. I. Morris, *Nationalism and the Right Wing in Japan* (New York, 1960) is a disturbing study. An analysis of the 1960 riots is made by

Herbert Passin, "The Sources of Protest in Japan," *American Political Science Review,* Vol. LVI (June, 1962), pp. 391–403. *Without the Chrysanthemum and the Sword* by Jean Stoetzel (New York, 1955) is the product of a French and Dutch sociologist's study of the changing Japanese youth. Two works of American scholarship are *Japan Between East and West* by Hugh Borton and others (New York, 1957) and Harold S. Quigley and John Turner, *The New Japan: Government and Politics* (Minneapolis, 1956), the latter a solid text. An assessment of Japan's role in the seas in the future is offered by Walmer E. Strope, "On Japanese Naval Rearmament," *U.S. Naval Institute Proceedings,* Vol. 82 (June, 1956), pp. 575–84.

The fall of China is still a subject largely in the area of journalistic speculation, but a beginning of scholarly study was launched by Herbert Feis, *The China Tangle* (Princeton, 1953), covering the period from Pearl Harbor down to 1946. An analysis which goes much further is Tang Tsou's *America's Failure in China, 1941–1950* (Chicago, 1963). William L. Neumann's *After Victory* (New York, 1967) deals with the planning for the postwar status of Japan and the Pacific.

INDEX

345

DATE DUE

MAR 30 1988			
APR 11 1988			

HIGHSMITH 45-102   PRINTED IN U.S.A.